THE FAMILY AND PUBLIC POLICY

Frank F. Furstenberg, Jr., and Andrew J. Cherlin
General Editors

The Time Divide

Work, Family, and Gender Inequality

Jerry A. Jacobs

Kathleen Gerson

HARVARD UNIVERSITY PRESS

Cambridge, Massachusetts

London, England

Library of Congress Cataloging-in-Publication Data
Jacobs, Jerry A., 1955–
The time divide : work, family, and gender inequality / Jerry A. Jacobs, Kathleen Gerson.
p.   cm.—(The family and public policy)
Includes bibliographical references and index.
ISBN 0-674-01153-8 (alk. paper)
1. Work and family—United States. 2. Hours of labor—United States. 3. Professional
employees—United States. 4. Women employees—United States. 5. Working class—United
States. I. Gerson, Kathleen. II. Title. III. Series.

HD4904.25.J3 2004
331.12′042′0973—dc22   2003056839

To Madeleine and Elizabeth (JAJ)
To Emily (KG)

Contents

Acknowledgments

When we began this project, we did not anticipate that almost a decade later we would be thanking so many people for their help and support. As our work has mushroomed, so has our debt to the many people who made this book possible, and made it better. Kathleen Christensen and the Sloan Foundation provided two invaluable research grants, which launched the project and sustained it along the way. Our deep thanks to Kathleen, whose enthusiasm and support sparked our commitment and kept us going. Many colleagues took time from their own crowded schedules to discuss our ideas and read and comment on earlier drafts. For the generous gift of their time and their incisive insights, we are especially grateful to Rosalind Barnett, Mary Blair-Loy, Suzanne Bianchi, Andrew Cherlin, Cynthia Fuchs Epstein, Frank Furstenberg, Arne Kalleberg, Demie Kurz, Annette Laureau, John Mollenkopf, Liana Sayer, and Eviatar Zerubavel. We are also grateful to Ellen Galinsky, Terry Bond, and all their colleagues at the Families and Work Institute for conducting the National Study of the Changing Workforce and sharing its rich data with us. We also wish to thank the folks at Harvard University Press—especially Michael Aronson and Donna Bouvier—for their help and dedication. For her excellent research assistance, we are equally grateful to Sarah Winslow. We also wish to thank Arlie Hochschild, John Robinson, and Juliet Schor, who provided helpful feedback and, more important, helped blaze the intellectual trail we have followed.

Several chapters were adapted from previously published articles, and we wish to thank the journals and their editors for this support. An earlier version of Chapter 3 was published as "Overworked Individuals or Overworked Families? Explaining Trends in Work, Leisure, and Family Time" in

Work and Occupations 28 (1): 40–63. An earlier version of Chapter 6 was published as "Hours of Paid Work in Dual-Earner Couples: The United States in Cross-National Perspective," *Sociological Focus* 35 (2): 169–188. We are grateful to Sage Publications and North Central Sociological Association respectively for permission to reprint portions of these articles.

Personal as well as academic concerns sparked and sustained our interest in the issue of work and family time. Indeed, as this book developed, we often noted the irony that writing it meant taking time away from our own families. The more we wrote about time pressures, the busier our lives became. And our employed spouses were often pressed for time as well in their own demanding jobs. Without their consistent support and understanding, as well as their insights into modern work-family dilemmas, we could not have written this book. Our deepest thanks and appreciation thus go to our partners-in-life, Sharon Jacobs and John Mollenkopf, and our children, Elizabeth and Madeleine Jacobs and Emily Mollenkopf. We hope that this book will contribute to creating a future in which Elizabeth, Emily, Madeleine, and their peers will enjoy far more opportunities and far fewer time divides than we write about here.

THE TIME DIVIDE

Introduction

The late twentieth century witnessed dramatic changes in the ways Americans organize their work and family lives. As men's earnings stagnated and women became increasingly committed to work outside the home, the breadwinner-homemaker household that predominated during the middle of the twentieth century gave way to a diverse range of work and family arrangements. Today, as a new century begins, we face a greatly altered family landscape, in which dual-income and single-parent families far outnumber the once ascendant two-parent, one-earner household.

These fundamental alterations in family arrangements and the gender composition of the labor force have created new challenges for the American workplace and new dilemmas for American families, most of whom cannot count on a full-time, unpaid caretaker to attend to children and the household. Women and men alike must now juggle the competing demands of work and family, often without institutional assistance or road maps to guide their way.

The rise of conflicts between the social organization of work and the demands of family life has raised a host of questions about the changing nature of work and family life and its consequences for workers and workplaces. Have workers' ties to paid work, and especially the time they devote to it, changed substantially, and if so, how? In what way does the structure of jobs and work settings shape the options and dilemmas facing American workers and their families? How do women and men experience these conflicts and dilemmas, and what are the implications for their families? And what organizational strategies and national policies can provide satisfying resolutions to the conflicts facing American workers and families?

These questions lie at the center of growing debates over the current

1

state and future prospects for family and work in America.[1] Central to this debate is the issue of time. Like money, time is a valuable resource that constantly provokes questions about how it should be allocated and spent. Unlike money, however, the overall supply of time cannot be expanded. There can only be twenty-four hours in a day, seven days in a week, and fifty-two weeks in a year. When time squeezes arise, it is not possible to create more time. It is thus not surprising that the starting point for understanding work and family change centers on the issue of time.

Are Americans working more than ever, and, if so, why and with what consequences?[2] The most commonly accepted answer to the first question is "yes." Analysts such as Juliet Schor (1991, 1998) argue that new social conditions have produced a rising tide of overworked Americans, whose private lives are being eroded by the new demands of greedy work institutions and rising consumer standards. Others have asserted an opposite— and, for many, counterintuitive—answer. Some economists and time-use analysts, such as John Robinson and Geoffrey Godbey (1999), claim that working time has not increased and leisure has not contracted. Still others, most notably Arlie Hochschild (1997), have focused on the "time binds" people confront, arguing that a cultural shift has led workers to view time at work as a preferable alternative to the complications of life in contemporary families. These debates have focused needed attention on the new conflicts and dilemmas that have arisen in the wake of work and family change. They have not, however, produced fully satisfying answers to the questions they raise. Indeed, efforts to summarize complex social trends with overarching generalizations that actually apply to only a minority may have unwittingly helped create some misleading assumptions about the nature of social change.

By addressing these central debates about the contours of working time, we offer a new perspective on the roots, shape, and consequences of Americans' changing ties to family and work. Since working time sets the boundaries within which conflicts and strategies develop, any consideration of work-family relationships must begin with this issue. Yet working time alone cannot tell the whole story. We also need to understand how the organization and culture of modern workplaces shape workers' experiences and responses. And we need to consider how social policies can help workers resolve the deepening dilemmas they face between attending to their work commitments and caring for their families. In each of these areas, we address core questions raised by the work and family transformations of recent decades and by the debates these changes have spawned.

To answer these questions, we present a multifaceted analysis of the complex and evolving links between working time, workplace arrangements, and work-family conflicts among American workers. We draw on a variety of evidence, including an original analysis of historical and cross-national data that places current trends in historical and comparative perspective and contemporary cross-sectional surveys that illumine workers' personal situations, perceptions, and preferences. Each of these sources sheds light on a different facet of the links among working time, workplace organization, and worker experiences. Combined, they offer a unique vantage point for assessing recent changes in and future prospects for balancing work and family life.

Historical Trends

To understand the causes and shape of changes in working time, Part One places recent trends in working time in historical perspective. We compare the situation of contemporary American workers to that of workers in earlier decades to resolve the puzzle of whether or not Americans are working more or less than they were in earlier periods. We also consider variations among contemporary workers to determine who is working more and who is not. By taking a careful look across the full spectrum of American workers and viewing their situation within the context of historical trends, we provide a broad overview of the ways that the contours of working time are—and are not—changing.

We offer a perspective on the "overworked American" debate that helps resolve the apparently irreconcilable differences between researchers such as Juliet Schor, who argue that working time has risen precipitously, and those such as John Robinson, who claim instead that a growth of leisure has taken place. Although each of these views provides a kernel of truth, each is incomplete. Just as the proverbial blind men reach different conclusions after touching different parts of the same elephant, this debate has become stalemated by the partial view presented by each perspective. To make sense of the contradictions in this debate, we move beyond a focus on general averages for all workers to examine differences among workers in their commitment to, and perspective on, work.

In addition to focusing on general averages in working time, the "overworked American" debate has also focused almost exclusively on the time demands and obligations of individuals. We argue, in contrast, that key changes over the recent decades are best understood in terms of the time available to *households*. Drawing on information from the *Current Population Survey* (U.S. Bureau of Labor Statistics 2002a) from 1970 through 2000, we find that the working time of couples has risen far more dramatically than that of individual workers. Contemporary households face a rising time squeeze not because individual workers are putting in substantially more time at work, but rather because households, whether headed by dual-earning couples or single parents, face a changing equation in the overall time available for paid work versus domestic pursuits. As revolutionary social and economic shifts have propelled most women into the workplace and left most American households depending on either two workers or one parent, deepening time dilemmas are a logical consequence of the clash between changing family forms and intransigent, time-greedy workplaces.

Worker Perspectives and Workplace Organization

After clarifying the nature of changes in working time, in Part Two we turn to other, more subjective aspects of work-family conflict. Beyond a statistical examination of whether or not Americans are working more or less than their counterparts thirty years ago, we seek to understand how workers experience contemporary time squeezes. Since overwork is in the eye of the beholder, we compare how much Americans actually work with how much they wish to work. Here, too, we find not one general trend, but important differences among workers—especially between those who would prefer to work less and those who would prefer to work more. We also examine how increased expectations placed on both workers and parents contribute to the experience of overload. Finally, we analyze how the formal organization of jobs and the informal culture of the workplace influence work experiences and opportunities for involvement at home. Again, we find that different work settings can either exacerbate or alleviate the conflicts workers face. Especially for those who put in long days at work, key aspects of the job, such as flexibility and autonomy, may be especially important. Regardless of how much time a worker devotes to the job, some measure of control over when and how to work can make a difference.

In expanding the focus beyond the issue of working time to consider the quality of workers' experiences and the workplace conditions that are more or less likely to help them balance their aspirations for work and their commitments at home, Part Two is especially concerned with the link between workplace conditions and issues of gender equity and parental involvement.[3] What are the roles of so-called family-friendly policies—both formal and informal—in shaping the options and strategies of workers? And what are the links—and the gaps—between workplace policies and the needs and aspirations of workers? Do family-friendly policies that allow workers greater control and flexibility in meeting their family demands also promote gender equality? Or do they ask workers to make a choice between parental involvement and job mobility? We thus pay attention to the options and trade-offs workers face, the way these options differ across work settings, and the arrangements workers would prefer if a wider array of supports and options were available.

To offer a closer look at how workers feel about their commitments and their options as well as the aspects of work organization most critical in helping or hindering efforts to integrate paid jobs with the rest of life, we draw on the 1992 and 1997 *National Study of the Changing Workforce,* a representative survey of more than 3,000 workers.[4] We find that workers' actual time at work does not necessarily reflect their desires. We also discover that there is a growing time divide between those working especially long weeks, who would prefer to work less, and those working relatively short weeks, who would prefer to work more. The concern for overworked Americans, while important, should not obscure the attention that also needs to be focused on those who cannot find sufficient work to meet their families' needs. Nor should we ignore the finding that most workers, whether they work long or short weeks, would like to find a balance that often eludes them.

The sense of overload that many workers feel is a response not just to long weeks but also to increased expectations on the job as well as at home. Yet we find little support for the argument that contemporary workers forgo family-friendly policies because they look to the workplace as a refuge from the difficulties of family life. Drawing on comprehensive information about the availability and use of a range of workplace policies, we find that most parents are seeking to combine work and family, not seeking to avoid family time. When we distinguish between career-costly options, such as working part-time or job sharing, and options that provide job flexibility but hold less risk to long-term career prospects, such as working at home occasionally, we find that most workers use family-friendly options that incur less risk to their long-term work trajectories. Beyond formal policies, workplace culture is crucial in helping workers feel either comfortable or disquieted at the prospect of using policies that may be available on the books but are rarely offered cost-free.

In theory, family support and gender equity are the organizing principles upon which family-supportive policies are built. Yet there is good reason to be concerned that in fact these policies pose dangers to both women and involved parents of either gender. Even when they exist on paper, making use of family benefits can entail risks to a work career. In the best of all possible worlds, neither mothers nor fathers would be penalized for taking care of their children. And surely such a world would not penalize women more than men. Yet there remains a nagging suspicion that "family-friendly" does not necessarily mean either "woman-friendly" or "parent-friendly."[5] Instead, using—and even asking for—family support at work can be dangerous to the work careers of the very people who are its purported beneficiaries.[6]

We thus find that workers perceive a trade-off between generous family-friendly policies and opportunities for advancement. Mothers and fathers alike fear that family-friendly workplace policies come with significant strings attached. As a result, workers feel that they are being forced to choose between family involvement and career building. These perceptions are well founded.

Time Dilemmas and Gender Equity through Public Policy

Transformations in the way Americans organize their work and family lives have created new avenues for women outside the home and new options for women and men to share parenting and paid work. Yet the organization of jobs and child care has been much slower to change. Alongside new opportunities, Americans are facing new conflicts between the demands of earning a living and the needs of the domestic sphere. These changes are not simple reflections of individual preference but point instead to an increasing gap between the goals most workers seek and the demands most employers impose. Because these dislocations are the result of large-scale and unavoidable social changes, only large-scale social policies can provide resolutions to the dilemmas they have created. In Part Three we turn our attention to considering what can be done to alleviate workers' binds.

Since good policy depends on an accurate analysis of the sources of the problem, we begin by putting the circumstances and experiences of American workers in cross-national and theoretical perspective. Comparisons with other postindustrial countries that share similar levels of economic development, but differ in the supports and obstacles confronting their workers, helps to highlight the distinctive features of American work patterns as well as to point the way toward policies the United States can and should consider.[7] Here we are concerned not just with the question of time, but also with broader issues of equal opportunity, gender equity, and parents' need to provide their children with economic security and quality care.

Are U.S. trends in working time unique or shared by other advanced postindustrial societies? Comparisons among ten developed countries, based on information from the Luxembourg Income Study (De Tombeur 1995), show that Americans work more hours than do workers in most other advanced societies. A larger range in working time can also be found among American workers. When the focus is on the working time of couples, the American pattern becomes especially distinct. American families also have shorter vacations, and American women are more actively involved in the labor force.

These comparisons also show that policies matter. The time dilemmas that American workers feel are not an unavoidable consequence of the inherent nature of work in postindustrial settings, nor do they simply reflect Americans' supposed cultural preference for overwork. By adopting a varied range of policies, other developed countries have been able to provide alternative resolutions to the time problems of modern workers and especially of dual-earner and single-parent families.

Yet none of these countries simultaneously achieves the twin goals of family support and gender equity. Indeed, the trade-offs between these goals are put in sharp relief by international comparisons. The Netherlands, for example, has the shortest work week, making it perhaps the most family-friendly of the countries we have studied. Dutch women, however, remain largely secondary players in the workforce, with most holding part-time jobs. The Netherlands has resolved the time bind problem at the expense of gender equality. Finland, in contrast, has moved farther toward gender equality, with Finish women working almost as much as men. With everyone putting in full work weeks, however, the pressures on family time are more severe and reliance on institutional supports more elaborate. Thus, simply copying the models set by other countries will not achieve gender equity and family support. Yet Americans can learn from the experiences of other countries and borrow selectively among the best alternatives to create a new framework that fits the diversity of American families and workplaces.

What form, then, does the American landscape take? No single trend nor cultural impulse nor set of technologies can capture the complicated social shifts and new personal dilemmas facing American families. Instead, our contemporary dilemmas and conflicts involve the emergence of several interconnected "time divides." Each is important, but none can be fully understood on its own. The *work-family divide* that now captures so much attention is perhaps the most obvious one to emerge as American households have come to rely on either two workers or one parent. Yet we have discovered a number of equally important but typically overlooked time divides. A growing bifurcation of the labor force, for example, has produced a new *occupational divide* between jobs that demand excessively long days and jobs that provide neither sufficient time nor money to meet workers' needs. Alongside this development, workers are experiencing an *aspiration divide* between the time they devote to work and their ideal working time. A *parenting divide* also continues to separate parents from other workers, leaving parents to face the tightest time squeezes with scant and often inadequate support. And last but certainly not least, we find a *gender divide* that leaves women confronting the most acute dilemmas and paying the highest price for their efforts to reconcile family needs with work demands.

These time divides are interconnected, socially constructed, and deeply anchored in processes of work and family change in the twenty-first century. Effective social policies depend on recognizing, understanding, and addressing all of them. Only by attending to the many time divides now emerging—between work and family life, between the overworked and underemployed, between the options and preferences of workers, between women and men, and between parents and other workers—can we address the social roots of our current dilemmas.

What policies can and should be enacted to provide workers, and especially working parents, not only with family-friendly and gender-equal work environments but also with assurances that they need not choose between their children's emotional welfare and their families' economic prospects? We conclude by considering a range of policies that focus on time and other factors as well. We discuss reforms that would help workers better integrate work and family and that would provide greater economic security, gender equity, and parental support. Most of the discussion of family-friendly policies up to now has centered on the need for more flexibility in working time. However important, this is only one of several strategies for reducing work-family conflict. Some policies, such as on-site day care or extending the school day and the school year, make it easier for parents to work more, or at least work more comfortably. Other policies, such as a reduced workweek and longer, mandatory vacations, help limit the extent to which the workplace dominates the rest of life. Policies thus differ in their economic consequences, the political support they are likely to garner, and the consequences they are likely to have for families and workplaces. We also need to consider how new technologies, such as fax machines, cell phones, palm pilots, and laptop computers, have double-edged possibilities—offering the power to enhance both worker flexibility and employer control. In light of the variations we have found in workers' needs and desires, we propose a range of policy options that offer ways to balance work and private life without compromising principles of gender equity and economic security. Reaching all of these goals means adding work-reducing policies to the mix of options that focus on providing more family support and more work flexibility.

The Myths and Realities of Work, Family, and Gender Change

In these pages we offer new evidence and a new perspective on the state of work and family life in America. By addressing ongoing debates and synthesizing a range of findings, we aim to puncture some prevailing myths and to sketch instead a more complicated picture of the nature and contours of contemporary work and family dilemmas. Yet we hope to provide more than just an analysis of puzzling intellectual problems. By offering a comprehensive, albeit more complex, diagnosis of the time dilemmas of today's American workers, we also hope to point the way toward policy reforms that will help Americans resolve the conflicts and dilemmas that the "overworked American" debate has so successfully brought to the fore. By employing a broad range of sources and methods and by adopting an approach that focuses on families as well as individuals, examining variations across the workforce for women and men, and moving beyond the issue of time to look at the structure and culture of the workplace, we seek to reframe the debate about work and family change.

Trends in Work, Family, and Leisure Time

1

Overworked Americans or the Growth of Leisure?

Many American families find their lives increasingly rushed. The tempo may vary from steady to hectic to frantic, but a large and growing group perceives that life moves at a faster pace than it did for previous generations. Are these perceptions accurate? In this chapter, we address the thicket of competing claims about whether or not daily life has become more hurried and less leisurely, and, if so, whether overwork is the main cause of this dilemma. Is the shortage of "time for life" real, or is it an ambiguous or isolated social trend that has become exaggerated by a lack of historical perspective and a persuasive concern for social criticism?

In important ways, these questions—and the prevailing answers—are too simple. No one trend can adequately portray the complicated changes taking place in the American labor force and among American households. A more complete account would recognize the diversity among workers and their families. In fact, while a large segment of the labor force *is* working longer and harder than ever, another group of workers is confronting the problem of finding enough work. It is true that Americans are increasingly torn between commitments to work and to family life. Less apparent, however, are the ways in which the American labor force is diverging, as some workers face increasing demands on their time at work and others struggle to find enough work to meet their own and their families' needs. Once this diversity, and indeed divergence, is acknowledged, the competing claims about whether Americans are working more or enjoying more leisure can be resolved.

For a growing group of American families, feelings of overwork are real and well founded. Workers in some households are putting in a great deal of time at work. And many who are not working especially long days are nevertheless facing the challenges of managing a two-earner or a single-parent household. The lack of time for family life is not simply a matter of questionable choices made by some individuals, but instead reflects the way choices are shaped by our economy and the structure of our work organizations. The experience of feeling squeezed for time reflects fundamental and enduring changes in the nature and composition of American society. From this perspective, the scarcity of time for the tasks of daily life is not just a personal problem, but a public issue of great importance.

The "Overworked American" Debate

Ordinary citizens, no less than scholars and political actors, are expressing increasing concern over the issue of time. Yet despite the widespread perception that time squeezes represent a growing social problem, students of time disagree about the scope, dimensions, and causes of this problem. In *The Overworked American*, Juliet Schor contends that contemporary Americans are working more than their predecessors at any time since the Second World War. Her claim—that the century-long decline in working time has reversed in recent years—touched a social and cultural nerve and helped focus public attention on the importance of work-family conflicts in American households. It has also helped undermine the ill-founded idea that Americans are not working as hard as their international peers in the global economy (see, for example, Goldberg 2000). And it has helped to draw attention to how changes in the family economy, which now typically depends on the earnings of women, have created a growing sense of overwork in many households.

Schor's contention about the general trend toward overwork has also sparked a national debate. A number of conflicting views have been offered about the "overworked American" thesis. Some have followed Schor's lead, pointing to the growth of overtime (Hetrick 2000) or the possibility that Americans are turning to the workplace as an alternative to the increasingly complex challenges facing them at home (Hochschild 1997). Others, such as officials of the U.S. Department of Labor, have argued in contrast that the workweek has remained essentially unchanged in recent decades (Rones, Ilg, and Gardner 1997). And some analysts, most notably John Robinson and his colleagues, have used "time-diary" data to argue that leisure time is actually more prevalent than ever (Robinson and Godbey 1999).

How can we make sense of these conflicting and apparently irreconcilable views? Untangling this plethora of competing claims requires examining the "overworked American" thesis and the evidence on which it rests.

Measuring Time

First, we need to consider the ways that time is measured. Researchers' conflicting perspectives may reflect differences in how they measure people's use of time. Various measures include self-reports of work activities, time diaries, beeper studies, and observational studies. Self-reports and time-diary studies are the most commonly used measures and are also the major sources of contention. Other alternatives, such as beeper studies and observational studies, are either rare or generally small-scale. We will begin by considering the less common approaches before turning to those relied on most often.

Beeper studies measure use of time by the recording of specific experiences as they occur. Outfitted with beepers that go off at random, participants are asked to record both their activities and their state of mind when the beeper sounds. Repeated measures result in a broad outline of both the use and experience of time. By getting as close as possible to the specific moment when events occur, beeper studies can provide a more contemporaneous and detailed approach to the measurement of time than time diaries. Because these studies are only just beginning, it is too soon to know if and how that potential can be achieved.[1]

All self-reports, including surveys and time diaries as well as beeper studies, are subject to distortion. People may be reluctant to report actions that may trigger social disapproval, such as smoking or watching long hours of television, and to exaggerate activities they think will be deemed worthwhile, such as helping their children with homework. Observational studies, in which an unbiased observer reports on what is really happening at the workplace or around the kitchen table, offer a way to circumvent the potential distortions of self-reports (Coltrane 1996; Lareau 2000; Levine et al. 2001). The observational approach allows researchers to delve beneath the surface of self-reports, but it can only take place on a small scale and is potentially disruptive to the very routines that are under investigation.

With all their strengths, observational and related types of measures cannot provide an overview of how time is experienced and used. For topics such as the length of the workweek, large national surveys provide standard, comprehensive information. The *Current Population Survey (CPS)*, which tracks the monthly unemployment rate, is the main source of self-reports on working time; but a variety of surveys, including the decennial U.S. Census and other workforce studies, use the same method. In addition to collecting information on who is employed, the *CPS* asks a minimum of 60,000 people a variety of questions about their lives, including how many hours they work, in what occupation and industry they are employed, and how much education they have completed. Every month, the *CPS* asks workers how many hours they worked in the previous week and, for those not at work (such as those who were on vacation that week), how many hours they usually work. The March surveys also include a series of questions about the longest job held in the previous year, including the usual hours worked in this job.

Critics claim that the *CPS* information is not accurate. John Robinson, the leading proponent of time-diary studies, argues that people have only a few seconds to decide how to respond and thus provide only hurried guesses (Robinson and Godbey 1999). He argues that those working long hours are especially likely to exaggerate the length of their workweek. He thus concludes that Schor's assertions, which are based on *CPS* data, are exaggerated because they are based on inflated estimates of working time. Despite the fact that U.S. Census Bureau studies reflect the employment experiences of many thousands of individuals tapped month after month, time-diary advocates believe that these official labor statistics are based on guesswork and exaggeration.

In contrast, Robinson maintains that time diaries offer more detailed and carefully collected information—an antidote to biased, inaccurate self-reports. Time diaries ask people to list their activities, usually from the previous day, in order. By including time spent doing housework and at leisure, time diaries make it possible to add the time people devote to unpaid work to the time they spend at paid employment to get a broader measure of working time. Unlike the *Current Population Survey*, time diaries thus allow researchers to address the issue of the double-shift or double burden of paid employment and housework.

Yet time diaries have their critics as well. Schor and Arlie Hochschild argue, for example, that the busiest people simply decline to fill diaries out (Schor 1991; Hochschild 1997). If so, Robinson's contention that leisure time is expanding reflects nothing more than the lack of time overworked Americans have to fill out forms to prove how busy they are.[2] If self-reports may overestimate time spent at work, diaries may underestimate the time pressures of the busiest workers and families.

In addition, since time-diary studies ask participants to choose the amount of detail they provide, their findings vary considerably across respondents. To encourage comprehensive answers, some self-administered time diaries provided space for thirty-three entries, not including nighttime hours. This would produce roughly one entry for each half hour, but respondents were able to report any activity that lasted as little as one minute followed by another that lasted for several hours. This procedure was used through 1985, after which the diaries were administered over the phone (Robinson and Godbey 1999, p. 68).

Who is right in this battle of charge and countercharge? We maintain that both approaches provide important information and that the claims of bias are exaggerated. Self-reports on working time and time diaries provide complementary information that, taken together, expand our understanding of how we spend our time.

In response to criticism that self-reports are unreliable and exaggerated, our analysis has found that they are actually remarkably valid and free of bias (Jacobs 1998). Though errors doubtless exist, they tend to average out in samples of many people. Since it may be psychologically easier to recall the usual times for leaving for work and returning home than it is to calculate the usual number of working hours, a comparison of these two measures is revealing. When commuting time is subtracted from usual departure and arrival time, it becomes possible to estimate the average time spent at the workplace as well as traveling there and back. And although reports of time away from home may be a bit longer than self-reports of working time, they probably include lunch breaks and other activities not strictly associated with work, but important and time-consuming nonetheless. In fact, reports of time away from home correspond remarkably well to self-reports of working time, which do not appear to be systematically inflated.

Those who lack a regular work schedule, moreover, do not appear to be especially prone to misestimates or exaggerations. Nor do employed mothers, who might feel more rushed and consequently apt to exaggerate their time on the job. And neither do professionals, whose personal identities may be tightly wrapped up in their careers. Across a range of groups, there is no evidence to support the claim that some groups of workers are especially prone to exaggerate their devotion to—or time spent at—their jobs. Self-reports of working time hold up remarkably well for a wide variety of demographic groups in a wide variety of job settings; there is little evidence of systematic bias. In short, official measures and reports on the workweek appear to be a reliable guide to trends in the time people spend engaged in paid work.

Time diaries and beeper studies illuminate how much time spent on the job is time spent engaging in activities that are strictly defined as work (Robinson and Godbey 1999; Schneider and Waite 2003). All time at the workplace is nevertheless time spent away from home and family life. The conventional definition of paid working time used in surveys and census studies is thus appropriate for understanding the work-family time divide.

Time diaries, too, do not appear to be riddled with bias. Do they miss the busiest people and underestimate working time? A close inspection provides little support for this claim. Participants who filled out Robinson's time diary also answered a short questionnaire, which included the standard self-report question about how many hours were worked in the previous week. His respondents' answers are comparable to *CPS* estimates about the labor force.

Time-diary studies find no shortage of busy respondents, just as Census Bureau statistics do not appear to overestimate working time. Robinson and Ann Bostrom (1994) have demonstrated that the self-reports of working time in their 1985 time-diary survey matched those of the *Current Population Survey* quite closely. By the time of their 1995 survey, time-diary respondents actually appear to be even busier than the average *Current Population Survey* respondent (Robinson and Godbey 1999, p. 326).

In the end, measurement issues cannot resolve the larger debate over time use. While each method possesses limitations, neither can be dismissed for this reason alone. Even if, as time-diary advocates believe, official labor statistics contain elements of guesswork and exaggeration, these surveys nevertheless reflect the employment experiences of many thousands of individuals for a sustained period of months, years, and decades. And although time diaries may systematically underestimate the time pressures of the very busiest people, they also offer a look at a wide scope of daily activities and pursuits. No clear winner emerges from this battle of charge and countercharge. Indeed, both approaches provide useful, if different, information, and the claims of bias in each are exaggerated. Self-reports on the workweek and time-diary entries provide complementary sources of information that can help us construct a fuller picture of how time is spent in daily life, but neither can resolve the debate about how and why the balance of work and leisure has changed.

The Overworked American Revisited

Putting aside the debate over measurement, let us take a closer, more careful look at the substance of the "overworked American" argument. To make her case for Americans' increasing working time, Schor estimates the annual hours worked by the average man and woman in the labor force and concludes that women's annual working time increased by 305 hours between 1969 and 1987, while men's increased by 98 hours (Schor 1991; see also Leete and Schor 1994).[3]

If the focus shifts from annual hours to the length of the workweek, however, a different picture emerges. Despite the broad resonance of the notion of increasingly overworked Americans, the average length of the workweek does not appear to have changed appreciably in recent decades. To the contrary, the American worker, on average, appears to be putting in about the same amount of time on the job as did his or her counterpart thirty years ago.

Figure 1.1 highlights the stability in the workweek since 1960, suggesting that the number of hours Americans put in during the average workweek has been virtually the same over the past several decades.[4] Employed

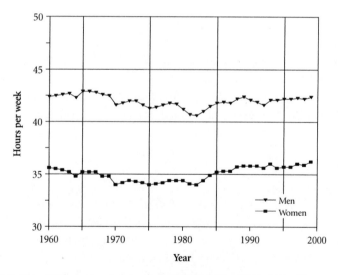

Figure 1.1 Trends in average hours worked, by gender, 1960–2000 (*Source: Current Population Survey*)

American men work an average of about 42 or 43 hours per week for pay, while American women who work for pay put in about 35 or 36 hours per week on the job. These numbers are supported by time-diary findings. Robinson and Godbey report that the average employed man works 42 hours per week, and the average woman works 37 hours per week (1999, p. 326). When it comes to measuring working time, the time diary and *Current Population Survey* results could hardly be more consistent.

These times have fluctuated by less than an hour or two over the last forty years. Remarkably little change has occurred from year to year, and the changes that have occurred most likely reflect the swings of the business cycle. The length of the average workweek dipped slightly during the recession of the early 1980s and climbed slightly during the sustained boom of the 1990s, but these valleys and hills were quite small. The consistency of the trends in Figure 1.1 also makes it clear that conclusions about changes in working time do not depend on comparing specific years to suit one's argument. Indeed, picking any two years will tend to point to the same conclusion.

There are many ways to look at trends in working time. The focus can move to wage and salary workers, excluding the self-employed. Agricultural work can be put to the side, on the grounds that working time on farms follows a different rhythm and is determined by different forces than those in the rest of the economy. Underemployed workers can also be put aside (as Schor does), on the grounds that the enforced "excess" leisure of this group should not be used to discount the excess toil of the rest of the labor force. The focus can be on the number of hours worked last week or on the usual hours worked in the longest job a person held last year. Making all of these, and numerous other adjustments, still leaves the basic story unchanged. However it is defined, the average workweek has hardly budged over the last thirty years.

How is it possible to reconcile the finding that the workweek has remained remarkably stable with the conclusion that working time has grown substantially? A small part of this puzzle can be solved by noting differences in historical perspective: Schor's analysis coincides with a period when the workweek was increasing, albeit slightly. A close look at Figure 1.1 shows a notable dip in working time during the severe recession of the early 1980s, with an apparent rise as it passed.   ·

The more fundamental explanation for such apparently conflicting findings rests, however, with the difference in focus between annual and weekly working hours. While the total annual hours worked is of course the product of hours worked per week and weeks worked per year, the idea of the overworked American conjures up images of endless work-filled days spilling over from one to the next, leaving little room for anything else as the week goes by. Yet the lion's share of the increase found by Schor reflects a general trend toward people working more weeks per year rather than more hours per week.[5]

Is Vacation Time Shrinking?

An increase in number of weeks worked per year may reflect a decline in vacation time for American workers. Most European workers enjoy legislative and contractual guarantees that afford them at least one month of vacation time each year, leaving U.S. workers with substantially shorter vacations than those in most other advanced societies (see Chapter 6). But have American vacations become even briefer over time?

Figure 1.2, which presents trends in vacation time from 1980 through 1997, suggests little change during the 1980s and early 1990s, although there was a slight *increase* in vacation time for those with ten years or less on the job. Vacation time generally increases with years of service, with those with one year or less receiving an average of nine days of paid vacation annually and those with five years receiving about fourteen. Ten years of service gives workers an average seventeen days of vacation time per year, while twenty years bestows an average of just over twenty days. Workers with one year, five years, and ten years on the job all saw nearly a one-day increase in vacation time between 1984 and 1997, while those with twenty years saw little change. Although these increases are slight and hardly noticeable, especially compared to the generous vacations Europeans enjoy, they belie the notion that a growing sense of overwork reflects declining vacation time.

These measures of vacation time have several drawbacks, however. For one thing, they reflect firms' reports on how much time workers are entitled rather than the actual time workers use. Second, they omit important categories of workers, including part-time workers, subcontractors, and other workers in less secure jobs who may receive little if any paid vacation time. The growth of part-time and, especially, contingent employment may have reduced paid vacation time for an important segment of the labor force, even while there has been little change in formally available vacation time for the "standard" workforce.

How much of the vacation time offered to employees do they use?

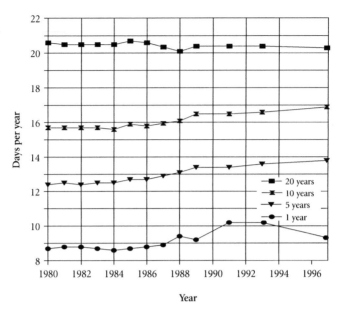

Figure 1.2 Vacation days per year, by years of service, 1980–1997 (*Source:* U.S. Bureau of Labor Statistics, Establishment Survey Data)

Table 1.1, which presents findings from the 1992 National Study of the Changing Workforce (Bond, Galinsky, and Friedman 1993), shows that most workers use nearly all of the vacation time they are offered.[6] Overall, Americans earn an average of twelve vacation days and use just over eleven per year, a figure well behind the four to five weeks that are standard in many European countries.

Since vacation time is often available only to full-time workers and may be offered only after a period of time on the job, the results in Table 1.1 are confined to self-described full-time employees who had been with their employer for at least one year. These workers earned just under three weeks of vacation (14.2 days) and used two and a half weeks per year (12.5 days). Men accumulated a bit more vacation time than did women, but women used a bit more than men. Professional and managerial workers earned nearly four weeks of vacation and used just over three weeks, in both cases about a week more than their nonprofessional counterparts. Vacation time is one clear case in which those at the top of the occupational ladder have more employment support than those in the lower ranks, even though these professionals may not use all the vacation time made available to them.

Table 1.1 Vacation days earned and used, by occupation and gender

Type of worker	Vacation days	
	Earned	Used
Total	12.0	11.1
Total full-time, with at least one-year tenure	14.2	12.5
Men	14.4	12.1
Women	14.0	12.9
Professional/managerial	18.1	15.7
Men	18.4	15.1
Women	17.7	16.4
Other occupations	12.4	11.4
Men	13.0	11.1
Women	12.4	11.4

Source: National Study of the Changing Workforce, 1992.

Americans enjoy substantially less paid time off from work than workers in many other advanced societies. This time is also distributed unequally throughout the labor force, with those in more highly paid professional and managerial positions enjoying more. Yet these findings do not point to a decline over time in the amount of vacation time available to American workers, who have never been afforded much paid time off compared to their European peers.

The Rise of Committed Women Workers

Despite the meager vacation time afforded American workers, it does not appear to be shrinking and thus cannot account for the overall increase in their annual working time. Instead, there is an alternative and fairly straightforward explanation: much of the growth in annual working hours reflects the growing attachment of women to the labor force. Over the period in which increases in average annual hours of work have occurred, women have streamed into the workplace and become increasingly committed to full-time, uninterrupted work patterns. Most of the labor force, and far more women, are working full-time year round today than were doing so several decades ago. Only a minority of jobs are designed for less than a full-year schedule, with teachers (who typically have two months off in the summer) and migrant farm laborers (who may work year-round but only work in particular jobs part of the year) standing out as two notable exceptions. While some jobs have paid vacations and others do not, most workers put in a full year. With the exception of those who hold seasonal jobs, workers are likely to work less than a full year for mainly temporary reasons. They may have started or ended a period at work during the year, or they may have been unemployed for a time. Neither of these situations represents an enduring commitment to part-time work.

Greater continuity in women's labor force attachment inevitably produces an increase in the overall number of weeks worked per year. While the *Current Population Survey* focuses on employment in the previous calendar year, it does not discern whether a worker intends to work for a short interval or for a sustained period. Many who are counted as part-year workers are in fact beginning a long period of employment, which just happened to begin at some point in the middle of the previous year. For the 2000 *CPS*, for example, over 60 percent of those who worked part-year (less than 50 weeks) in 1999 were still employed in March 2000.

The churning associated labor market entries and exits thus may account for much of what is taken as part-year work. As women's labor force participation climbs, labor market interruptions decrease, and employment spells that begin in the middle of the calendar year decline as well. One consequence is an increase in the number of weeks worked per year.

The same is true for men. Labor force participation varies over the life course, with somewhat lower levels among young men (under age twenty-five) and older men (over fifty-five or sixty). In those life stages with lower participation, there are also fewer weeks worked per year. Small changes in weeks worked per year for women and men thus reflect cyclical changes in the labor market and changes in workers' personal demographic characteristics, such as age and education.

Figure 1.3 shows that women's labor force participation has inched upward in lockstep with the proportion of employed women working full-time, full-year over nearly the past fifty years (from 1950 through 1998). The serial correlation between these two measures is, indeed, nearly perfect ($R = .965$). Since the number of weeks worked per year reflects the degree to which work is continuous or discontinuous, combined with the amount of occasional or seasonal work, the expansion of annual workweeks is closely connected to changes in the demography of the labor force and especially the rise of committed women workers.

In sum, the expansion in the number of weeks per year worked by the average American worker is largely a consequence of women's determined

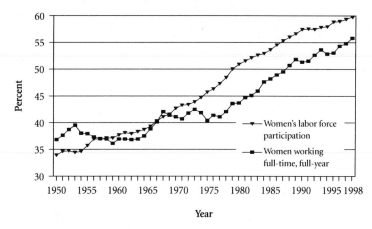

Figure 1.3 Women's labor force participation and percent working full-time, full-year, 1950–1998 (Source: *Current Population Survey*)

and steady march toward greater commitment to economic independence and work outside the home. The vast changes in work commitment and the rise of time squeezes for families cannot be understood without first acknowledging the revolution in women's lives.

An Increase in Leisure Time?

If the "overworked American" thesis needs to be reformulated, then what should we make of the competing argument made by John Robinson and Geoffrey Godbey (1999) that the period between 1965 and 1985 witnessed an increase in leisure time? Eschewing the use of national surveys (including the *Current Population Survey,* on which Schor's results are based) in favor of time diaries, Robinson and Godbey report that Americans' leisure time increased from 35 hours per week to 40 hours per week during these two decades.

In making the case for a growth in leisure, Robinson and Godbey point to the expansion of certain segments of the nonworking population, including demographic groups that are more likely to enjoy relatively high amounts of leisure time. Increasing proportions of men are retiring at younger ages, for example. At the other end of the age distribution, a growing group of young adults in their twenties are remaining in school for longer periods. Since students and retired men have more apparent leisure than does the average worker, the growth of these groups would point to an increase in leisure time in the general population, even with no change in the average workweek.

This argument, however, overlooks the growth in women's work participation, which has more than offset such changes. Indeed, a larger proportion of the adult population is in the labor force today than at any time since the Second World War. The ratio of employed individuals to the whole population (age sixteen and above) rose from 56.1 in 1950 to 64.3 in 1999. Similarly, the percentage of the population in the civilian labor force rose from 59.2 to 67.1.[7] And if the growing fraction of the population aged sixty-five or above were removed from the picture, the growth in the employed population would be even steeper. Any overall changes in working time thus apply to a growing, not a shrinking, share of the population.

The rise in the labor force participation rate masks two contrary trends: a sharp increase for women and a gradual decline for men. Since 1970, men's participation has fallen from 80.0 percent to 75.6 percent, while women's has jumped from 42.6 percent to 59.6 percent. The leisure-time puzzle must thus be understood in the context of historically high labor force participation rates, which point more toward the expansion of work than the growth of leisure.

Overwork, Growing Leisure, or Both?

On the surface, the "overworked American" thesis and the "increase in leisure" thesis seem irreconcilable. After all, everyone enjoys a limited and equal amount of time to apportion among a range of activities. Changes in work and leisure should thus involve a zero-sum trade-off: any increase in work time should decrease leisure time. And since no one measure of these trends can be considered definitive or clearly superior, data quality alone cannot solve the puzzle or provide a clear winner among competing perspectives. Once we recognize the vast diversity among workers, however, it becomes possible to resolve the apparent contradictions between these arguments and find a kernel of truth in each. Workers vary in their work and domestic circumstances, and both of these dimensions make a world of difference, not only in how much time they give to the different domains of their life but also in how they feel about this balance.

The "growth of leisure" thesis rests on an average workweek estimated for the entire population. While this may seem to be a good place to begin, time-use differences across groups are so large that the average amount of leisure is, in the end, not a particularly meaningful figure. Robinson and Godbey report, for example, that women as a whole devoted about 4.8 hours per week to child care in 1995 (1999, p. 329), but this average applies to almost no actual women, since those with children spend far more time caring for children than those without children. Similarly, Jonathan Gershuny reports that the average woman in the United States puts in about three hours per day in paid employment (Gershuny 2000, p. 172). Yet only a handful of women working part time actually fit this average, which includes a large number of women who are employed eight or more hours a day and another large number who do not work for pay at all.

The focus on averages across varied groups partly reflects the fact that time-diary studies generally rely on small samples, which makes trend analysis difficult for comparatively small but important groups, such as single mothers. And since U.S. time-use diaries provide information on only one day per person, the workweek must be constructed by averaging the experiences of different people. As a result, it is no surprise that time diary studies tend to report homogenized results.

Even if we consider the entire population, the evidence suggests that leisure has stopped growing and begun to decline in recent years. Liana Sayer (2001) reports that women's total working time—including paid work, housework, child care, shopping, and commuting—dropped from 480 minutes per day in 1965 to 430 minutes in 1975 and then rose to 507 minutes in 1998. Men also experienced an increase in working time, from 441 minutes per day in 1975 to 481 minutes in 1998, leaving them with only slightly less working time than the 491 minutes they put in during 1965. Over the last twenty-five years, the trend does not appear to be toward more leisure, and the overall change is not only quite small but actually rests on a 1965 baseline from a small and disputed survey.[8]

The fundamental point that needs to be understood is that the apparent increases in leisure stem from declines in housework rather than paid work (Bianchi et al. 2000). Time-diary researchers rightly insist that housework—including cooking, cleaning, and shopping—should be recognized as real, though unpaid, work.[9] Although child care is often treated as a separate activity, it is also lumped with housework when activities are divided into the four broad categories of paid work, unpaid work, personal care (including sleeping), and leisure.

Sayer reports that women devoted almost two fewer hours per day to housework in 1998 compared with 1965, while men increased their involvement in housework by an hour per day in the same period (Sayer 2001). The growth of leisure thus reflects a decline in women's attention to housework added onto a relatively unchanging paid workweek. Robinson and Schor focus on trends in two different types of work and thus reach different conclusions by touching different parts of the elephant.

The decline in housework, moreover, reflects shifts in the demographic composition of the population as well as changes in the behavior of people within various groups. As Robinson and Godbey note, some groups perform less housework than others. Single women, for example, do less housework than married women, and women and men without children do less than parents. Because the average age of marriage has increased, the age at first birth has increased, and the number of children per household has declined over the past thirty years, it is not surprising that overall time spent in housework would also decline (Cherlin 1992). It is also not only possible but likely that some families are postponing parenthood and having fewer children because work is so demanding (Robinson and Godbey 1999, p. 9; see also Gerson 1985). The extra time available to young adults without children may itself reflect a concession to the voracious demands of paid work.

From a life-cycle perspective, these demographic trends point to changes that give people more leisure time without reducing their time on the job or the demands that paid work entails. Parents, especially mothers, may feel a significant time crunch as the work of caring for children and the domestic household increases. The time crunch on parents may worsen even as more people postpone parenthood and so limit the amount of time spent in this life stage.

The decline in housework is noteworthy even if it does not provide an adequate solution to the problem of time squeezes. It may represent, as time-diary researchers suggest, a growing release from unsatisfying domestic chores as rising incomes allow families to purchase appliances that lighten housework and services that replace it. There may be much to recommend social and cultural changes that lessen the pressure to maintain a spotless home, but the decline in housework may reflect new pressures as well as liberation from earlier ones. Many working parents, for example, may still not have time to spend in domestic activities they deem important. Indeed, we will see in Chapter 5 that a large minority of workers report feeling so busy and drained from work that they are unable to keep their living space in order. It is important to pay attention to people's experience of time as well as to how they allocate it.

Demographic diversity means that leisure is not an evenly distributed resource, even if paid working time remains stable overall. Certain key groups (such as working parents) may experience time squeezes and a dearth of leisure, while other groups (such as young singles and empty nesters) may enjoy more time to spend as they choose. Even those who argue that leisure time has grown also acknowledge that working women and parents, and especially employed mothers, are spending a great deal of time engaged in either paid or unpaid work.

To understand the nature and scope of a growing time crunch, we need to look beyond national averages to focus on specific groups, such as working parents, who are the most likely to be pressed for time. When parents are placed at the center of attention, a strikingly different picture emerges. Sayer (2001) reports that total working time (paid plus unpaid work) for mothers was 504 minutes per day in 1965, declined to 463 minutes in 1975, and then rose to 547 minutes in 1998, while fathers' combined working time declined from 500 minutes in 1965 to 494 minutes in 1975 and then rose to 540 minutes in 1998.

Time-use studies have also found that parents are spending more, not less, time with their children, even though the average number of children per household has fallen. The time mothers devote to child care rose from an average of 87 minutes per day in 1965 to 104 minutes per day in 1998, while fathers' time went from 21 minutes to 57 minutes (Sayer 2001; see also Bianchi 2000). The growth in reported time parents spend with children may in part reflect a desire to conform to growing expectations for women to practice "intensive mothering" and for fathers to become more involved with their children (Hays 1997; Coltrane 1996; Gerson 1993). Even if these cultural injunctions prompt some people to inflate reported times, they still create a context that encourages most parents to devote much time and attention to their children.

These increases contradict concerns that employed parents, and especially working mothers, are spending insufficient time with their children. And these findings are more pronounced among the most educated, who as a group are also likely to be putting in the most hours at the workplace (Gershuny 2000). Time squeezes may create stresses and dilemmas for families, but parents appear to be making a strong effort to fit family time into their crowded lives.

People often find themselves "multitasking," and time spent with children is often divided time (Sayer 2001). When time diaries ask people "what else were you doing" in addition to the primary activity, the time pressures on working parents emerge more clearly. In 1975, parents spent between 30 and 40 percent of their time with children doing something else as well. By 1998, mothers spent nearly 70 percent of their time with children and fathers spent 63 percent of such time engaged in other activities (Sayer 2001, Table 7.3, p. 222). Being rushed appears to be one of the leading complaints children have about their parents (Galinsky 1999).

Although time diaries do not chart parents' feelings, multitasking provides a clue to the ways that they feel pulled in several directions at once. Cooking dinner while talking to a child about the school day, perhaps with the television on in the background, may be perceived as either a relaxing start to the evening or a harried conclusion to a difficult day. In either case, having respondents simply record the time devoted to one "main" activity is not all we need to know.[10]

Time diaries therefore offer useful information, but they do not readily answer some important questions. Their small samples make it difficult to chart trends for specific groups that may be especially vulnerable to time squeezes, such as single mothers. They do not tap how intensely people work nor how people feel as they conduct their varied activities.[11] Observational and other studies indicate, for example, that women are not only more likely than men to spend time with their children; they are also more likely to take primary responsibility for housework, parenting, and arranging child care (Lareau 2000; see also Peterson and Gerson 1992).

Most important, most time diaries rely on information for a single day and must thus create a "synthetic week" by combining the experiences of seven different people, including five who report on a weekday and two who report on a weekend day (see Gershuny 2000 for some exceptions).[12] These weekly averages generated from daily diaries of different individuals do not provide a picture of a week in the life of an individual or a couple. Nor can they tell us who is likely to put in an especially long or an especially short workweek. We thus need to be careful about drawing definitive conclusions from this information alone.

In addition, because analyses of time-diary studies tend to focus on national averages, they do not provide a more complex map of the social and demographic geography of time use. This variety can only be gleaned by paying attention to groups whose experiences of work and leisure are likely to differ in important ways. Adopting such a lens makes it clear that while the *average* workweek has not changed significantly, notable shifts have occurred in the distribution of working time across particular groups of workers.

To fully understand changes in work and leisure time, we must also focus on households as well as individuals. Even if the average in individual working time has not changed, the shift from single-breadwinner to dual-income households means that couples may experience a marked increase in the length of their shared workweek.[13] The growth of single-parent homes, most headed by mothers, also points to the emergence of a time crunch. Whether or not single mothers are working longer days, the absence of an unpaid worker at home leaves them pressed for time and overburdened. And even if dual-earning couples and single parents are not significantly more pressed for time than they were thirty years ago, they now represent a much larger proportion of American families and households.

Debates about whether work or leisure has expanded therefore cannot be resolved by pointing to "the average American." It is entirely possible for leisure to have grown for some groups—especially those at the beginning and end of their work careers—while contracting for others. It is also possible for some groups—especially those in their peak years of family building—to experience severe time crunches even without a significant rise in time spent at paid work. We thus need to focus on the vast diversity in the circumstances of American workers.

Trends in the Workweek since 1970

There is little doubt that workers are facing new and unprecedented challenges in meeting the demands of family and work. The transformation of family structure and household composition in the closing decades of the twentieth century have clearly created a significant time bind for many workers. This time squeeze is both less general and more varied than overarching arguments about national trends have implied. To understand the dynamics of change and its diverse consequences, we need to examine the full range of situations among a varied group of workers.

The *Current Population Survey* measures working time in several ways, including average weekly working time for the job (or jobs) held the previous week and average time spent at work in the prior year. The question "How many hours did you usually work per week in the job (or jobs) held last week?" makes it possible to ascertain a current job's time demands. To make certain that including time at all jobs held in a year does not produce appreciably different results than focusing on time at a current job, we also looked at time spent at work in the prior year.[14]

Figure 1.4 presents the full distribution of working time in 1970 and 2000 for men and women. While the forty-hour workweek remains the modal pattern, with just over 40 percent of both men and women reporting working this amount of time in 2000, it has become less typical than it was thirty years ago. For men and women alike, the forty-hour standard has declined by about 10 percentage points, with increases at both the higher and lower ends of the spectrum. (See Rones, Ilg, and Gardner 1997 for additional evidence of the growing dispersion in working time.) Choosing different years for comparison produces only a small increase or a small decline. There is, in sum, little support for the notion that there has been a general and markedly upward trend in the length of the average workweek.

If it seems surprising that the average length of the workweek has remained largely unchanged since 1970, it is important to remember that this apparent stability masks some important shifts. Variation around the average has increased, marking the emergence of both longer and shorter workweeks for different groups of workers.[15]

Table 1.2 compares working time in 1970 and 2000 for nonfarm wage and salary workers employed for at least one hour in the survey week. We use the standard of fifty hours per week to illustrate the prevalence of long workweeks, which can constrain the amount of time families have to spend together. A fifty-hour workweek, for example, translates into ten-hour days on the job each day for a five-day workweek. If one adds a half hour for lunch and the average forty-five-minute round-trip commute that Americans generally have, the day stretches to more than eleven hours. That might mean leaving for work at 7:00 A.M. and not returning home until 6:00 P.M. Being home to send a child off to school is challenging under this schedule, and of course it would be impossible to be home when a child returns from school. Few after-school programs run as late as 6:00 P.M. While many day-care centers are open from 7:00 A.M. until 6:00 P.M., few parents would want to leave their young children at day care for that long a day. Live-in nannies give working parents more leeway in their schedules, but even for professional couples this remains an expensive and

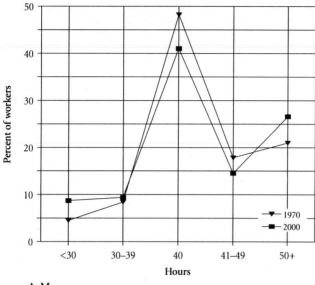

A. Men

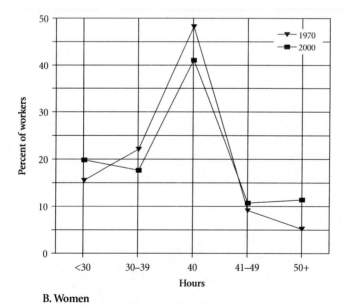

B. Women

Figure 1.4 Hours worked per week, 1970 and 2000. A: Men. B: Women. (*Source: Current Population Survey*)

Table 1.2 Total hours worked, by education, occupation, age, marital status, and gender

	Men			Women		
	Mean hours last week, all jobs	Percent < 30 hours	Percent 50+ hours	Mean hours last week, all jobs	Percent < 30 hours	Percent 50+ hours
Total, 1970	43.5	4.5	21.0	37.0	15.5	5.2
Total, 2000	43.1	8.6	26.5	37.1	19.6	11.3
Selected groups, 2000						
Occupations						
Managerial, professional, technical	45.6	5.8	37.2	39.4	14.8	17.1
Other	41.8	10.0	21.3	35.7	22.4	8.0
Education						
Less than high school	38.8	15.2	13.5	34.5	24.9	5.3
High school graduate	42.6	7.1	21.5	36.7	18.7	8.0
Some college	42.2	11.1	24.8	36.0	22.5	9.3
College graduate	46.0	5.3	38.8	39.5	15.6	19.5
Race						
White	43.6	8.5	29.2	36.8	21.1	12.1
Black	41.5	9.6	19.3	38.2	13.8	10.1
Hispanic	41.2	8.2	17.0	36.9	17.0	6.6
Asian American	41.5	9.6	21.7	37.6	18.0	12.0

Source: Current Population Survey (CPS).

undesirable option. A fifty-hour workweek thus is difficult for working parents to reconcile with the standard daily schedule of children.

These comparisons point to the general stability in the average work-week, but they also show that the percentage of men and women working longer and shorter workweeks has grown during the same period. In 2000, over one quarter of men (26.5 percent) worked fifty hours per week or more, up from just over one in five (21.0 percent) in 1970. The rise in long weeks is more pronounced for employed women, for whom the proportion working fifty hours or more per week rose to more than one in ten (11.3 percent) from 5.2 percent in 1970. At the other extreme, almost one in ten employed men (8.6 percent) worked thirty hours per week or less in 2000, compared to 4.5 percent in 1970, while about one fifth of working women (19.6 percent) were employed for thirty hours or less, compared with 15.5 percent in 1970. While the average workweek may not have expanded, a modest but growing bifurcation of working time has developed among workers.

Long days on the job impinge on family time. Of those working fifty hours or more per week, about half (49.5 percent) regularly work on the weekends. In addition, 15 percent report that they usually work seven days per week, with the rest reporting one weekend day as part of their usual schedule. A majority (52.2 percent) of men working fifty or more hours per week report working on the weekends. Women, in contrast, are more likely to try to confine their time on the job to weekdays, with "only" 42.4 percent of those working fifty-plus hours coming in on the weekends.[16]

Who are most likely to work especially long weeks? Table 1.2 shows that long workweeks are most common among professionals and managers. Over one in three men (37.2 percent) who work in professional, technical, or managerial occupations work fifty hours or more per week, compared to one in five (21.3 percent) in other occupations. For women, the comparable figures are one in six for professional and managerial positions versus less than one in fourteen for other occupations.

These occupational differences can also be seen in sharply graded educational differences, again as shown in Table 1.2. Nearly two in five American men with four or more years of college work fifty hours per week or more, compared to around one in eight men with less than a high school degree. Among women, nearly one in five of the college-educated work fifty or more hours per week, compared to around one in twenty of those with less than a high school degree. While more educated workers are more likely to participate in national discussions about the contours of working time, they actually represent only one part of a larger and more complex puzzle about transformations in work commitment. Their experiences are just one aspect, albeit an important one, of a labor force that is growing increasingly segmented (Coleman and Pencavel 1993a, 1993b; (U.S. Bureau of Labor Statistics 2000; Wilensky 1963).[17]

It is important to note that while highly educated men and women are most likely to work long weeks, people in other occupations with less education nonetheless comprise the majority of such workers. Overall, professionals and managers represent just under half (45.7 percent) of all fifty-hour workers (results not shown in table). But since they comprise roughly one third (32.0 percent) of the labor force, they are clearly overrepresented among the "overworked." Similarly, 43.7 percent of those working fifty or more hours a week have a college degree, far more than the 28.3 percent of the labor force comprised by this group.

It is tempting to see these educational and occupational differences as a straightforward reflection of the richer rewards given to those with advanced degrees (Freeman and Bell 1995). From this perspective, the dispersion of working time reflects the tremendous inequalities in income opportunities. In what has been characterized as a "winner take all" economy (Frank 1995), highly educated workers certainly stand to gain more by working longer weeks.

Yet many forces are promoting a bifurcation of working time, and it would be dangerously misleading to attribute all of the difference to matters of personal taste and choice—a view implying that the longer work schedules of the highly educated represent neither a mystery nor a social problem. Personal taste may play a part, but there are strong reasons to conclude that this difference between the overworked and the underworked is far more than a simple reflection of workers' preferences. We show later, for example, that many with long workweeks would prefer to work less, while many with short workweeks would prefer to work more. (See Chapter 3 for a full discussion of the gap between worker realities and preferences.) International comparisons, moreover, reveal that these educational differences are not consistent across countries, and these differences are not the greatest in the countries with the most income inequality.

The growing bifurcation of working time also reflects structural incentives and constraints that make it appealing for employers to divide the labor force. Labor legislation that distinguishes between "exempt" and "nonexempt" workers contributes to the long workweeks of professionals and managers, who are rarely unionized and typically not protected by the provisions of the Fair Labor Standards Act of 1938. Because employers are not required to pay overtime to professionals who work more than forty hours per week, and because extra hours of work by exempt employees do not cost additional wages at all, employers face no strong incentive to limit such workers to a forty-hour workweek.

The structure and distribution of benefits, such as health care and other services, also give employers incentives to divide the labor force. By hiring part-time workers with no benefits and simultaneously pressuring some full-time employees—especially salaried workers—to work longer hours, work organizations can lower their total compensation costs. The unintended consequence of these cost-limiting strategies is a division of the work force into those putting in very long workweeks and those putting in relatively short ones. As the cost of benefits has become an increasing portion of an employer's total compensation expense, such considerations are likely to influence the way jobs are structured. In sum, it is neither possible nor convincing to attribute the growing time divide among American workers simply to purely personal, private preferences. A set of institutional arrangements also gives employers strong incentives to treat workers in different occupational niches differently.

The racial breakdowns in Table 1.2 show small differences that differ for men and women. White men work two hours more per week on average than do black, Hispanic, and Asian American men, and the differences are more pronounced among those working fifty hours per week or more. White women trail Asian American and black women by two and one hours, respectively, and put in about the same number of hours per week on the job as do their Hispanic counterparts. White women are more likely to work part-time, but they are also more likely to put in long workweeks compared to black and Hispanic women.

The differences between white men and their black and Hispanic counterparts narrow roughly one hour per week when education, age, occupation, and marital and parental status are taken into account, but these differentials in working time are not completely erased (see Table 1.3). The shorter workweeks of Asian American men are not completely due to differences in these attributes of workers and their jobs.

For women, the story is reversed. When these factors are taken into account, the difference between groups grows. Among those similar in age,

Table 1.3 Race and ethnic differentials, 2000

Race	Mean hours		Odds of working 50 hours +		Odds of working less than 30 hours	
	Uncontrolled	Controlled	Uncontrolled	Controlled	Uncontrolled	Controlled
Men						
Black	−2.06*	−1.15*	.573*	.746*	1.094	1.069
Hispanic	−2.55*	−1.61*	.459*	.619*	.963	.991
Asian American	−2.01*	−1.78*	.665*	.617*	1.177	.965
White	—	—	—	—	—	—
Women						
Black	1.47*	1.58*	.807*	.869	.584*	.545*
Hispanic	0.06	1.16*	.526*	.804*	.754*	.638*
Asian American	1.13*	1.99*	1.118	1.188	.750*	.629*
White	—	—	—	—	—	—

Source: Current Population Survey.

* $p < .05$

educational background, marital status, and occupational position, white women work one to two hours less per week than do their minority female counterparts. Since they are more likely to be highly educated and to hold professional and managerial positions where working days are longest, white women might be expected to work longer weeks. Their higher participation in part-time work, however, offsets this effect and lowers their overall average.[18]

Although the average American workweek has not changed dramatically over the past several decades, a growing group of Americans are clearly, and strongly, pressed for time. These workers include employees who are putting in especially long days at work each week, often against their desire, and people in dual-earner and single-parent families who cannot rely on a support system anchored by a nonemployed member. The intransigence in the structure of work and the rise of highly demanding jobs, especially at the upper levels of the occupational hierarchy, present dilemmas and problems for many workers. And, increasingly, women and men alike face challenging work without the traditional, unpaid spouses once taken for granted by husbands in upwardly mobile careers and highly demanding jobs. Yet employers have not readily responded to these changed realities, assuming that devoted workers have—or should have—unpaid partners who are home full-time to take care of the many domestic tasks on which not only family life but successful careers and secure communities depend. In the context of these dramatic social shifts in Americans' private lives, it is no surprise that many Americans feel that they are squeezed for time and working more than ever.

A "time bind" has clearly emerged in the contemporary United States. It is, however, rooted as much in the changing nature of family life and women's commitments as in the expansion of working time for individuals. Working parents in dual-earner and single-parent households have always faced a time bind, and the principal change over the past thirty years has been a marked growth in the number of people living in these family situations. The time squeeze created by spending more hours at paid work is, moreover, not universal, but rather is concentrated among professionals and managers, who are especially likely to shape the terms of public discussion and debate. Although there are also less affluent workers who put in substantial overtime or who work at two (or more) jobs, this group represents a smaller proportion of blue-collar workers than do overworked

Americans who are professionals and managers. These trends suggest that while it is important to address the new challenges and insecurities facing American workers and their families, we should be careful to move beyond generalizations to focus on the variety of dilemmas workers are encountering.

2

Working Time from the Perspective of Families

While debates over the growth of work-family conflict tend to center on the experiences of employed parents and dual-earner couples, analyses of trends in working time typically focus on individual workers. This chapter takes a closer look at families and households; instead of individuals, we look at the combined working time of all adult family members.

Families Rather Than Individuals

Focusing on families rather than individuals provides a fuller, potentially more fruitful lens for making sense of the changing balance of paid work, family work, and leisure time.[1] Certainly dual-earner couples, especially those with children, and single-parent families are the most likely to feel squeezed between the demands and rewards of work and the needs of family life. Single parents, who are predominantly mothers, are likely to experience even greater time squeezes than are dual-earner couples, who can call on each other for help, at least to some degree. What links these two types of households is not the amount of working time *per se* but rather the common ground they share: neither can rely on an unpaid caretaker at home. The experiences of these groups are at the core of the debate over the causes and consequences of work-family conflict.

Given their importance, overall trends and variations in how dual-earner couples jointly allocate time between work and other activities have received surprisingly little attention. While numerous studies have offered detailed examinations of the time couples allocate to housework and related domestic tasks, relatively few have focused on the amount of time dual-earner couples jointly devote to paid work.[2] And even fewer have investigated single-parent homes, where there is no adult partner with whom to share household tasks.

Most analysts argue that the rise of work-family conflict reflects an increase in the amount of time individuals are working; a focus on the combined hours of employed couples, however, points to a different explanation. If more members of a family are in the labor force (or, alternatively, fewer are available at home), each family member is more likely to feel squeezed between home and work. A rise in the proportion of households with either two earners or one parent can thus create new time binds among more people even if the average time individuals spend working has not increased. Dual-earner couples in 1970 may have felt similar time pressures, but there were simply far fewer such couples than there are today. As two-income households have become the norm, a once unusual experience has become typical.

Because, as we have seen, there are good reasons to doubt dramatic changes in the average length of the individual workweek (even if some workers are putting in very long weeks), the widespread transformation in households has likely played a larger role in fueling the growth of time binds across a broad range of workers. We know little, however, about the relative importance of family versus workplace change in the lives of workers, and we know even less about how these changes vary across the labor force. Has the combined working time for couples increased? How does working time vary among couples, and how has it changed?

Measuring Couples' Working Time

To answer these questions, we turn again to the *Current Population Survey* to compare working time in 1970 and 2000.[3] We looked at married couples in which both spouses were between the ages of 18 and 64.[4] And although many studies focus only on wage and salary workers, we included the self-employed as well. Our concern is with working time, not with the employer-employee relationship, so there is no reason to exclude self-employed workers who face similar time constraints. We did, however, exclude agricultural workers, since the organization of working time on farms differs in fundamental ways from the structure of work in other employment settings. It would be misleading to allow the historical decline in the size of the agricultural sector to overshadow other, more significant trends.

We divided couples into four exhaustive and mutually exclusive categories: dual-earner couples, male-breadwinner couples, female-breadwinner couples, and couples with neither spouse employed. Couples were assigned to one of these four groups according to whether each spouse had worked at least one hour in the previous week. For each spouse, we ascertained his or her education and age, and for each household, we also considered the number and ages of children in the family.[5] We analyzed households headed by single mothers and single fathers similarly.

Trends in Working Time among Different Types of Households

To understand the changes in working time that families have experienced, we need to know what changes have occurred in the distribution of types of households as well as how working time has changed for different kinds of households. Table 2.1 sheds light on both of these matters. First, it compares the proportion of American couples living in each of the four types of families—dual earner, male breadwinner, female breadwinner, and neither employed—in 1970 and 2000. Not surprisingly, these comparisons show a marked shift from the male-breadwinner family of mid-century to the dual-earner couple that predominated by the end of the century. In 1970, the male breadwinner remained the modal type among couples, with 51.4 percent of couples falling into this category. In contrast, husbands and wives were both employed in just over one third (35.9 percent) of married couples. By 2000, however, dual-earner couples represented a solid majority (59.6 percent) of married couples. In the context of this family transformation, it is no mystery that integrating work and the rest of life has emerged as a major social concern.

While it is clear that dual-earner and single-parent families have replaced the male-breadwinner model in both numbers and social significance, it is less clear that working time within these different household arrangements has also shifted. To understand this aspect of the process of change, Table 2.1 also compares the number of hours devoted to paid employment for each type of couple. Among all couples, paid working time performed by both husband and wife rose from 52.5 hours per week in 1970 to 63.1 hours per week in 2000—a substantial increase, to be sure. In addition, the proportion of families working very long workweeks (100 hours per week or more) tripled, from 3.1 percent to 9.3 percent of all couples (not shown in table). As a group, married couples clearly have less time away from paid work today than they did three decades ago.

Table 2.1 Trends in joint hours of paid work by husbands and wives, 1970 and 2000, non-farm married couples aged 18–64

	1970				2000			
	% of couples	Mean hours last week, all jobs	Husband's hours	Wife's hours	% of couples	Mean hours last week, all jobs	Husband's hours	Wife's hours
Total (all couples)		52.5	38.9	13.6		63.1	41.5	26.4
Both work	35.9%	78.0	44.1	33.9	59.6%	81.6	45.0	36.6
Husband only	51.4%	44.4	44.0	0.0	26.0%	44.9	44.9	0.0
Wife only	4.6%	35.5	0.0	35.5	7.1%	37.2	0.0	37.2
Neither works	8.2%	0.0	0.0	0.0	7.2%	0.0	0.0	0.0
Wife's education								
College grad.	20.2%	81.2	45.8	35.4	31.3%	83.3	45.9	37.3
Some college	18.1%	77.0	44.5	32.6	30.2%	81.3	45.2	36.0
H.S. grad.	16.4%	77.6	44.0	33.6	31.5%	80.8	44.4	36.4
< H.S. grad.	15.9%	77.8	43.5	34.3	7.0%	78.3	41.8	36.5
Children								
None ≤ 18	33.4%	79.5	43.2	36.4	42.7%	83.5	44.7	38.8
Some ≤ 18	66.6%	76.9	44.8	32.1	57.3%	80.2	45.2	34.9
1 ≤ 18	23.6%	78.3	44.3	34.0	22.5%	81.1	44.8	36.3
2 ≤ 18	21.0%	76.5	45.1	31.4	24.1%	80.0	45.5	34.5
3+ ≤ 18	22.0%	75.9	45.1	30.8	10.7%	78.4	45.4	33.0

Source: Current Population Survey, 1970, 2000.

A closer look, however, reveals that the growth of working time among married couples cannot be traced to significant increases in working time for each household type. It is instead a consequence of the expansion in the overall proportion of couples that fit the dual-earner pattern. The smallest changes occurred among male-breadwinner couples. By 2000, these "traditional" households were putting in 44.9 hours per week on average on the job, a slight increase from the 44.4 hours these husbands averaged in 1970.

Working time for women who act as sole breadwinners in intact marriages also grew only slightly, rising from an average of 35.5 hours a week in 1970 to 37.2 in 2000. More important, over this same period, sole female breadwinners in married-couple households remained a small minority of married couples. The influx of wives into the labor force did not induce many husbands to stay home, but rather increased the number of earners in most families.

If dual-earner couples constitute the fastest-growing household type, they also show the largest increase in working time. Husbands and wives in these marriages jointly devoted 81.6 hours per week in paid employment, up just over three hours per week from the 78.0 hours per week reported in 1970. The proportion reporting very long workweeks also rose sharply, from 8.7 to 14.5 percent (not shown on table). The major cause of this growth in the combined working time for dual-earner couples is the increase in wives' paid working time. While husbands' mean hours at work rose by only 0.9 hours during this period, wives' time work rose by 2.7 hours (36.6 hours per week in 2000 versus 33.9 in 1970). The relative emphasis in paid working time between husbands and wives thus also shifted during this period as wives became more strongly committed to work outside the home.

Two components thus account for changes in the working time of couples: shifts in the distribution of marriages across various family types and changes in the working time of individuals in the same types of marriages. But what is the proportional effect of each? Increases in the total amount of time dual-earning couples are working contributes to some of the rise, but the major influence is the fact that two-earner families account for more households. If, for example, we hold joint working time constant at 1970 levels for each marriage type and substitute the 2000 distribution of marriage types, the total working time for married individuals would have risen from 52.5 to 60.5 hours. Put differently, of the 10.3 additional hours worked in 2000 by all couples, 8 can be attributed to the shift from single-earner to dual-earner couples. In percentage terms, over three quarters (77.7 percent) of the growth in working time among married couples is due to the growth of dual-earner households, while the remaining quarter (22.3 percent) represents an increase in couples' working time, particularly among dual-earner couples. Thus, although there has been a slight increase in the total amount of time dual-earner couples devote to work, the principal source of change has been the rise in the proportion of couples who fit the dual-earner pattern. Actual increases in the paid working time of couples are real, but they are also modest compared to the sharp growth in the size of this group.

A growing number also appear to be putting in extremely long workweeks—one hundred hours or more. These couples are clearly working longer than their historical predecessors and are certainly likely to feel overworked and squeezed for time. Yet they do not represent the average. The fundamental point is that even dual-earner couples with typical workweeks are—and have always been—stretched thin.

The major change of the last generation has been a dramatic growth in the number of people whose families depend on women's earnings (whether or not they depend on a man's earnings as well) rather than a basic shift in the working time of individual workers. If there is scant evidence for a general shift in the relative balance between work and family among couples in which both partners work, the rise of widespread work-family conflict has a more straightforward explanation: the rise of women's employment and the demographic transformation of family life, with little in the way of countervailing shifts in the time men spend away from the job or the way that jobs are organized.

Accounting for Working Time across Couples

Although dual-earner couples as a group show only a small increase in their average working time, the number of couples whose joint work hours are very high has grown precipitously. Who are the couples putting in so much time at work, and how do they compare to others? Do they face more difficult circumstances because they are juggling child rearing with very long work hours, or are they more likely to be working long hours because children are less likely to be present in the home? To answer these questions, we need to understand how and why couples allocate their time in different ways. Do important social dimensions, such as education, occupation, and child situation, help explain why some couples put in very long hours and others do not?

Understanding work commitment for individuals provides clues to understanding households as well. Studies have found, for example, that demographic factors such as education, age, and the number of children help account for who is spending more or less time at paid work. Those with more education are likely to work longer weeks, as we saw in Chapter 1. Working time also tends to peak for workers between the ages of thirty and fifty-five, with older and younger workers putting in less time. Having children makes a difference, too, especially for women. While having children at home makes relatively little difference in men's paid working time, it tends to pull women away from long workweeks.

If these insights about individuals also apply to households, it is reasonable to find that working time has grown as the general educational levels have increased, the aging of the baby boom generation has placed a large fraction of workers at the height of their working years, and family size has declined. Taken together, these large-scale demographic trends provide powerful forces that have pushed more people toward increased work commitments.

Do these demographic forces explain changes in couples' joint paid working time? Table 2.1 makes it clear that the growth in working time has been concentrated among couples with the most education. Couples in which the wife had completed four years of college were working 2.1 hours more in 2000 than in 1970, while couples in which the husband had not completed high school were working 0.5 hours more.[6] A 3.4 hour difference in favor of the most educated couples in 1970 grew to become a 5.0 hour difference by 2000.[7] These changes principally reflect the growing hours of working women. Employed wives with at least some college increased their working hours by nearly two hours per week during this period.

Although some families are putting in more time at work than did their counterparts several decades ago, this trend appears to be modest. It is sharpest among one group—couples in which the combined working time of both workers adds up to a very long workweek. Since these couples are more likely to be highly educated, they occupy a disproportionate share of high-profile occupational positions among professionals and managers. The high visibility of this group has no doubt enhanced the national attention given to the problem of overwork.

Whether measured as a rise in the proportion of couples that consist of two earners or as a rise in the amount of time such couples are devoting to paid work, the growing work commitment of married women is the major cause of increases in married couples' working time. And since married men's working time has remained fairly stable or at most grown modestly, women's movement out of the home has not been offset by a comparable shift away from paid work among men. In this context, it is not necessary to postulate a dramatic increase in the working time of individual workers to understand why families feel squeezed. The gender transformations of the late twentieth century have propelled women into the world of paid work without providing new supports for the unpaid domestic work that earlier generations counted on wives and mothers to perform.

Explaining Changes among Dual-Earner Couples

The rapid growth of dual-earner households is the major cause of the rise of paid working time in families, but an absolute increase of roughly three hours per week has also contributed to growing time squeezes and work-family conflicts. Yet it is not clear why this absolute rise in working time has occurred. Do these longer hours stem from changes in the characteristics and orientation of the people who are working, or do they reflect changes in the nature of the jobs people hold?

A closer look at dual-earner couples and their circumstances helps untangle these forces. Table A.1 in the Appendix presents a simple model of working time for dual-earner couples, in which the basic demographic factors of age, number of children, education, and occupation for both husbands and wives accounts for two thirds of the increase in working time from 1970 to 2000.[8] This means that the three-hour increase in working time is due largely to changes in the kind of people who have become dual earners. Compared to their peers in 1970, dual-earner couples in 2000 are slightly older, more likely to have a college degree, more likely to be in managerial occupations, and have fewer children under age eighteen. Once these changes are taken into account, the growth in time on the job is reduced to just over one hour per week. This model cannot account for much of the variation among workers' time on the job, but it does account for most of the change that occurred during this period.[9]

Changes in both working time and household arrangements thus appear to be intertwined with other social and economic shifts. Dual-earner couples increasingly consist of comparatively older and better educated workers who hold relatively well rewarded positions. The growing time divide among workers is linked to other social and economic divisions that separate workers by education, occupation, and economic opportunity as well. Those putting in longer workweeks may face time squeezes and domestic conundrums, but those putting in shorter ones likely face other difficulties, such as insufficient income and blocked work opportunities. If so, then working time is linked to other social and economic inequalities, and overwork is only one among a more complicated set of economic and demographic shifts.

Dual-Earner Parents and Working Time

If families' working time is expanding, the greatest concern centers on the potential consequences for children. It is thus important to know to what extent those putting in long days on the job are also juggling work demands with parenting and child rearing. Have couples with children at home increased their combined working time, or are they more likely to be cutting back from paid work in order to care for their children?

To answer this question, Table 2.1 presents trends in the hours of paid employment for working couples with and without children. In 2000, dual-income parents worked 3.3 hours less per week than did couples without children, a difference only slightly greater than the 2.6 hours that separated working parents and childless couples in 1970. Working hours also declined slightly as the number of children increased. For those with one child under 18 in 2000, couples worked an average of 81.1 hours per week; those with three or more children worked 78.4 hours.

The reduced time among working parents is not gender neutral, however. Working hours for husbands actually increase slightly with the presence of children and as the number of children rises. The overall drop in working time among couples with children thus primarily reflects reduced working time among mothers. In 2000, fathers with three or more children worked 0.7 hours per week more than did husbands without children, while mothers with three or more children worked 5.8 fewer hours per week than married women without children. These differences are not substantially different than the situation in 1970, when fathers with three or more children worked 1.9 hours more than their childless counterparts, and mothers with three or more children worked 5.6 hours less. For those couples with one or two children (who account for most dual-earner parents), the patterns are similar, but the differences are generally smaller.

To examine the situation of employed parents more carefully, Figure 2.1 presents trends in paid working hours among dual-earner parents. Compared with 1970, fewer couples in 2000 can be found concentrated around the 80-hour average. Instead, more couples are located at each end of the spectrum, working either notably long or notably short hours. For couples no less than individuals, therefore, the historical trend points toward greater diversity and bifurcation among workweeks.

The combined working time of dual-earner parents is slightly less than that of childless couples, but the degree of change over time is slightly larger. Between 1970 and 2000, the joint hours in paid employment of working couples increased by about 4 hours for those with children and by 3.3 hours for those without. The percentage of couples putting in very long workweeks (one hundred hours or more) rose for both groups, but the rise was less pronounced for parents in both absolute and percentage terms. The percentage of childless couples working at least a hundred hours a week rose from 9.5 to 17.5 percent, while the percentage of working couples with children rose from 8.2 to 12.2 percent (not shown in table). Again, the trend toward more time at work holds for parents as well as for

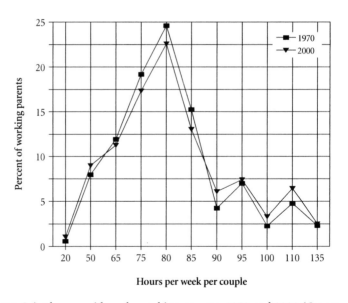

Figure 2.1 Joint hours paid work, working parents, 1970 and 2000 (*Source: Current Population Survey*)

couples without children at home, but it appears to be less pronounced for those with the largest family obligations.

The transformation from male-breadwinner to dual-earner marriages has not extinguished gender differences in the work consequences of parenthood. The arrival of children still tends to push men toward stronger work participation while pulling women toward somewhat less involvement, creating a larger gender gap in their level of work commitment compared to childless couples. These differences are nonetheless greatly attenuated compared to the once dominant pattern in which women withdrew altogether from paid work when children arrived. While the transition to parenthood continues to have different consequences for women and men, the magnitude of this difference is diminishing.

Whatever may be fueling the rise in working time, it is not concentrated among parents. The move toward more work involvement, whether among women or men, thus does not appear to reflect a desire among parents to escape the contemporary difficulties of rearing children. To the contrary, employed mothers continue to spend less time at the workplace than their childless peers, and employed fathers today do not spend substantially more time at work than men who are not fathers.

Single parents, who are overwhelmingly mothers, constitute another growing group. Over one fifth (21.9 percent) of families were headed by women in 2000, more than double the 1970 percentage (9.9 percent) (U.S. Bureau of the Census 2002). These parents are truly caught in a time bind: they need to work as much as possible to support their families and also need to spend as much time as possible with their children.

How do single mothers balance these competing demands? Figure 2.2 demonstrates that here too the story is one of greater diversity in working time rather than a shift toward a longer workweek. The proportion of single mothers working the modal forty hours has declined by nearly ten percentage points (from 45.3 to 37.4 percent), while increases have occurred at both the high and low ends of the scale. And even though the percentage of families living in these circumstances increased, their average workweek remained unchanged, at 38.5 hours per week in both 1970 and 2000.

Single fathers remain a much smaller group than single mothers (albeit a rapidly growing one). The proportion of families headed by single fathers doubled, from 1.2 percent in 1970 to 2.4 percent in 2000 (U.S. Bureau of the Census 2002). Single fathers doubtless face the same time dilemmas as single mothers do. Single dads in fact work just about the same average

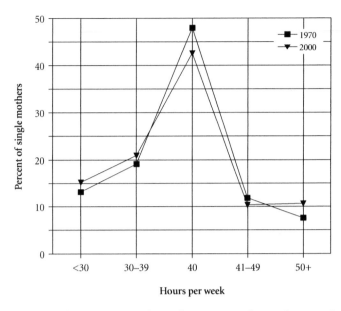

Figure 2.2 Hours of paid work, single mothers, 1970 and 2000 (*Source: Current Population Survey*)

number of hours a week as do single moms—36.8 hours per week for single fathers in 2000, a drop of two hours since 1970. The range of working time has grown for single fathers, as it has for the other groups. Being a single parent poses a daunting time challenge, which neither mothers nor fathers can escape.

To clarify the causes and contours of changes in working time, we believe the focus should be on whole families rather than on individual workers. This perspective makes clear that overall increases in working time reflect changes in family composition, especially the growth of dual-earner couples and single parents, rather than steep rises in the time individual workers spend at their paid jobs. Although we have not emphasized single parents, we have no doubt that their time binds are likely to be as high as—or higher than—those of dual-earning couples even if they do not spend especially long hours at work. And while overall changes in working time are modest, the last several decades have witnessed the emergence of a segment of employed couples who are putting in very long workweeks of a hundred hours or more. These couples are more likely to be highly educated workers, who tend to occupy the most visible and prestigious jobs and occupations. Finally, while parents do not appear to be putting in more time at work than other groups, a gender divide persists between fathers, who tend to work more than their childless counterparts, and mothers, who tend to work less.

The implications for family welfare and gender equality are worth noting. Rising time deficits stem from transformations in family composition and gender relations, which in turn reflect basic social-structural and economic changes. Developments such as the erosion of the single-income "family wage" and the growth of women's commitment to an adulthood not confined to the home are deeply rooted and apparently irreversible. They do not, however, indicate that parents prefer work over family life, but suggest instead that new generations are seeking a balance between home and work that remains elusive.

The central problem caused by this family and gender transformation can be better understood by comparing the major changes in women's lives with the more intransigent situation for men, whose work commitments have remained comparatively stable and whose domestic involvement has not increased sufficiently to offset women's rising work commitment. This situation has left dual-earning families to cope with persisting family demands in the context of rising work obligations, and it has left employed single mothers facing even greater time squeezes.

The future of families' and children's well-being will depend on developing policies that accept the irreversibility of this demographic transition. There is, to be sure, much to welcome in these changes. Women's expanded opportunities have benefited both women and their families in myriad ways. When a mother works, average annual household income rises by $10,000 per child in a two-parent home, and by $11,000 in a single-parent home.[10] These earnings provide families with important and often essential economic resources. And nonmaterial benefits, such as enhanced marital satisfaction, can be added to the obvious financial ones. Rosalind Barnett and Caryl Rivers (1996) find that dual-earning couples are, in their words, "happier, healthier, and better off." As Rosanna Hertz (1986) shows, they are also likely to be more equal. And despite the concern over children's welfare, it is increasingly clear that children also derive benefits from having an employed mother.[11] The good news about women's employment should not, however, blind us to the dilemmas that emerge when arrangements at work are slower to change. Dual-earning and single-parent families, in particular, face considerable challenges and need often elusive supports.

Unfortunately, the full incorporation of women, especially mothers, into the world of paid work continues to evoke ambivalence. One recent survey found, for example, that close to half of all of Americans (48 percent) believe that preschoolers suffer if their mothers work (National Opinion Research Center 2002). Another, conducted by the Families and Work Institute, found that even among employed parents, more than two out of five (42 percent) are concerned that many working mothers care more about succeeding at work than meeting their children's needs (Galinsky 1999, p. 11). Despite families' rising work pressures, cultural pressures for "intensive mothering" persist (Hays 1997). Whether or not they hold a paid job, mothers face conflicting social expectations that are difficult to meet. These cultural and political contradictions take an especially ironic turn in the push to require poor single mothers with dim employment prospects to work at a paid job while continuing to castigate middle-class mothers with better job opportunities for spending too much time in paid employment.

To a lesser but still important degree, fathers also face intensifying cross-pressures. Despite the erosion of the male "breadwinner wage," which leaves households increasingly in need of women's earnings (Levy 1999), men face significant barriers to family involvement. Resistance continues to greet individual fathers who want to spend less time at work to care for children. For all the attention focused on employed mothers, social policies that would help bring men more fully into the work of parenting get limited notice or support.

Employed parents and other workers must also contend with high expectations about how to spend their time on the job. Even as family time has become squeezed, competitive workplaces may be creating rising pressures at the office. Time at work is clearly important, but it is not the whole story. The structure of jobs and the organization of time also matters, even for those workers putting in the same number of hours.

In short, whether they are mothers or fathers, parents who aspire to balance and share the important work of earning a living and caring for a new generation face clashing, potentially irreconcilable expectations and demands. We believe that the pressures facing American families today stem not from too much change but from too little. Despite women's growing need and desire to build a life beyond the domestic sphere, it has proven difficult to overcome the "stalled revolution" that leaves women facing blocked opportunities at work and men with more limited involvement at home (Hochschild 1989). Ultimately, the problem of family time deficits cannot be solved by chastising parents (particularly mothers) for working too much. We need a workplace transformation commensurate with the family transformation that has already taken place.

Integrating Work and Family Life

Do Americans Feel Overworked?

Even if the average workweek has not changed substantially, a growing group of Americans are clearly spending more time at paid work than their counterparts did several decades ago. Even more important, a revolution in women's commitments has created a whole new group of workers and transformed American households, leaving women and men alike facing new time squeezes in the home. These historical changes are dramatic and important, but they cannot, taken alone, tell us how workers feel about their changed circumstances. Does more time at the workplace reflect a preference for public over private pursuits in an era of family upheaval, or does it reflect the constraints of high job demands and inflexible work organizations? More important, how would workers prefer to combine their varied commitments at home and at work, and how do their ideals compare with the alternatives they are offered?

Certainly, we cannot assume that workers' choices are merely a reflection of their own personal preferences. In a myriad of ways, the world of work is organized and structured by forces far beyond any individual worker's control.[1] It is thus not sufficient to know how the behavior of workers has changed. We also need to ask whether, and to what extent, contemporary work patterns reflect the preferences of workers or the demands and constraints of the options they are offered.

In this chapter, we shift from a focus on historical changes in worker behavior to examine the situation of contemporary workers. We take a closer look at workers' preferences for apportioning their time as well as the actual time they devote to work.[2] While there may be some workers who look to work as an escape from private life, at least at some point in their lives, there is little reason to conclude that a general pattern of this kind is emerging. To the contrary, many of those who are putting in long work-weeks would actually prefer more time for private pursuits; only those working relatively few hours would prefer to work more. Most workers wish neither to escape family life through work nor to focus solely on family at the expense of work commitments. Instead, the general trend appears to be a growing desire among workers across a wide spectrum of work and family situations to find a reasonable and fair *balance* between the economic and social rewards of the workplace and family-centered pleasures and challenges.

Reconsidering Workers' Preferences

As families diversify and workers face new challenges, people feel increasingly torn between their public and private worlds. Whether they are working more or less, workers confront new pressures and dilemmas as they attempt to cope with the conflicts that inevitably arise between family and work. These conflicts are real and growing. Yet it remains unclear whether they stem from workers' preferences to spend more time at work or, alternatively, from a growing gap between what workers prefer and what they feel they must do.

Some have argued that the emergence of time binds reflects a widespread cultural shift in which workers increasingly look to work as an escape from the complexities of contemporary family life. From this perspective, workers' preferences are at the heart of changes at work and at home. Arlie Hochschild's study of Amerco, a fictionally named American company, shows in illuminating and powerful detail how some workers cope with complexities at home by spending more time at work (Hochschild 1997). The average employee at Amerco, however, works nearly one day per week more than the average American worker. This makes Amerco a great place to study the coping strategies of overworked parents, but it is not an ideal vantage point from which to generalize about overall trends in labor force behavior and cultural changes in America. Nearly all the vignettes presented by Hochschild describe workers who put in fifty or more hours per week, from the sixty-hour-per-week executive to the "over-time hound" assembly-line worker. As we have seen, this is an important and growing segment of the labor force, but it does not represent the average worker.

To reach broad conclusions about general cultural, structural, and individual change, we need a broader look at workers in a range of work settings. How are workers' experiences embedded in larger social and economic forces, and how do workers' options and perceptions vary with their circumstances?

It is equally important to understand the ways in which workers experience a conflict between what they prefer and what they feel compelled to do. Personally held values and preferences, whatever their content, rarely provide a full explanation of a person's actions because few people have the opportunity to enact their fondest desires—especially at the workplace, where so much is influenced by organizational rules, incentives, and constraints. To understand how workers develop strategies for juggling home and work responsibilities, we need to place both workers' desires and their actions in the context of work structures and organizations.

In addition, stressing personal preferences and cultural values overlooks other possible explanations for the accommodation people strike between family and work. Without denying the importance of cultural influences outside the workplace, a range of structural, economic, and demographic forces also play a role in shaping workers' options and choices. We need to reconsider the meaning of "culture" in the context of growing work-family conflicts. Wider cultural values, for example, are often contradictory. When cultural messages simultaneously stress both "the work ethic" and "family values," people feel torn because it is difficult, if not impossible, to enact conflicting virtues at the same time. Also, competing cultural values cannot serve as a roadmap (or, in Ann Swidler's words, a "tool kit") for action.[3]

While wider cultural values vary and conflict, the workplace has its own culture.[4] Workplace cultures influence the way workers experience their jobs and perceive their options. The culture is likely to be shaped most forcefully by those at the top of an organization, thus forcing workers at the middle and lower rungs of the hierarchy to adjust as best they can.[5]

Workers must adjust their work and family commitments in the context of specific job demands and the larger workplace structures and cultures in which those jobs are embedded. A range of demographic factors, which influence where workers are placed in the economy, the labor market, and the family life course, also shape the conflicts workers face and influence their ability to respond. It is difficult to untangle the extent to which a choice to put in very long days on the job reflects an individual's preference for work over other activities and to what extent it is a response to real or perceived pressures and constraints at the workplace. Examining the link between actual time at work and workers' desires offers a way to uncover the mix of preferences and constraints that shape a worker's commitments. And comparing workers in a range of companies, who inhabit varied workplace structures and cultures, helps capture the ways that different workplace arrangements engender a variety of worker strategies.

Worker Needs and Employer Expectations

There is reason to conclude that more workers are feeling overworked even if average work hours have not increased substantially. While the structure of work has not changed significantly, workers' private lives have undergone dramatic transformations, making employed parents feel squeezed in ways that are altogether new. Yet the debate has focused on historical trends in actual time spent at paid work rather than on how workers *feel*. And since most national surveys do not gather information on preferred work schedules, it has been difficult to address this subjective aspect of change.[6]

Some have suggested that since most workers are currently putting in a few minutes less than were their counterparts in 1950, they do not feel overworked (Kneisner 1993). Such a conclusion not only ignores the widespread and fundamental changes that have taken place in family structure, but also overlooks the question of what kinds of work schedules contemporary workers desire. How Americans feel about their current commitments matters as much as the historical trajectory in working hours.

We have seen how the labor market is increasingly divided into longer work schedules for workers in demanding jobs while there is less economic support for workers in jobs with fewer hours. In contrast, changes in the lives of workers have left them in greater need to integrate family and work. Just as employers face incentives to divide the workforce, workers, especially employed parents, face new pressures to secure good jobs that also give them more time and flexibility for life outside the workplace. Employers' expectations and demands thus may be increasingly at odds with workers' needs and preferences.

Changes in family structure have transformed the lives of workers in several ways. As men have faced stagnant wages and women have become increasingly committed to work outside the home, most households now rely on women's earnings. These economic transformations have fueled women's need and desire for secure, well-paying jobs and left dual-earner and single-parent households to cope without an unpaid worker at home. Women are thus likely to prefer good jobs with reasonable hours, and fathers who share breadwinning responsibilities with an employed partner also need flexible hours and some measure of control at work.

These profound changes in the private lives of women and men are thus generating changes in worker preferences that may not fit with the supply of jobs. While people face new needs for balance and flexibility in their working lives, employers have good reasons to offer jobs with either long or short workweeks. This forces workers to choose between time and income—a difficult decision that clashes with the exigencies of the new family economy.

Ideal versus Actual Working Hours

If changes in the shape and character of the labor force are clashing with economic forces that influence the structure of jobs, workers are indeed likely to feel caught in the conflict. This clash between job demands and private needs can take several forms. Many may feel compelled to work more than they would wish, while others are likely to wish to work more than they are able. As workers' circumstances vary, so do the kinds of time binds workers experience. Yet so many now face family time squeezes that those who desire to put in less time at work are likely to outnumber those who wish to work more.

The 1997 Changing Workforce survey (Bond, Galinsky, and Swanberg 1998) provides a wide array of information about workers' actual and preferred commitments to work, family, and personal pursuits, which makes it possible to examine the contours and causes of actual and ideal working time. This survey is distinctive in terms of the range of questions asked regarding workers' values and preferences and in its focus on the links, tensions, and conflicts between work and family. People were asked how many hours per week they usually worked at their principal job and also at any additional jobs they held. They were also asked: "Ideally, how many hours, in total, would you like to work each week?" Thus, because people were asked about their ideal as well as their actual working hours, we can examine whether their overall level of work reflects their desires. We can also ascertain whether variation in preferences across groups of workers corresponds to variations in actual work levels.

Comparing people's actual and ideal hours also makes it possible to measure the difference between a worker's usual time on all jobs and his or her ideal working time. Table 3.1, which compares ideal hours to total hours worked for employed women and men, demonstrates that most American workers experience a significant gap between how much they work and how much they would like to work. One fifth said that their actual and ideal hours correspond precisely; but fully three in five felt that their usual workweek was longer than their ideal hours, and an additional one in five preferred to work more than they currently do. (The unemployed should be added to this group of underworked Americans, but the Changing Workforce survey only includes the currently employed.)

The vast majority of those who preferred fewer working hours wished to work at least 5 hours less per week. Nearly all of those who wanted to work less preferred to work at least 5 hours less per week. Nearly half (over 47 percent of both men and women) wished to work 10 hours less per week, and over one quarter wanted to work at least 20 hours less.

While women work an average of about 6 fewer hours per week than men, the difference between their actual and ideal hours is quite similar. Women and men wished to work less by approximately the same amount.

Table 3.1 Comparison of total hours worked and ideal hours, by gender

	Men	Women
Total hours usually worked (all jobs)	47.3	41.4
Ideal hours	37.5	32.1
Difference (actual − ideal)	9.8	9.3
Percent wanting to work less	60.2	60.1
Percent ideal equals actual	20.5	21.4
Percent wanting to work more	19.3	18.5
Percent wanting to work at least 5 hours less	58.4	58.6
Percent wanting to work at least 10 hours less	47.4	48.8
Percent wanting to work at least 20 hours less	28.3	27.9

Source: National Study of the Changing Workforce, 1997.

Note: All percentages are of total male and female samples, respectively. Thus, 60.2% of men reported wanting to work less; 58.4% wanted to work at least 5 hours less. This is not 58.4% of those who wanted to work less, but rather is 58.4% of the total. In other words, the great majority (58.4% over 60.2%) of those men who reported wanting to work less reported at least a 5-hour gap between their actual and ideal working hours.

Men preferred to work 9.8 fewer hours, compared to 9.3 fewer hours for women (a difference that is not statistically significant). If both groups were able to realize their wishes, the gender gap in hours worked—which, at about 6 hours per week, is not large—would probably not change significantly.

Whether or not contemporary Americans are actually working more than earlier generations, the majority seem to *feel* overworked—at least compared to their ideals. Excessively long workweeks certainly do not emerge as ideal or an aspiration. But neither are short workweeks desirable to those who wish to work more.[7]

The proportion of people wishing to work less appears to have grown during the 1990s. In 1992, when the Changing Workforce survey was first administered, workers expressed the desire to work about five hours less per week, on average; by 1997, that figure had jumped to over nine hours per week. The overall proportion wishing to work less also grew from just under half to over 60 percent for both men and women (see Jacobs and Gerson 2000). It appears that American workers no longer prefer longer workweeks.

Understanding the Gap between Work Ideals and Realities

Though it is clear that there is a gap between workers' ideal working time and workplace realities, the reasons for people's sense of having to spend either too much or too little time at work depend on their personal and occupational circumstances.

Number of Working Hours

The relative size of the groups wishing to work more or less is likely to vary with the number of hours worked. That is, a sizable proportion of those putting in long days at work are likely to wish for shorter workweeks, and a sizable proportion of those with comparatively short weeks are likely to wish for more.

Figure 3.1 shows that the gap between ideal and total working hours is clearly linked to the number of hours a person works. Those who work few hours on average prefer to work more, while those who work many hours on average prefer to work less. The great majority of both men and women working over 50 hours per week would prefer shorter schedules. Indeed, 80

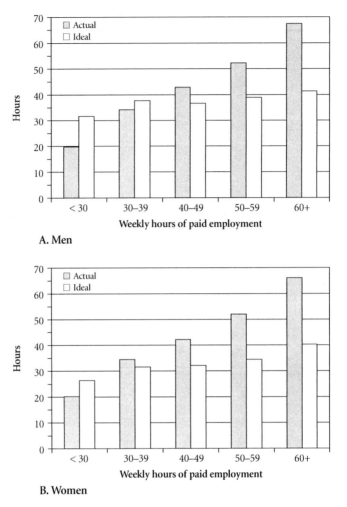

Figure 3.1 Actual and ideal working time, by weekly hours of paid employment. A: Men. B: Women. (*Source:* National Study of the Changing Workforce, 1997)

percent of men and almost 90 percent of women who worked over 50 hours per week wished for fewer hours. The difference between actual and ideal was substantial: those working between 50 and 60 hours per week preferred working over 13 fewer hours (13.35 for men, 17.72 for women), while those working over 60 hours preferred a full 25 hours less. While individual aspirations vary within each group, only 6.4 percent of women and 17.6 percent of men wished to work more than 50 hours per week—

even though over one third of men (37.6 percent) and nearly one fifth of women (19.8 percent) reported putting in that much time.

The gap between ideals and realities is another indication of how the labor force has become increasingly divided. A growing time gap separates not only the overworked and the underemployed, but also the options and desires of workers in each of these groups.

Since those putting in excessively long days feel overworked, a taste for overwork does not appear to explain why they put in so much time at work. Conversely, a taste for leisure cannot account for the equally important group who cannot obtain as much work as they would like or need. These disjunctions between actions and ideals demonstrate that workers' choices often do not reflect their actual desires. When it comes to structuring employment options, we need to ask whether employers are heeding the needs and preferences of their employees or whether, in contrast, there is a growing divergence between workers' preferences and the jobs made available to them.[8]

Education and Occupational Position

Since those working the most hours are more likely to be highly educated and employed in managerial, professional, and technical positions, these well-educated and well-positioned workers are also more likely to experience the greatest gap between long workweeks and a shorter ideal. (See Table 3.2.) Actual hours worked increase with educational level, while desired hours tend to decline. The gap between ideal and actual hours is highest among the most educated workers of both sexes.

In an interesting twist, desired hours are highest among male high school dropouts, who feel they must work relatively long days at low rates of pay to earn an adequate income. In contrast, actual hours worked are highest for college graduates and those with graduate training, who also express the largest gap between actual and ideal hours. Over two thirds of women and men with at least a college education want to work fewer hours (not shown in table).

A similar pattern can be found among workers in different occupations. Professional, managerial, and technical workers are most likely to feel overworked (results also presented in Table 3.2). Women in these positions would prefer to work 13 hours less than they do, while women in other occupations want to work about 7 fewer hours. Male professionals want to

Table 3.2 Total hours worked and ideal hours, by education, occupation, age, marital status, and gender

	Men			Women		
	Total hours	Ideal hours	Difference	Total hours	Ideal hours	Difference
Education						
Less than high school	44.8	39.7	5.1	37.7	33.2	4.5
High school graduate	48.0	37.8	10.2	40.2	32.6	7.6
Some college	45.4	36.1	9.3	40.2	31.7	8.5
College graduate	48.6	37.8	10.8	42.8	32.0	10.8
Some graduate education	50.0	38.4	11.6	47.0	32.1	14.9
Occupation						
Managerial, professional, and technical	48.9	37.3	11.6	43.9	30.9	13.0
Other	46.4	37.7	8.7	39.6	33.0	6.6
Age						
16–25	41.8	37.1	4.7	37.8	36.0	1.8
26–35	47.7	38.4	9.3	42.7	32.9	9.8
36–45	49.5	37.6	11.9	41.7	31.4	10.3
46–55	48.0	36.8	11.2	42.5	31.1	11.4
56–65	44.9	35.7	9.2	40.2	32.4	7.8
Marital status						
Married (or living with partner)	48.2	37.8	10.4	40.9	30.8	10.1
Not currently married	45.7	37.1	8.6	42.0	33.8	8.2
Married, employed spouse	48.1	38.2	9.9	41.4	30.4	11.0
Married, nonemployed spouse	48.3	37.3	11.0	38.5	32.8	5.7
Children						
With children under 6	49.3	38.9	10.4	39.4	30.0	9.4
Without children under 6	46.8	37.3	9.5	41.8	32.5	9.3

Source: National Study of the Changing Workforce, 1997.

work just under 12 hours less, while their counterparts in other occupational categories wish to work about 9 hours less. And while professionals and managers tend to put in longer workweeks than others, their *ideal* work schedules are not longer. Men who are professionals and managers wish to work about the same amount of time as other male workers. Women professionals and managers prefer to work about 2 hours less per week but actually work 4 hours more than women in other occupations.

Occupational position is a key factor in shaping the needs and desires of both men and women. Despite the persistent view that female professionals are less committed to work than their male counterparts, workers of both sexes appear to be looking for a reasonable balance between paid work and other pursuits. Those who put in long hours, regardless of gender, would like to cut back, while those who face shortened workweeks would like to work more. The most highly educated and well remunerated professionals and managers face the greatest demands to put in many hours at work. Rather than insulating one from overwork, well-paid jobs that offer advancement may actually increase the pressures to work more as well as the penalties for working less.

It could be argued that since those with the highest levels of education and income are working as much as, if not more than, other employees, these choices simply reflect a reasonable preference to enhance financial and career opportunities through hard work. Yet affluent workers, no less than other workers, face economic and other workplace constraints. Our analysis supports the widespread conviction and case histories presented elsewhere that exceptionally long workweeks are routinely required for career advancement, but not necessarily desired by those who experience them (see, for example, Epstein et al. 1999).

Age and Life Stage

Personal circumstances shape people's needs for time and money. Family responsibilities raise the stakes for both, increasing economic obligations as well as time demands at home. Changes in personal circumstances that are linked to age and life stage are thus likely to shape workers' perceptions and feelings.

Does age determine the size of the gap between actual and ideal hours? If work-family conflict is the principal force driving the desire for fewer hours, the biggest gap between actual and ideal hours is likely to be found among those in their late twenties, thirties, and early forties, the years during which people are most likely to marry, become parents, and shoulder the responsibilities of caring for young children.

Table 3.2 shows that the gap between actual and ideal hours does indeed reach its peak for men and women in these family-building and career-launching years, although the differences between age groups in ideal working hours are small and often statistically insignificant. For men, actual working hours increase until ages thirty-six through forty-five and then begin to fall somewhat. Ideal hours remain roughly constant. The gap between actual and ideal hours thus grows for men until age forty-five, but remains high thereafter. Among the thirty-six to forty-five age group, the gap is nearly 12 hours. Over two thirds of this group of men prefer fewer hours. Yet it appears that the fathers of young children are not the only group who feel this way. Men in their fifties (whose children are more likely to be older) are nearly as likely to express a desire to work less.

For women as well as men, ideal hours are remarkably consistent across the age groups. The gap between ideal and actual work hours peaks at 11 hours among forty-six- to fifty-five-year-olds, and it only drops 3 hours for women over fifty-five. From age twenty-six through fifty-five, over 60 percent of women wish to work fewer hours.

For women and men alike, the desire to work less is not restricted to the prime child-bearing and -rearing years. Nor is there a clear generational shift. An interest in working less is as strong among the middle-aged as among the youngest workers. Age and cohort position undoubtedly combine to influence these results. Younger workers in the current period may thus favor a more balanced work schedule than did previous generations at the same point in their life course (Gerson 2002).

When gender differences emerge, they suggest that men in their fifties may be seeking more leisure, while women in their thirties may be seeking more time for family care. Perhaps more telling, however, gender differences within age groups are generally small. As women continue to develop ties to paid work that resemble the long-term, uninterrupted commitment once reserved for men, women and men appear to be developing common strategies for building work careers over the life course.

The gap between ideal and actual working hours thus seems driven more by the shifting demands of work than by age differences *per se*. During their thirties and forties, as men and women are trying to build their careers, their time at work necessarily increases. Since their desire to work more hours does not show a corresponding rise, a gap between ideal and actual work time emerges. In lieu of basic changes at the workplace, women and men alike experience "life stage squeezes" as work demands continue unabated while family pressures mount (see Oppenheimer 1980; Estes and Wilensky 1978).

Marriage, Children, and Gender

The life course has grown increasingly fluid and unpredictable, and age may simply be too crude a measure to reveal the dynamics between personal circumstances and work constraints. Regardless of the age at which people choose to marry or have children, family commitments are almost certain to increase the need for domestic time. Marriage and parenthood should thus influence the gap between ideal and actual working time.

Gender also shapes the pressures and dilemmas of private life; marriage and especially parenthood are likely to affect women and men in different ways. Although men's participation in domestic work has increased in recent decades, women continue to bear a greater share of the load, especially when children arrive. And amid the growing strength of mothers' work commitments, fathers continue to face pressures to provide primary economic support for their families (see, for example, Gerson 1993). This means that, while both men and women are likely to feel torn between family and work, they are also likely to feel this conflict in different degrees and to respond in different ways.

Despite the growing convergence between women's and men's work commitments, they continue to face different pressures as parents. And though women and men express roughly equal desires to work fewer hours, a more complicated relationship emerges between gender and family situation in Table 3.2. First, married and single workers of both sexes differ in their ideal working hours. Married women work almost 1 hour less per week than women who are not married, but they would like to work 3 hours less. The gap between actual and ideal working time is thus 2 hours greater for married than for single women. Ideally, married women would prefer to work 10 hours less per week, while single women would prefer to work 8 hours less per week.

In contrast, married men work more than single men, by about 2.5 hours per week. Married and single men wish, however, to work about the same amount of time.[9] Married men thus experience a larger gap between actual and ideal hours (10 hours per week) than do single men (8 hours per week). For both women and men, married life adds to the feeling of being squeezed for time, but they have somewhat different reasons for feeling this way. Married men feel torn because they are spending more time on the job than single men. Married women are prone to cut back slightly in their working time, but would like to cut back more.

Within marriage, differences emerge among women living in different family situations, although they are not as large as might be expected. Women with employed husbands work about 3 hours per week less than those few whose husbands do not work, but this small difference is not statistically significant. Women in dual-earner marriages want to work 30 hours per week instead of the 41 hours they actually work, creating a sizable gap of 11 hours per week. For those with husbands who are not employed, the gap is 6 hours (and, again, the difference between the two is not statistically significant).

Women with preschool children show a similar pattern. These women work 39 hours per week on average, but would prefer to work 30 hours per week, for a gap of 9 hours per week. For women without children under six, there is also a 9 hour per week differential, which is statistically indistinguishable from the gap for those with preschool children. Having preschool children and employed husbands thus shapes women's desired and actual working time, but does not create a dramatic change in the gap between the two.

Marriage and parenthood also influence men's actual and ideal working time but, as in the case of women, in only modest ways. Surprisingly, men whose wives are employed do not differ from those with nonemployed partners in either actual or ideal working time. Having preschool children does increase the total number of hours worked per week for men, but it also increases their desired working time. The fathers of young children are thus likely to conclude that their family's financial needs require them to put in more time at work. And since actual working time increases by more than desired time, a higher proportion of these men want to work less.

To some extent, the modest gap in women's actual and ideal working time reflects the fact that they have already made strategic adjustments to avoid work-family conflict. After all, their average working hours are lower than men's at the outset. The larger pattern nevertheless suggests that family circumstances are as important as gender and that both mothers *and* fathers with young children want more time away from work than do other groups. Marriage clearly creates a context that pulls both women and men toward personal commitments outside of work. Yet we find little support for the oft-stated argument that married women with young children are the primary group wishing to work less. In fact, about half of married men and women across a range of family situations express such a desire. While some have argued that the arrival of children increases the number of hours that both mothers and fathers spend at the workplace, we find that women with small children cut back on their time at paid work, but to a smaller extent than in previous generations. The larger message in these findings is that all parents, whether they are mothers or fathers, need job arrangements that enable them to strike a balance between the economic and caretaking work that parenthood entails.

Alternative Measures of Preference and Ideals

Trying to ascertain "true" preferences and ideals is difficult at best. Not accustomed to thinking in such ways, people may be only dimly aware of their preferences when asked to express them. And even when they have given these matters a great deal of thought, their answers will depend on how the question is asked. In the case of working time, a key point is whether the question tries to capture the trade-off between hours and earnings. Lost income may be the immediate cost of working less, but lost promotion opportunities and reduced job security may represent truer and far greater long-term costs. Since working time is inextricably linked to other aspects of work, self, and family well-being, it is difficult to imagine a change in working time while holding all other things equal. For example, in earlier research on work and family choices, women and men routinely specified that their ideal of working less holds only if such an option does not lower their income or their chances of finding satisfying work in the future (Gerson 1985, 1993).

The measure of "ideal hours" used in our analysis does not ascertain what, if any, trade-offs workers are willing to make to reach their ideals or what circumstances would enable them to do so. And since we are exploring the types of trade-offs society should promote, this measure has advantages. It is worthwhile to know what aspirations people would hold in a more ideal world, even if they are not attainable today.

Other studies have attempted to build the notion of trade-offs into their analysis, and the answers to their questions are telling. These studies, even with their alternative ways of posing questions about ideal working time, also find that many American workers would prefer to work less. Questions that explicitly raise the issue of trade-offs, however—that is, ones that specify that cutting back hours would result in less income and other negative consequences—find that a smaller proportion of people respond that they would want to work less (and a larger proportion respond that they would want to work more). Yet among those putting in the longest workweeks, the wish for fewer hours is sustained whether the question skirts the issue of trade-offs or includes it.

In 1998, the *General Social Survey* (National Opinion Research Center 2002) asked several questions about ideal working time, including the following:

> Suppose you could change the way you spend your time, spending more time on some things and less time on others. Which of the things on the following list would you like to spend more time on, which would you like to spend less time on, and which would you like to spend the same amount of time on as now?

Of employed individuals, 32.0 percent preferred to work less, 34.7 percent wanted to work the same hours, and 20.8 percent wished to work more. (Another 12.5 percent couldn't decide or did not answer this question.) These answers are broadly similar to the "ideal hours" question we examined, with a 3 to 2 majority preferring a shorter workweek (Reynolds 2001).

The answers shift markedly, however, when the issue of wages is added, as it is in another question in the same survey:

> Think of the number of hours you work and the money you earn in your main job, including any regular overtime. If you had only one of these three choices, which of the following would you prefer—work longer hours and earn more money; work the same number of hours and earn the same money; work fewer hours and earn less money?

When the options are posed as trade-offs between time and money, working less becomes less attractive. In this case, 28.6 percent wished to work more, 50.5 percent preferred to work the same hours, and only 8.9

percent wanted to work less.[10] (Again, 12.0 percent could not choose or gave no answer.)

Financial concerns thus appear to be a major obstacle to working less. Indeed, there would be little demand for a shorter workweek if significant financial costs were attached to such a change. But the question of how much less work—or how much less pay—matters remains unanswered. To better understand this trade-off, the 1992 Changing Workforce survey asked: "Would you be willing to give up a day's pay each week for an extra day of free time?"

Responses to this question suggest that there is substantial interest in working less. Of working respondents in 1992, 24.3 percent said that they would trade a day's pay each week for an extra day of free time, and another 3.3 percent said that it depended on the circumstances. Thus, when ambiguity about the extent of the trade-off between time and money is lowered, people are more willing to volunteer that they would prefer to work less.[11]

In the 1992 Changing Workforce study, those who reported working longer than their ideal hours were asked, "Could you afford to work less?" The majority (60.9 percent) said that they could not. The 1997 survey also asked those who wanted fewer hours why they didn't work less. Nearly half (46.8 percent) said that they needed the money, by far the most common response. Another sizable group (18.7 percent) explained that their employer would not allow it. Financial considerations clearly—and not surprisingly—play a major role in shaping preferences for working more or less.

When people are asked about preferred working time without an explicit mention of the costs of making such a change, a significant minority express the desire for a shorter workweek. Whether the question is posed in terms of ideal hours or simply as an ideal allocation of time among a variety of activities, the finding remains. When the potential price of such a change is included, the proportion expressing interest in working less declines, although the extent of the decline varies. The inclination to work less remains consistently concentrated among those working the greatest number of hours, just as the desire to work more remains concentrated among those working the least.

A sustained public effort to reduce the workweek would speak to the needs of many workers, but only if it were attentive to the potential cost in forgone income and productivity. If a shorter workweek spurred productivity and minimized the loss of wages, it would surely be more attractive than vaguely worded survey questions can convey. Reducing the length of the workweek only makes sense, however, in the context of a wider range of policies that also support workers, provide for families, and enhance job flexibility.

Where do the intrinsic rewards of work fit into this picture? Many professionals love their jobs, as do workers in many other settings. In a study of financial professionals, Mary Blair-Loy (2003) finds that many of the women she interviewed were deeply devoted to their work, a devotion that was often difficult to reconcile with their equally fervent devotion to their families. Without discounting the intrinsic rewards of work, however, there are limits to how much time any job should require. Moreover, recent trends are clouding the appeal of professional jobs.

Put simply, the professions, as well as many other occupations, are not what they used to be. Kevin Leicht and Mary Fennell (2001), following Eliot Freidson (1986) and others, point to the various ways that professional autonomy has been undermined by the rise of bureaucratic organizations and the constraints of market forces. Some of the recent increase in working time among professionals may reflect the devotion that comes from immersion in challenging work, but perhaps it is more likely due to the forces impelling professionals to work harder regardless of whether those added hours add to or detract from the personal gratification that comes from engaging in interesting work.

Divided Options, Shared Aspirations

Although much of the debate concerning overwork in America has focused on the time women and men are spending at the workplace, we have looked closely in this chapter at how contemporary workers *feel* about their time at work. The concept of overwork depends as much on ideals as on actual working time, and we have found a notable gap between what workers do and what they would prefer. Most workers experience a significant time divide between their circumstances and their aspirations.

Yet this does not mean that all, or even most, workers feel overworked. Workers disagree considerably about whether they would like to work more or less. This disagreement makes it clear that the perception of overwork is not a general problem, but is nevertheless an important one to those whose jobs require that they put in very long workweeks and those whose family responsibilities are at their height. Far from using work to avoid family time, these workers would prefer more balance in their lives, with more time for private and family pursuits.

The problems of overworked Americans should also not blind us to the difficulties faced by those workers who cannot find sufficient employment to meet their own or their families' needs. As we have seen, many of those with relatively short workweeks would actually prefer to work more. Essentially, the gap between ideals and realities, rather than overwork *per se,* is the core problem for contemporary workers. Among women and men alike, most aspire to a balance that neither the overworked nor the underworked can achieve. Thus, in order to make sense of the experiences and challenges facing workers and their families, we need to look not just at historical trends to examine the discrepancy between what workers do and what they want, between their current circumstances and their aspirations.

These findings also point to the emergence of another kind of time divide that separates the overworked and the underworked. A bifurcation of the labor force can be seen in the differences between those working long and short weeks. We have consistently found that workers in high-demand jobs would prefer to work less. It is only at the opposite end of the occupational spectrum, where less educated workers in blue-collar jobs are more likely to face underemployment and economic squeezes, that workers would prefer to work more. And since there is no evidence suggesting that most of those putting in either very many or relatively few hours are acting on personal preferences, these circumstances are more likely to reflect the options offered by employers than the desires of workers.

The growth in long workweeks among some groups of workers does not appear to be driven by a broad cultural shift in workers' wish to spend ever more time at the workplace. For those spending more and less time than they would like at paid work, the labor market is not producing employment options that reflect their preferences. Indeed, a majority of workers would prefer a different work schedule than the one they have, and those putting in the most time were the most likely to wish to work less. We need to pay attention to the mix of job opportunities workers face and how these options meet, or fail to meet, the needs and aspirations of workers on both ends of the spectrum.

If we look carefully at who is most likely to feel overworked, we also find that a range of forces are reshaping job options in ways that are colliding with family needs. Those who are most likely to need time away from work to care for children and tend to family needs are also those most likely to feel overworked. Gender is an important factor here, with women still assuming the lion's share of family work. Nevertheless, despite the differences in the circumstances of mothers and fathers, both women and men wish to have more time for private pursuits. At the same time, they are both facing a bifurcation of work into overdemanding and underdemanding jobs. We believe that the problems of integrating parenting with satisfying work cannot be solved by recreating a distinct, separate, or unequal set of options for women and men.

While workers are divided in their options and constraints, they are remarkably united in their aspirations. Across gender, class, and family situation, most workers agree that work and family are equally important life commitments that need to be combined and integrated, not avoided. Whether they are women or men, overworked or underworked, most want a job that is economically sustaining and personally satisfying, yet not overwhelming. Most Americans want a reasonable balance between work and the rest of life. The problem appears to be that many simply do not possess the resources or social capacity to enact this desire.[12]

The debates about overwork and work-family conflict should be expanded in several ways. First, we need to look at what workers need and prefer as well as what they do. And rather than focusing only on whether or not Americans are overworked, we should assess the ways in which Americans increasingly face a divided labor market in which some experience overwork while others are not able to work as much as they would like. As Barry Bluestone and Stephen Rose point out, we need to "unravel the economic enigma" of both overwork and underemployment (Bluestone and Rose 1997). Rather than focusing on the mean, or average, worker, we need to examine the dispersion among workers in the time they spend at work. Overworked Americans sacrifice family and leisure time, while underworked Americans experience economic hardship and thwarted opportunities. Since each of these situations is problematic in its own way, generalizing from only one overlooks the experiences of many and leads to limited understanding of the more general dynamics of social change.

We also need to clarify how economic and social changes have created a gap between employer expectations and worker needs. Employers may benefit from dividing jobs into categories that distinguish strongly and weakly committed workers. And on the surface, the rise of long workweeks for some and contingent, part-time jobs for others may appear to provide an innovative solution to the dilemmas faced by working parents and non-traditional families. In the context of workers' needs and desires, however, such changes are likely to intensify workers' dilemmas rather than resolve them. Women and men alike need jobs with sufficient time demands to allow them to support their families economically but not with so many hours that they cannot meet their families' and their own needs for time and attention.

If workers are forced to choose between well-rewarded jobs with expanding opportunities and jobs that allow them to take their family commitments seriously, neither families nor the economy are likely to fare well over the long run. And if this division of jobs serves to further divide men and women workers, the problems of work and family life will be exacerbated. We have found that men and women alike need employment that offers both job opportunity and family time. The social and economic fabric of American society can only benefit when working parents are able to balance paid employment and family life without endangering their economic security or long-term work prospects.

To resolve the conflicts created by a growing time divide, we need to develop work structures and cultures that can sustain workers in this new family age. First, however, we need to discover the conditions of work, beyond the dimension of time, that can make a difference in the lives of those who must cope with work-family conflicts every day.

4

How Work Spills Over
into Life

Most Americans face a gap between their aspirations and their actual time at work, and for most, this gap reflects a desire to work less. Yet this is just the tip of the iceberg, alerting us to more deeply felt experiences of personal conflict.

In this chapter, we rely on the 1992 and 1997 Changing Workforce surveys to look at how and to what extent workers experience conflicts between work and family and to explore their strategies for coping with these multiple obligations. We also examine workers' ideals for allocating their time between work, family, and personal pursuits. And, given this backdrop, we address the debate about whether work is more likely to interfere with family life or, in contrast, family is more likely to spill over into work.

Beyond Time

Whether the arena is the job or the home, the intensity of work is as important as the amount of time it takes. And while difficult to measure, both work and domestic demands may well have intensified in recent decades. Subtle changes in the amount of time spent at work may obscure more basic changes in the effort, energy, and concentration expected on the job. And what is expected from parents, if not housework *per se,* may also have expanded, at least for some social groups. Many Americans may feel torn between work and family not just because their households increasingly juggle competing responsibilities, but also because job expectations and parenting standards have become more demanding.

There is little question that improvements in labor productivity over the course of the twentieth century helped raise living standards for most

Americans. These changes stemmed, at least in part, from the emergence of new technologies that allowed workers to produce more in a shorter period of time. There is good reason to conclude, however, that increasing expectations for more concentrated effort accompanied these changes. British labor historian Chris Nyland (1989) has suggested, for example, that historical reductions in working time have involved a gradual rise in the intensity of work. For each reduction in the length of the workweek, he argues, there were concomitant increases in worker productivity. If so, many late-twentieth- and early twenty-first-century workers would find it impossible to work the way they do following a nineteenth-century schedule. That is, workers in contemporary automobile plants, for example, would strain mightily to maintain the pace they manage over their eight-hour day for the twelve hours their counterparts worked in an earlier era. Many modern jobs are mentally demanding, rather than physically draining.

Nyland also suggests that increased productivity explains why briefer workweeks have failed to bolster employment. Since resourceful employers find ways to increase productivity when the workweek is reduced, there are fewer gains in employment opportunities than might be expected. Of course, if shortening the workweek fails to increase employment, as some reformers may have hoped, this "failure" actually is due to the success of fewer hours in stimulating higher productivity. (We discuss this issue further in Chapter 8.)

In addition, corporate downsizing, especially since the 1980s, may have increased the scope of many white-collar jobs (Cappelli 2001). And high-performance employment systems put pressure on fewer employees to produce more at a lower cost. These rising pressures at work have emerged alongside the growth of dual-earner couples, many of whom are likely to hold such high-demand positions. The result is a collision between the expectations of employers and the ability of workers to maintain the pace that has come to be expected.

A subtle but nevertheless real expansion in parenting expectations and standards, especially among middle-class mothers and fathers, may be compounding this trend in work demands. Sharon Hays (1997) suggests, for example, that mothers are increasingly responsible not simply for the care and sustenance of their children, but for all aspects of their emotional and intellectual development. And while this transformation in the definition of good mothering began in the early period of industrial development, it has expanded during the postindustrial period. Women have faced rising opportunities and pressures to build committed ties outside the home, but they are also confronting rising expectations not just for their children's physical and emotional well-being but for their children's social success as well. Parenting standards this diffuse and demanding leave little room for personal pursuits, much less for simply relaxing.

While Hays stresses the cultural contradictions facing contemporary mothers who are expected to practice "intensive mothering" even as they chart paths outside the home, it is clear that expectations for fathers have increased as well. The "good father" is no longer a benevolent but absent breadwinner, but is instead expected to be intimately involved with all aspects of his children's lives, from playing and changing diapers to shuttling them between activities to helping with their schoolwork. Needless to say, not all fathers meet these standards, but they have nevertheless taken root. And despite the obstacles, fathers are taking these rising expectations to heart. While middle-class fathers may have received the most attention, fathers from all backgrounds have shown a steady increase in parenting involvement over the past several decades.[1]

Further evidence of a rise in parenting, and especially mothering, standards can be found in the work of Annette Lareau (2002), who finds that middle-class parents are striving to nurture their children's development through a "concerted cultivation" that requires them to enroll children in a range of ever-evolving age-specific activities. As many middle-class parents find themselves shuttling their children from soccer practice to piano lessons, child-centered activities can come to dominate family life and create a frenetic domestic pace. Lareau finds that after-school activities often cut into the workday, make it difficult to share dinner, and can take up significant portions of the weekend as well.

The intense involvement with their children expected of middle-class parents makes the long hours they put in at work more problematic. In other words, they have to deal with more hours and higher expectations on the job and also come home and help their children with class projects or shuttle them to sports practice and music lessons. Still, middle-class parents have more resources to deal with these higher expectations, including not only more money but also more flexibility in their jobs, than working-class parents can count on (Heymann 2000).

Structural and demographic shifts are also contributing to rising parental pressures. While smaller families may lower parental demands—and indeed may reflect a demographic adjustment to the challenges of child rear-ing—smaller families also mean that fewer older children are around to take care of younger ones. As family size contracts, the amount of parental attention focused on each child may thus increase. And since smaller fami-lies and residential expansion leave children more geographically isolated from each other, parents are less likely to rely on the casual emergence of unscheduled, unsupervised play. Concerns about crime add further to a perceived need for parental supervision. The unstructured play of the 1950s and 1960s has given way to a wide array of more structured activities that require parental time and attention.

The needs of elderly parents or other relatives are another factor in the caring equation. Advances in longevity have created a burgeoning popula-tion of elderly, who tend to spend at least some of their years in a state of dependency. Thirty-five million Americans were aged sixty-five or over in 2000, a 12 percent increase from the 1990 level. The number of elderly Americans is expected to reach over 80 million by 2050, which will take them from the current 12.6 percent of the population to 20.3 percent (U.S. Bureau of the Census 2002). The care needs of the elderly are less uniform and less predictable than those of young children, since the nature, onset, and duration of illness range so widely. Thus, heart attacks can result in an abrupt loss of life; cancer may ravage its victims for months or years; and Alzheimer's disease can exhaust even the most dedicated caregiver over an extended period.

The term "the sandwich generation" was introduced to capture the chal-lenges of a group simultaneously facing the needs of their frail parents and their young children.[2] Those caught in this situation recognize how dif-ficult it can be. Fortunately, attending to the needs of elderly parents tends to begin when people reach their late forties and fifties, and thus for many families occurs after the heaviest child-care needs have passed. Later in this chapter we examine elder care in addition to parenting responsibilities as factors affecting work-family conflict.

The emergence of "nonstandard" work hours has added to the growing complexities of integrating work with family time. Pointing to the rise of such work shifts, which involve nights, weekends, and other periods for-merly considered private time, Harriet Presser (2003) maintains that we are moving toward a twenty-four-hour, seven-day-a-week economy in which employees are increasingly working evenings, nights, and rotating shifts as well as weekends. Nearly one fourth of all married couples with at least one earner contain a spouse who works nonstandard hours. The percentage is even higher for those with children, and it rises to 30.6 percent for couples with children under age five. Whether they lack child-care options and the funds to afford them or simply believe that children should be cared for by their own parents, these couples appear to be engaging in a strategy of "tag-team" parenting. Yet such strategies can exact a heavy toll on relationships and family life and are associated with higher rates of separation and divorce. These shifting work schedules, along with new technologies such as e-mail and cell phones, contribute to the sense that work is increasingly spilling over into family life, even as family needs become more diffuse and complex.

Conflicts between Family and Work

Many workers find that their paid work leaves too little room for the rest of life. But how many people experience such conflicts, and how often? Based on findings from the National Survey of the Changing Workforce (Bond, Galinsky, and Swanberg 1998), Figure 4.1 provides a sense of how individual workers experience work and family conflicts.[3] Several points are made clear from this figure. First, large numbers of American workers are concerned about work-family issues. Second, since workers and their families are remarkably diverse, and since work-family issues are manifested in many ways, the extent of concern varies widely depending on the specific issue considered. Third, work-family issues are not confined to women. Indeed, Figure 4.1 shows that men are just as likely as women to express these concerns.

A slight majority of workers experience at least some conflict in balancing work, personal life, and family life (55.5 percent of women and 59.8 percent of men). Over two-fifths (47.1 percent of men and 42.0 percent of women) reported experiencing either "a lot" or "some" interference between job and family. Over one third (34.7 percent of men and 37.9 percent of women) feel "used up" at the end of the workday often or very often. A similar fraction feel unable to get everything done at home because of their job. Indeed, these findings suggest that perceived time pressures account for at least some of the historical decline in housework. Americans are living in larger homes, but spending less time on them. Purchasing services fills some of this gap, but a large minority lack the time to attend to the daily demands of paying bills, keeping their house or apartment in order, and maintaining their homes and cars.

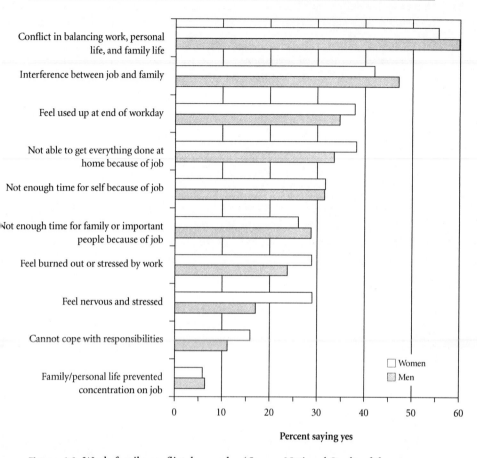

Figure 4.1 Work-family conflict, by gender (*Source:* National Study of the Changing Workforce, 1997)

Between one quarter and one third also felt that their jobs left insufficient time for themselves or their families. Here, men report slightly more work-family conflict than do women, although the difference is not statistically significant. Work-family conflict may be acute for women, but it is not restricted to them. Certainly, time squeezes are not simply a "working mother's" problem, although the popular debate is often framed in this way. Men, for example, work longer hours and are also are more likely to travel for work. And despite the rise of dual-earner households and committed women workers, men continue to feel breadwinning obligations that make it difficult to participate fully and equally in family life. Even more than women, men are reluctant to leave work early for routine child-care activities or to refuse assignments for personal reasons (Kmec 1999).

Of course, women also experience acute work-family conflicts. Indeed, these conflicts often prompt them to adjust their working hours and make other work choices to accommodate the demands of home and children. While such adjustments may reduce the experience of conflict, they nevertheless stem from and reflect the existence of structural conflicts between family and work.

Whether or not parents make adjustments that involve pulling back from work or working more, many women and men feel there is little time left for themselves in the squeeze between work and family life. These conflicts also leave many workers feeling they have too little time for their families. About one quarter (23.7 percent of men and 28.9 percent of women) reported feeling burned out or stressed by work often or very often, although relatively few were willing to concede that these tensions left them unable to cope: just over one tenth said they could not cope with their responsibilities often or very often, and less than one in ten reported that family life prevented them from concentrating on their job.

The answers of so many people to such a wide range of questions makes it clear that many men as well as women are facing not only changes in, but conflicts among, their multiple ties. Although the gender gap is in most instances small and not statistically significant, this does not mean that women and men experience these conflicts in entirely, or even predominantly, the same way. The psychological costs of work-family tension, for example, appear to take a greater toll on women, who are more likely to report feeling "nervous" or "stressed" than men (29.0 percent for women versus 17.0 percent for men). The psychological consequences of work-family tension, such as feeling "used up" at the end of the workday or feeling emotionally drained from work, also appear to fall more heavily on women than men (or at least are more often reported by women).

The popular debate does everyone a disservice, however, by continuing to focus on the problems of working mothers. Not only does it ignore the conflicts and stresses faced by all parents, but it leaves both men and women workers unable to seek or demand more creative, egalitarian solutions. Women are left facing trade-offs that require them to choose between their families and their own economic prospects on the one hand and their children's care on the other. Many make short-term adjustments that will have longer-term consequences; others may choose to postpone or forgo motherhood altogether. Although the experiences of childless women cannot be captured in a study of working parents, they represent the other side of the balance sheet when work and family collide amid persistent gender inequities. If some women adjust work commitments to meet family needs, others avoid those demands by having no children at all. Whether the choice is to forgo work or childbearing opportunities, both strategies emerge from a constrained and unequal set of options.[4]

Fathers also face trade-offs, but usually of a different sort. They remain constrained by organizations and cultural definitions that leave them little room for cutting back from work to care for children or share more family responsibilities equally with their partners. The perceived sacrifices and adjustments may vary, but women and men both pay a price.

Busy work schedules can have very specific, tangible effects on family life, such as altering rituals and routines like dinnertime. Shared family dinners, for example, appear to be on the decline in American society. Drawing on information from the late 1980s, Harriet Presser (2003) reports that in single-earner families, most (64.1 percent) mothers and about half (47.4 percent) of fathers have dinner with their children every night of the week, but only a third (36.7 percent) report that both parents are always present. Each of these figures drops four or five percentage points among dual-earner couples. Single mothers are also less able to have dinner with their children every night—only two in five (42.7 percent) report being able to do so. Most of this is a consequence of the parents' schedules, but some is due to the busy schedules of teenagers. To make inferences about teenagers, Presser compares children under thirteen with those under eighteen and finds that family dinners are more common with younger children. Families can prosper without having dinner together, but family dinners are nevertheless an important event whose erosion may signal changes in other rituals as well.

Perceptions of Ideal Allocations between Work and Family

Although most workers do not experience extreme levels of work-family conflict, almost half appear to experience at least some.[5] These figures taken alone, however, may understate the scope of the dilemma because they do not tell us how workers would *prefer* to allocate their time. Do they wish to spend more time with their families, more time working, or more time on personal pursuits beyond the bounds of either family or work?

The answer to this question is not obvious. If people perceive that work offers the pleasures once sought at home while home now poses the problems once found at work, then most would probably prefer to spend more time on the job. Yet we expect that those who experience conflicts would, if given an opportunity, devote more time to family and personal life. To understand how Americans are experiencing work-family conflict, we need to know not only how they are currently balancing the various aspects of their lives but also how they would do so if they had more options.

Figure 4.2 offers some insight by comparing the actual and ideal balance between family, self, and work for women and men. Both women and men would prefer, on average, to devote a larger percentage of their time to family and personal pursuits than they currently do. Similarly, each group would prefer to spend a smaller percentage of time at work. In considering their ideal balance between family, work, and self, women say they wish to spend 13 percent less time at work and 4 percent more time with their families. Men display a similar outlook, wishing for 14 percent less time on the job and 7 percent more time on family activities. Both groups, on average, would also like to have considerably more time available for pursuing

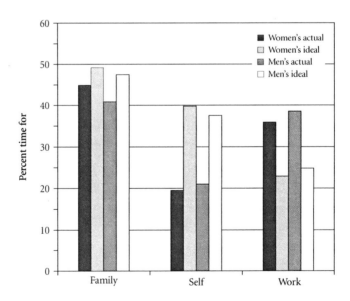

Figure 4.2 Actual and ideal work-family balance (*Source:* National Study of the Changing Workforce, 1997)

individual and personal activities, with women wishing for 20 percent more time and men hoping for 15 percent more.

The gap between the actual and ideal figures grows as workers' hours increase (results not shown). Those who work fifty hours per week or more are most likely to report that their actual distribution of time to work is too high and to family is too low. For both men and women, these are the workers most likely to report that their ideal balance is far from their actual balance. These preferences, moreover, are consistent with other findings, which also show that men and women who put in the longest days on the job are most likely to report a preference for working less (see Chapter 3).

If workers could act on their wishes, it appears that they would create a new balance in which work would occupy less time and family life would get more attention. While there are surely exceptions, most workers are not going to work to flee their homes. Rather, in the competition among work, family, and self, it is the self that may be losing. The costs of work-family conflicts appear to have settled on working women and men who, in their desire to meet both work demands and family needs, have less time to care for themselves.

Spillovers between Home and Work

Work may spill over into family life, and family life may spill over into work life, but which is more common? Despite the fact that findings from study after study suggest that the spillover from job to family life is more prevalent, much public debate focuses on concern that family needs interfere with jobs. To untangle these closely connected relationships, it is important to examine not only the degree and intensity of conflict, but also the direction of interference. Certainly family needs can and do spill over into work, but the more pressing concern may be not how family needs interfere with the performance of workers, but rather how work—at least as it is currently structured for most people—makes it difficult to attend to family concerns.

Spillover from Home to Work

How and to what extent does taking time off for personal or family issues interfere with work responsibilities and commitments? Figure 4.3 offers a

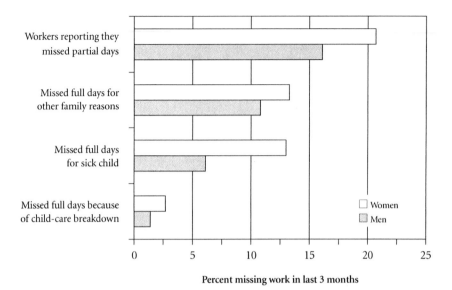

Figure 4.3 Days of work missed, by gender (*Source:* National Study of the Changing Workforce, 1997)

look at this dynamic. It shows that, while missing partial days is not an unusual occurrence, with about one in six men and one in five women reporting having at least one such absence in the last three months, it is less common to miss full days because of family reasons, a breakdown in child-care arrangements, or a sick child. Gender differences do emerge in missed days from work: women are more likely than men to stay home with a sick child or to fill in when child-care arrangements break down. As Heymann (2000) points out, parents are aware that inflexible jobs often mean that family needs cannot be met—a teacher's appointment cannot be scheduled or a doctor's visit cannot be made. Indeed, the fact that we find limited spillover from family to work is a testimony to the inflexibility of current workplaces. In a world where most parents are also workers, we should both expect and welcome some degree of engagement in family life at the workplace.

Who feels the most tension between work and family? Parents do! Figures 4.4 and 4.5 compare parents and non-parents, using the same questions presented in Figure 4.1. For eight of the ten items in Figure 4.4, mothers of children under eighteen are more likely to voice concerns than are women without children. Only two indicators, "feel used up at end of

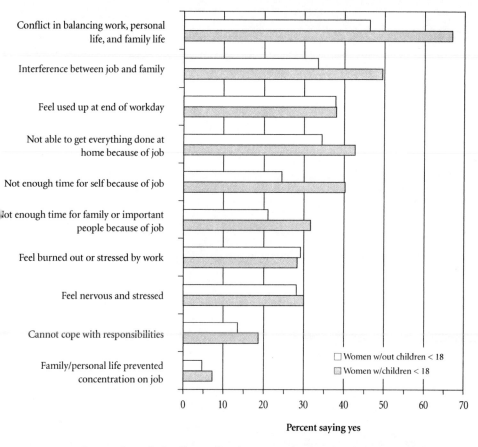

Figure 4.4 Women's work-family conflict, by parental status (*Source:* National Study of the Changing Workforce, 1997)

workday" and "feel burned out or stressed by work," did not vary by women's parental status, and these measures focus more on the experiences of jobs than on work-family issues *per se*. Fathers differed on five of the ten measures: "conflict in balancing work, personal life, and family life"; "interference between job and family"; "not able to get everything done at home"; "not enough time for self"; and "not enough time for family" (Figure 4.5). While parents experience more conflict than nonparents, the difference between mothers and women without children appears greater than those between fathers and other men.

Having children at home clearly increases the sense of conflict, but the

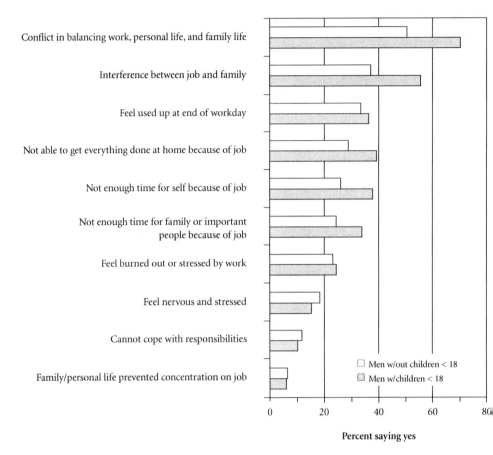

Figure 4.5 Men's work-family conflict, by parental status (*Source:* National Study of the Changing Workforce, 1997)

age of children does not appear to matter. Few differences emerge when older children (aged 6–18) are separated from younger ones (0–5). The nature of parental stresses may change as children age, but they do not necessarily diminish, as many parents of teenagers will attest (Kurz 2000).

Spillover from Work to Home

The spillover from family to work is real, especially for parents, but it is not as pronounced or severe as the opposite dynamic, in which work spills over into the home. Table A.3 in the Appendix offers some insight into these processes. This table summarizes the results of separate regression equations for men and women, analyzing a range of factors that might account for job-to-home spillover. To untangle the relative influences of individual attributes, working time, and workplace arrangements on spillover from the workplace to the home, it uses a composite measure of "negative" spillover.

The American labor force is increasingly diverse, so it is important to understand how workers with varying resources living in varying family situations cope with job demands and structures that may not be as varied or flexible as they would like. In addition to individual resources, we need to know if job structures and arrangements influence the experience of work-to-home spillover. Working time, of course, is likely to be important, but what about a worker's job schedule or level of personal autonomy at work? Do these matter as much, or more, than one's personal situation? To explore these relationships, we need to look at such factors as working time and intensity and job flexibility. And since feeling satisfied with one's life choices may be more important than the choices themselves, we also need to know if job satisfaction makes a difference in the perception that one's work interferes in negative ways (Gerson 2001; Hoffman et al. 1999). Table A.3 in the Appendix shows the relative influence of each of these factors for women and men, beginning with a worker's personal situation, moving on to work time and intensity, and then exploring the role of job flexibility and satisfaction.

For women, personal circumstances make a difference, but so do work conditions. Younger women workers and those with children under 18 experience more conflict than older workers and those without dependent children, but so do women who work many hours per day, bring work home, work at nonstandard times, and generally feel under pressure at work. On a more upbeat note, work flexibility, especially in the form of increased autonomy and a supportive workplace culture and supervisor, lessens the perception of conflict, interference, and stress.

It is surely unsurprising that having dependent children increases women's sense of conflict, but it underscores the importance of these concerns. Mothers with young children are one of the fastest-growing groups in the paid labor force, and their rising numbers increase the pool of workers for whom work-family issues are so salient. The meaning of a decline in perceived conflict as women age is more ambiguous. As women grow older, they may develop strategies to cope with work-family challenges, but they may also have simply adjusted to and become less likely to object to the conflicts they face. In any case, after controlling for other measures, it appears that a woman's educational level does not affect her sense of conflict.

Women who work longer hours per day and who often bring work home also experience more work-family conflict. While it is not surprising to find that time and intensity on the job contribute to spillover, it underscores the importance of paying attention to the time workers spend at work and the pressures they face to work even while not "officially" at the workplace. As the physical and temporal boundaries of jobs continue to blur, there is good reason to anticipate that the incursion of paid work into family time and private space will become even more common and more problematic (Galinsky, Kim, and Bond 2001).

Job schedules and a perceived sense of pressure also make a difference for women. Those who worked nonstandard shifts, which do not coincide with a regular daytime schedule, experienced added spillover from work to home. And women who frequently work under pressure were much more likely to experience work-family conflict than were those who feel less pressure at work. Beyond the amount of time a job extracts, the intensity and timing of work also shape how a job affects life at home. If growing numbers of workers face more intense and pressured work arrangements along with less standard schedules (as Presser 2003 has shown), the sense that one's job is spilling over and interfering with private life is likely to grow. While Presser and others (for example, Garey 1999) have noted that some parents of young children seek out evening and night shifts so as to ensure that one parent is always available for child care, the effect of such nonstandard schedules can make it difficult for parents and children to spend time together as a whole family.

Finally, work flexibility also matters. Greater flexibility and autonomy at work can help lessen the conflicts experienced by women workers. Those with more autonomy on the job and those who enjoy more family-friendly workplace cultures and supervisors are less likely to experience negative spillover from their jobs. As important, higher job satisfaction also reduces perceived conflicts, but even taking this into account, work structure remains consequential. The importance of supervisor support in our findings is telling, for it suggests that family-supportive policies depend on the discretion of individual supervisors. Work organizations can take measures to lessen the consequences of work spilling over into life, but only by insuring that family supports are provided at the lowest levels.[6]

Men's experience of spillover from work to home emerges from similar circumstances. Like women, younger men and those with children under eighteen experience more spillover, as do those working more hours and those who are under more pressure from their jobs. Like women, men who are more satisfied with their jobs, who have more control over their schedules, and whose supervisors are more supportive experience less spillover.

Since most married women have an er..ployed partner and since employed men are likely to contribute less to the work of the household than their partners, having an employed husband makes little difference in shaping women's perception of work-family conflict. While one might expect that having an employed wife might make more of a difference for men, our results do not support this conclusion. Instead, the attributes of people's jobs make the clearest difference. Among factors associated with family structure, the presence of children in the household has the strongest influence on workers' perception of spillover from job to home.

In several cases, differences between men and women may be real, but they do not appear to be statistically significant. Men thus report having more control over their work schedules than do women, and having this control reduces stress for men, but the gender difference is not statistically significant. And having a child under eighteen at home appears to increase spillover for women more than for men, but the gender difference here is also not quite significant. In general, it appears that common features of jobs impinge on the lives of working men and women in similar ways. Taken together, the factors we examined account for a substantial proportion of the variation in the level of spillover—30 percent for women and 28 percent for men.

Clearly, the difficulties of integrating family and work are not confined to women and are not simply a "woman's problem." These conflicts have structural roots, and they emerge from the institutional conflicts that confront any worker who must blend family responsibilities and the demands of a rigid or encroaching job. If more women experience these conflicts, or if women experience them more intensely, that is because women are more likely to face these difficult circumstances.

Elder Care and the Sandwich Generation

In the Changing Workforce survey, 37.9 percent of working women said yes to the question "During the past year have you worried about an elderly relative while at work?" while 11.0 percent reported that they provide care to an elderly relative or dependent adult because of a handicap, illness, or old age. For employed men, 34.8 percent worried about an elderly relative (which is not statistically distinguishable from the figure for women), but men were less likely than women to provide care (7.4 percent).

Concern over the health of elderly relatives is more common than actual caregiving. Caring for elderly relatives typically occurs later in life than caring for young children, but the overlap between the two will rise as people have children at older ages. For working women in the Changing Workforce sample, just under half (43.7 percent) had children under age eighteen to care for, one in ten (11.0 percent) had elder-care responsibilities, and one in twenty (4.0 percent) had both. From the children's point of view, the chances of having one's parents also caring for grandparents are roughly one in ten. From the grandparents' point of view, however, roughly one third of their adult children have their own children under age eighteen to care for.

We examined the influence of elder care on the sense of work-family conflict and found the results instructive. We did not include elder care in the model of work-family conflict (reported in Appendix Table A.3) because it failed to be statistically significant. We did find that the story differs for men and women. For working women, the initial results showed that providing elder care has a significant effect on the perception of work-family conflict. However, when job demands and supervisor support are taken into account, elder care by itself is no longer a statistically significant factor. In other words, having a supportive supervisor and a job that is not overly stressful enables working women to handle the demands of elder care. For men, the provision of elder care has no discernable influence on stress, even before other factors are taken into account.

Work Matters

Taken as a whole, the picture that emerges suggests that family does not interfere with work as much as might be expected—and certainly not as much as work interferes with family. The burden falls heaviest on workers at particular life stages and especially when children are growing up. Since most workers will experience and ultimately pass through these stages, there is good reason to structure jobs and work careers to lessen the short-term burdens and long-term consequences of raising the next generation (or caring for an aging one). And since work structure matters, we should pay attention to how job arrangements can alleviate stresses and minimize negative aspects of spillover, especially for those women and men in the high-demand stages of child rearing.

Have job pressures increased over the past generation? It is not easy to answer this question. Not only are such pressures experienced subjectively, but also researchers rarely ask the same question over time so that trends may be assessed. The available evidence nevertheless corroborates the argument that jobs today are more demanding, at least on average, than they were several decades ago. When asked, for example, "How much would you say your job and your family life interfere with each other?" people in 1997 reported a higher level of interference than those in 1977, even after taking various control factors into account (Winslow 2002).

These findings are broadly consistent with John Robinson and Geoffrey Godbey's contention that a gradual increase has occurred from the 1960s through the 1990s in the proportion of Americans who report feeling rushed all of the time, with a concomitant decline in the proportion saying that they had free time on their hands (Robinson and Godbey 1999, p. 232). While these questions were not directly linked to workplace experiences, changes at the workplace could well be an important factor contributing to this trend.

Once considered separate spheres, the domains of work and family can no longer be so easily divided. The notion of distinct but complementary spheres has been replaced by a growing concern that the demands of work are increasingly at odds with the needs of families, most of whom now depend on either two earners or one (female) parent. Yet the organization of work continues to be based on the principle that work commitment means uninterrupted, full-time, and even overtime attention for a span of decades. This clash between family needs and workplace pressures has produced a new image based not on the notion of separate spheres, but on work-family conflict.

The experience of conflict is common, if not universal. Working parents—especially mothers—are consistently more likely to voice concerns about the challenges they face trying to meet their responsibilities at home and at work. Those who work the most hours, not surprisingly, feel these stresses most acutely. And the nature of the job matters, too: those in jobs with a great deal of pressure, low autonomy, and little support for family issues are most apt to feel that their jobs spill over into their private lives.

How can these conflicts be alleviated? Given the time that most people must devote to work, we need to know what kind of workplace arrangements make a difference in workers' abilities to resolve the conflicts they face. We also need to know if workers perceive that serious costs or risks are associated with options that are ostensibly designed to ease their plight. We need, in short, to better understand what kinds of work arrangements and conditions—beyond the matter of working time—help to alleviate workers' conflicts. In the next chapter, we explore how the structure and culture of the workplace can either exacerbate or alleviate the conflicts workers face.

5

The Structure and Culture
of Work

Focusing on working time alone neglects an equally important aspect of work-family conflict: the actual conditions of work. Since most workers have limited control over the amount of time they work, it is critical to determine whether other circumstances at work can help lessen the experience of conflict.

To discover how workplace structure and culture shape workers' experiences, we again draw from the 1992 Changing Workforce survey (Galinsky, Bond, and Friedman 1993). First, we explore how the structure and culture of the workplace can either exacerbate or alleviate the conflicts workers face. Especially for workers who must put in long hours, aspects of a job such as flexibility, autonomy, and control are likely to matter as much as working time. Next, we examine the supply of and demand for family-supportive options, such as flexible scheduling and child-care services. How widespread are these options? Do workers use them when they are offered? Would workers use them if they were offered? Finally, we consider the hidden costs of family-supportive workplace policies. Even when such options are formally available, workers may conclude that taking advantage of them entails unspoken, but very real, penalties and dangers. What are the conflicts between "family-friendly" and "high-opportunity" work environments? Do workers perceive that making use of policies that provide for family support is at odds with their long-term prospects for job or career?

Assuming that work arrangements offering flexibility, autonomy, and control can help workers resolve conflicts between family and work, we need to understand how such arrangements can be implemented fairly. The challenge is to develop social and economic policies that lessen current dilemmas without sacrificing either gender equity or children's wel-

99

fare. If the principle of equal opportunity is at odds with the principle of parental support, family-friendly workplace policies run the risk of reinstituting old inequalities in a new form.

Flexibility at the Workplace

For many workers, especially those with little ability to limit their working time, flexibility and autonomy at work may matter as much as—or more than—actual working hours. Although there are many intangible features of workplace culture that are difficult to measure, the degree of flexibility a worker possesses in scheduling her or his work hours is one that can be studied. Furthermore, not only is control over scheduling important in its own right; it is also likely to be linked to other circumstances at the workplace, such as a sense of having autonomy and feeling support (Glass and Finley 2002). For full-time workers in particular, forty-five flexible hours may seem less onerous than thirty-five rigidly scheduled ones. Indeed, many workers may be willing to work more in exchange for greater flexibility.

Flexibility gives workers some sense of control over when (and, in some cases, where) they work. It also provides workers with greater discretion over how they meet their family responsibilities and so enables them to better integrate the public and private aspects of their lives. S. Jody Heymann (2000) has shown, for example, how rigid work schedules make it difficult for parents to attend teacher's conferences and to help with the care of their chronically ill children. Despite the often criticized notion of "quality time," there are good reasons to believe that workers with flexibility and control over their working conditions will derive greater pleasure from work and be happier, more supportive family members. Indeed, decades of research have consistently shown that satisfaction with work and good child-care arrangements are critical factors affecting the welfare of employed parents and their children.[1]

In order to determine who has flexible schedules and whether this flexibility makes a difference, we examined answers to the question "Overall, how much control would you say you have in scheduling your work hours—none, very little, some, a lot, or complete flexibility?" We discovered that the overall perception of personal control is remarkably similar for women and men. Forty-four percent of women and 42 percent of men respond that they have "none" or "very little," while another 26 percent of women and 27 percent of men say they have "some." At the other end of the spectrum, 30 percent of women and men report having "a lot" or "complete flexibility." At this general level, gender does not appear to be linked to job flexibility, as some have suggested (for example, Glass 1990). Our findings are in line with those of other studies using the *Current Population Survey* on flexible work schedules (Beers 2000; U.S. Bureau of Labor Statistics 2002b).

Although one might expect that flexible schedules represent an adjustment or accommodation to long workweeks, there appears to be no strong or significant link between working time and flexibility. Among men, no relationship emerges between control over scheduling and hours worked.[2] Women who work long hours report less flexibility than those with less demanding jobs, but the relationship is not strong ($r = -.13$). Work flexibility is thus not simply a reflection of overall hours worked.

A closer look reveals some hidden effects of gender beneath the apparently similar and generally weak link between working time and control over scheduling. Figure 5.1 shows a curvilinear relationship between workers' perceptions of flexibility and the number of hours they usually work in their main job, but the extent of the curve differs by gender. It is not sur-

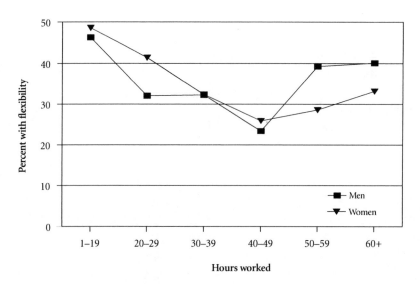

Figure 5.1 Scheduling flexibility, by gender and hours, 1993 (*Source:* National Study of the Changing Workforce)

prising that a high percentage of both women and men with relatively short workweeks report more flexibility. Nor is it surprising that the percentage who report flexibility declines steadily for both women and men as hours increase until the number of hours reaches forty to forty-nine. Part-time work is, almost by definition, more flexible. While flexibility may be an unintended by-product of fewer working hours, many may opt for shorter hours as a strategy for obtaining flexibility.

Among workers who have very long workweeks, however, men and women diverge in unanticipated ways. While men who work fifty or more hours per week report substantial increases in flexibility, women in this situation experience this rebound to a much smaller degree. For men, working relatively short or long workweeks bestows flexibility, leaving those in the middle relatively squeezed. For women, however, there is no such reward for working more hours. Women at the high end of the spectrum lack the autonomy and control that similarly situated men enjoy.

The lack of flexibility available to highly committed women workers signals difficulties for women (and their families) on several fronts. Most obviously, it implies that those workers most likely to be shouldering heavy burdens at work and at home are less likely to have the flexibility they need. Equally problematic, we suspect that committed working women's lack of control at work likely reflects a hidden consequence of the glass ceiling, which limits women's upward mobility. While men who put in many hours at work may enjoy the rewards of achieving positions of authority, women who do the same are less likely to attain sufficient status to control their schedules.[3]

Since job conditions and workplace support appear as consequential as working hours in shaping workers' experiences, it is important to discover the structural and personal factors that either enhance or diminish perceptions of control over work scheduling. Do work conditions remain consequential even when more personal characteristics, such as family situation, are taken into account? Economists, especially those who emphasize the role of human capital in labor-market processes, argue that men and women make contrasting work choices because they prefer a different balance between family and work (see, for example, Becker 1981). They contend that men prefer to maximize earnings and job success to support their families, while women with children are willing to sacrifice economic reward and upward mobility in order to invest more time in family pursuits. This argument implies that women, especially married mothers, are more likely to choose more flexible jobs while men, especially married fathers, are more likely to make work choices based on other criteria.

Gender and Family Situation

Is work flexibility linked to gender and family situation? The answer appears to be "no." When the simple association between family attributes and flexibility at work is examined, we find no link to such key indicators as being married and having children in the household.[4] Moreover, having an employed spouse has no influence on either women's or men's own work flexibility, and neither does a spouse's number of work hours. For women, there is also no link between placing a higher importance on a husband's job and choosing flexible work. And men who place more importance on a wife's job are less, rather than more, likely to experience flexibility in their own jobs.

There is thus no support for the contention that women choose and men eschew flexible work in order to reproduce a gendered division of work in the home. Family obligations may increase the pressures on working parents, but neither mothers nor fathers enjoy more flexibility to meet these demands. And our research suggests that jobs in female-dominated occupational categories, such as clerical, sales, and health-care occupations, are generally less flexible than those in male-dominated occupations, especially in the professional sector.

The Relative Importance of Individual, Family, and Workplace Conditions

Since few have the power to choose the conditions of their work based on their private needs, it should come as no surprise that family situation is not linked to work flexibility. Despite the rise of dual-earner and single-parent homes, employers, far more than workers, set the conditions under which parents combine work and family.

The crucial importance of work conditions becomes especially clear in Table A.4 in the Appendix, which presents the multivariate relationships between workplace flexibility and a range of individual, family, and workplace factors. Even after such personal attributes as age, education, job experience, and family situation are taken into account, work structure and culture remain consistently important factors linked to job flexibility.

Are hours on the job linked to control over scheduling? One might expect that long workweeks would mean less control over one's schedule, and indeed women do report this type of trade-off. But the association is quite small for women and is not evident for men.

Do those with more family obligations sort themselves into jobs with more scheduling flexibility? We were unable to find much evidence to support this common assumption. Among men, those with children at home and those whose wives held paid jobs reported having less control over their schedules than did other men. For women, marital and parental status were not statistically significant. This evidence reinforces the conclusion that those who need flexibility the most are often unable to find it.

We were surprised that older workers were not located in more flexible positions. There was no age effect for men, and older women actually tended to have slightly less scheduling flexibility. Seniority might be expected to enhance flexibility, but our examination of the effects of length of time in a particular job and tenure with the firm did not bear this out.

Which jobs are the most flexible? In general, the higher the status of the job, the more employees are able to control schedules—but there are exceptions. Among men, education enhances flexibility, and white-collar positions are more flexible than blue-collar jobs. For women, education *per se* does not enhance flexibility, but the impact of being in a white-collar position is sharper for women than for men. Thus, for both men and women, either education directly or employment in more prestigious occupations, which is closely associated with education, is tied to greater scheduling flexibility. For both men and women, union and public-sector jobs tend to have more fixed schedules and thus reduced scheduling flexibility.

Supportive supervisors and workplace cultures are another factor in job flexibility: those having supportive supervisors are more likely to have flexibility.[5] Yet it is job autonomy—control over the content of one's job—that provides the most powerful link with workplace flexibility. Job autonomy increases the percent of explained variance from 13 to 19 percent for men and from 11 to 18 percent for women. When autonomy is taken into account, the relative importance of such factors as workplace culture and supervisor support appears to diminish. However, all of these contextual factors are highly intertwined and tend to occur together as aspects of the overall work environment, and they have similar consequences for men and women in similar situations.

We stress the similarities in the influence of job attributes for men and women because there is a tendency to exaggerate the differences. Indeed, the focus on gender differences often leads people to forget the tremendous overlap in the experiences of men and women. Nonetheless, there are some interesting differences that are worth noting. Men with long work commutes report less scheduling flexibility, while women do not. This finding may reflect the fact that women's commutes tend to be somewhat shorter than men's. Also, women with supervisory responsibility report sharply higher scheduling flexibility than other women. This effect is not evident for men, perhaps because men in nonsupervisory positions have more flexibility than do their female counterparts. Men who are employed in jobs that are eligible for overtime report less scheduling flexibility, while the opposite is so for women.

These results highlight the different types of work-family challenges posed by different types of jobs. Professional and managerial positions often demand many hours at work but sometimes offer scheduling flexibility not available in clerical and assembly-line jobs. Many pink- and blue-collar jobs offer more regular, but more rigid, schedules and pay wages that are too low for these workers to buy the extra services available to the affluent. In setting the work-family policy agenda, we thus need to address the problems of all workers and not focus exclusively on the issues facing busy professionals.

Workplace structure and culture make an important difference in workers' lives. Employers' support for flexible work arrangements, especially in the form of understanding supervisors and a supportive workplace environment, give both women and men more control over how to balance work and family life. And while similar work conditions affect female and male workers in similar ways, men are more likely to obtain privileges at the workplace that give them more felicitous work circumstances.

Family-Friendly Workplace Options

Workplace conditions, especially flexibility over working hours, are as important to busy Americans as time spent working. Control over working hours is nevertheless only one part of a larger package of family-supportive policies that offer workers the chance to ease their work-family conflicts and gain more discretion about how to meet their multiple obligations. Other possible family-friendly options include job sharing, shorter workweeks, parental leaves, child-care services, and elder-care support.

Our findings reveal strong worker support for family-supportive workplace policies. A large proportion of workers who have these benefits use them (though it should be noted that many of these benefits are situation specific: not everyone needs them all of the time). In addition, a substantial proportion of those who do not have family benefits express a willingness to trade other benefits and even, in many cases, to change jobs to receive them. Clearly, there is a high demand and perceived need for supportive workplace policies.

Even though workers want and often use family support policies, there remains the possibility that many are reluctant to take advantage of these options because they fear that doing so will entail costs and sanctions. Indeed, such options might be used more if they were perceived to be free of career- or job-threatening penalties. In other words, family-supportive workplace policies may be formally available but informally frowned upon. In this section, we aim to gain a clearer picture of what types of family-supportive options are currently available to workers, as well as what workers would like to have available and what obstacles prevent them from taking advantage of opportunities that either exist or might be developed.

Flexible Scheduling

Information on the availability, use, and demand for a wide range of family-supportive benefits can be found in Table A.5 in the Appendix. When it comes to flexible scheduling, it appears that a large proportion of the workforce (almost 86 percent) has the discretion to change their working hours "as needed," but far fewer can set their own hours (29 percent) or change them daily (40 percent). Differences across groups of workers are generally small and inconsistent. However, there are some notable exceptions. Professional men, including those with children under six, are most likely to be able to set their own working hours (about 40 percent), but professional men with young children are the least likely to report being able to change their hours daily (23 percent compared with 40 percent for the total workforce) or to change their hours as needed (74 percent compared with 86 percent for the workforce). Among women, professionals with children under six are the least likely (26 percent) to be able to set their hours and are also disadvantaged in terms of changing their hours daily (38 percent). Here is more evidence that, at least among professional and managerial workers, those most likely to need flexible scheduling have a more difficult time getting it.

There is, however, some good news. Professionals with young children have comparatively more access to such benefits as extended breaks, working more one day in order to work less the next, and working at home. However, it appears that these benefits accrue to professional status and, to a lesser extent, gender rather than family status. In general, professional men fare better than either professional women or nonprofessional workers. Among professional men, 63 percent can take extended breaks at work (compared to 41 percent for nonprofessional workers), 50 percent can vary the length of the work day (compared to 41 percent for nonprofessionals), 39 percent can work at home regularly (compared to 13 percent for nonprofessionals), and 25 percent can do so occasionally (compared to 8 percent for nonprofessionals). Women professionals fare better than nonprofessionals, but not as well as their male counterparts, who enjoy an advantage when it comes to being able to take extended breaks and working at home occasionally.

Among those who can take extended work breaks, vary the length of the workday, and work at home, a very high proportion do so. Among all groups, the percentage making use of these options does not drop below 63 percent and reaches as high as 88 percent. When given a choice, both women and men with young children seem to prefer more time at home and less time socializing at the office. This finding seems commonsensical, but it is worth mentioning because it casts additional doubt on the argument that parents are avoiding time with children in order to socialize at work. Indeed, the high proportion of workers who take advantage of the opportunity to work at home and vary the length of their working day suggests a strong demand for work arrangements that allow people to integrate work and family life more thoroughly and flexibly.

Part-Time Work and the Willingness to Trade Pay for a Day Off

Professional women, especially those with young children, are the most likely to enjoy the options of part-time work and, to a lesser extent, job sharing. Compared to their female peers, professional men with young children are much less likely to have the option to work part-time (59 percent for women compared to 45 percent for men) or to be willing to trade pay for the opportunity to work less (38 percent for women compared to 15 percent for men). Women appear to be more able to cut back on their careers, but this discrepancy in the options of men and women does not bode well for women's ability to gain equality.

Part-time work is a less popular option than flexible scheduling or working at home, because of the high immediate and long-term costs of working part-time. As shown in Table A.6 of the Appendix, only 16 percent of all workers would trade a benefit and only 11 percent of workers would change jobs to obtain part-time work. However, among professional women with young children, 32 percent would trade another benefit, although only 15 percent would change jobs in order to work part-time.

Child-Care Services

While unpaid parental leaves are required by law and are almost universally available, child-care services are notable by their lack of availability (see Table A.6 in the Appendix). Only a small percentage of workers are offered either child-care (or elder-care) referral services, employer-sponsored child care, or child-care vouchers. Among professionals with children under six, these figures remain low. Among women in this category, 24 percent have access to a referral service, 19 percent to employer day care, and 3 percent to vouchers. Among men, the percentages are comparable: 26 percent, 14 percent, and 7 percent.

Among professional workers with young children who have child-care benefits, a large minority takes advantage of them. Thus, 31 percent of women and 38 percent of men make use of child-care resources and referrals. In addition, 42 percent of mothers and 47 percent of fathers use employer sponsored day care. Finally, 40 percent of mothers and 16 percent of fathers use child-care vouchers. Though less than half of professional parents use the child-care resources offered by their employers, a sizable number do. After all, professionals are likely to have the financial and social resources to arrange child care privately. In this context, it is notable that so many rely on employer services.

The Demand for Family Benefits among Those without Them

What about the majority of workers, who do not enjoy family-supportive benefits such as flexible scheduling, the choice of working at home, and child-care services? Many not only desire these benefits but would be willing to trade other benefits and even change their jobs to get them. This is especially so for professional mothers with young children (see Table A.6).

Among workers who do not have flexible schedules, about 28 percent would be willing to trade other benefits and 26 percent would be willing to change jobs to get flexibility. For professional women with children under six, the percentages rise to 49 percent and 32 percent, respectively. Only 12 percent of professional fathers would give up another benefit for flexibility, but 29 percent would change their job.

The chance to work at home is also in high demand. Among all workers, 21 percent would trade other benefits to obtain such an option, and 22 percent would change jobs. For professional mothers, the percentages rise to 48 percent and 32 percent. For fathers, again we find less interest than among mothers: while only 18 percent of professional fathers would trade another benefit for the chance to work at home, 24 percent would change jobs for this option.

Finally, child-care services and resources appear to be a popular idea among those parents who are not offered them. Thus, 18 percent of professional mothers and fathers with young children would trade another benefit to get child-care resources. More important, 49 percent of mothers and 31 percent of fathers would trade for employer-sponsored child care, and 40 percent of mothers and 35 percent of fathers would trade for child-care vouchers.

Clearly, the desire for family-supportive options among workers, especially among mothers and fathers with young children, is high. With the exception of benefits that entail high economic and other costs, such as part-time work, a large percentage of workers use family-supportive benefits when they are available. When they are not available, a large percentage would be willing to trade other work benefits and even change jobs to obtain them. Again, we find little support for the argument that workers prefer to spend their time at the workplace rather than with their children. Instead of supportive workplaces pulling workers away from strife-ridden families, family-supportive workplaces tend to enhance workers' family involvement. When workers lack such support, they often wish they had it and are prepared to give up other perquisites to get it.

The Hidden Costs of Family-Supportive Policies

Workers, especially parents with young children and employed partners, clearly benefit from family-supportive arrangements. Support for such options as work flexibility, autonomy, and control over scheduling is high. And most workers who do not have these benefits wish they did. When, for example, the option to work more one day and less the next is available, 75 percent of workers take advantage of it (including 81 percent of professional women and 74 percent of professional men with children under six). Similarly, among those who are allowed to work at home occasionally, 79 percent choose to do so (including 88 percent of professional women and 84 percent of professional men with young children).

When given a genuine choice, both women and men, especially those with young children, prefer more flexibility at work and more time at home. When the option is available, a high proportion of workers take advantage of the opportunity to work at home and vary the length of their working day. Similarly, when flexible scheduling is not available, a remarkable number of women and men appear willing to make other work sacrifices to obtain it. In contrast to the notion that workers are pursuing personal gratification at work rather than meeting the needs of their families and children, this picture suggests instead that they are striving for more flexible and fluid options for integrating these no longer so separate spheres.

Despite the large and often unmet desire for family-supportive work arrangements, however, many workers may be fearful that taking advantage of family-friendly policies will be costly. A relatively low interest in part-time work, for example, suggests that workers are reluctant to use options that might threaten their economic and career prospects. Thus, only 16 percent of workers would be willing to trade other benefits and only 11 percent would be willing to change jobs to have a part-time option. Among professionals with young children, the part-time option remains equally unattractive, with only 15 percent of women and 5 percent of men willing to change jobs.

Such options might be more popular if they were believed to be free of career- or job-threatening penalties. It is thus crucial to understand whether workers perceive family-friendly policies to be formally available but informally stigmatized. By doing so, we gain a clearer picture not only of what workers need but also what obstacles prevent them from meeting or even expressing these needs to those in a position to provide them.

The costs of choosing to work less than exceedingly long workweeks can be particularly acute for professional workers. In *The Part-Time Paradox,* Cynthia Epstein and her colleagues report, for example, that lawyers must endure both short-term disapproval and longer-term career sacrifices for challenging "time norms" that expect them to work far more than forty hours a week (Epstein et al. 1999). They show how work organizations stigmatize those putting in less than very long working hours as "time deviants," creating intractable double-binds for committed workers who also wish to be involved parents. In high-pressure occupations such as law, where eighty-plus hours a week is common, the once-standard forty-hour workweek has come to be defined as part-time. These time norms exact a toll on those who resist them as well as those who do not, forcing all to choose between occupational success and time for private life (see also Epstein and Kalleberg forthcoming).[6]

In theory, family support and gender equity are the organizing principles upon which family-supportive policies are built. And many workers appear prepared to make substantial sacrifices in order to obtain them. Yet these policies may also pose dangers, since making use of family benefits can entail risks to a work career. If such policies target only women, they threaten to recreate earlier forms of gender inequality in a new form. "Mommy tracks," for example, ask women to forgo upward mobility in order to combine motherhood and work (Schwartz 1989). Such policies force women to confront an unfair choice between motherhood and a career, while excluding men from the expectation that they have parental responsibilities. "Gender-neutral" family policies may appear less pernicious. Buy if they stigmatize parental involvement, both involved mothers *and* fathers are disadvantaged. It is a dubious social policy that rewards parents of either sex for subordinating family needs to work and career.

The economic costs of parenting remain sizable. Michele Budig and Paula England (2001) estimate that mothers are paid 7 percent less for every additional child they have. But this figure substantially understates the cost of parenting because it compares individuals who worked the same number of hours. The principal way that motherhood affects earnings is to reduce working time, including pushing mothers to withdraw from the labor force. Ann Crittenden (2001) is in the right ballpark when she suggests that the cost of becoming a mother in terms of lost lifetime earnings can easily exceed half a million dollars for a middle-income woman and well over a million dollars for a woman with a college degree. The economic losses to women in less rewarded jobs may be lower in absolute numbers, but they are surely as (or more) important to their families' welfare.

In the best of all possible worlds, neither mothers nor fathers would be penalized for taking care of their children. And surely such a world would not exact a higher price from women than from men. Yet the evidence suggests that "family-friendly" does not necessarily mean either "woman-friendly" or "parent-friendly." Despite the heralding of policies to ease the plight of employed mothers, options that provide family support at the expense of career advancement exact significant costs to anyone who might choose them. In contrast, policies that not only provide for a fluid balance between family and work but also safeguard the work opportunities of the person who uses them are more than just family-friendly. By protecting the rights of employed women and acknowledging the needs of work-committed parents of either sex, such policies would be genuinely woman-friendly, parent-friendly, and child-friendly. The rise of family-supportive policies, however, has more often been conceived in terms of "mommy tracks" that penalize employed mothers and exclude fathers altogether.

Since employers are reluctant to admit that their policies are offered at great cost, it is difficult to ascertain the exact nature of the risks workers take when they seek or use family-supportive options. It is, however, possible to uncover whether or not workers perceive that formally available policies contain informal but heavy sanctions. Moreover, the perception of risk, regardless of its objective validity, is crucial in shaping how workers weigh their options and make their choices. We thus examine the relationship between workers' perceptions of whether their workplace culture is family-supportive and their perceptions about advancement opportunities for women and other groups.

As Table 5.1 reveals, workers with supportive workplace cultures typically report having supportive supervisors as well, and for women, the link is especially strong ($r = .44$). Yet family-friendly workplaces do not appear to provide the best opportunities to advance. Having a supportive workplace culture is thus negatively related to women's perceptions for both white and African-American women's chances for advancement. Equally noteworthy, these women also report that such workplaces do not necessarily provide good opportunities for white and minority men as well. Perhaps most significant is the fact that women's perceptions of their *own* chances for advancement are negatively related to their beliefs that their workplaces are family-supportive.

When the focus is supervisor support for family-friendly arrangements rather than the general level of supportiveness at the workplace as a whole, the same pattern emerges; here, in fact, the relationships are even stronger. The negative link between supervisor support for family-friendly arrange-

Table 5.1 Relationship between family-friendly workplace culture and self-reported chances for advancement

	Workplace culture	Supervisor support
Women		
Workplace culture[a]	1.00	.44
Supervisor support[b]	.44	1.00
Chances to advance:		
White women	−.12	−.21
Minority women	−.17	−.28
White men	−.07	−.07
Minority men	−.15	−.22
Respondent's own chances	−.18	−.31
Men		
Workplace culture[a]	1.00	.46
Supervisor support[b]	.46	1.00
Chances to advance:		
White women	−.12	−.17
Minority women	−.15	−.18
White men	−.09	−.19
Minority men	−.14	−.21
Respondent's own chances	−.18	−.32

Source: National Study of the Changing Workforce, 1992.

a. Workplace culture is a composite of 4 items designed to tap whether the respondent's working environment is sensitive to work-family issues.

b. Supervisor support is a composite of 9 items designed to tap whether the respondent's supervisor is attentive to workers' needs and concerns.

Note: All correlations statistically significant, $p < .05$.

ments and women's perceptions of their own chances for advancement is the strongest ($r = -.31$). Moreover, these patterns are virtually identical for men. Men also perceive that having a family-supportive workplace culture and a supportive supervisor is less likely to result in chances for advancement for *any* group. They agree with women that having a supervisor who is supportive of family needs is also less likely to enhance their *own* chances for advancement ($r = -.32$).

Do these perceptions persist when other factors are taken into account? While a family-supportive workplace culture remains negatively associated with chances for advancement, the effects become attenuated as other factors, such as autonomy, are added (Jacobs and Gerson 1997). When supervisor support is included, the effect of workplace culture disappears altogether, but the effect of supervisor support remains. This pattern occurs for women whether they are asked about advancement opportunities for themselves or for other women, and it holds for men as well.

Women and men alike thus tend to perceive that family-friendly workplace policies come with costly strings attached. Their concern about being forced to choose between family-supportive options and career building are probably well founded. The *New York Times* has reported, for example, that the companies with the best record for promoting women are not the same as those that have the most supportive family policies (Dobrzynski 1996).

Genuine family support in the workplace must move beyond organizations' mere tinkering at the edges; we need to restructure the basic assumptions on which they are built. At its core, a workplace that is "woman-friendly" and "parent-friendly" also needs to support the careers of those who wish to invest time in the unpaid work of caring for their families even as they strive at work.

Creating Flexible and Egalitarian Workplaces

While the debate over work and family change in America has focused largely on the issue of overwork, working time is only one of several important ingredients contributing to both work-family conflict and gender inequality. Workplace structure and culture matter, and workers who enjoy job flexibility and employer support are clearly better off than those who do not. Most full-time workers desire more time for family and leisure than they now enjoy and strongly support family-friendly workplace options. Unfortunately, they also perceive that the benefits these policies offer can only be gained at considerable cost.

Gender inequality persists in institutional arrangements, yet women and men increasingly face similar dilemmas. As women build ever-stronger ties to the workplace and families confront the time squeezes posed by dual-earning arrangements, mothers and fathers must cope with conflicts that ensue not simply from family demands but more fundamentally from intransigent job constraints. When women and men face similar circumstances, their responses are also similar. Yet, more often than not, men and women confront different options and pressures. In the struggle to resolve work-family conflicts, persisting gender inequality continues to place

women at a disadvantage. Women shoulder more responsibility for domestic work, and they also face larger obstacles at the workplace, including
less autonomy and flexibility on the job and more pressure to make career
sacrifices by cutting back time at work, at least temporarily.

If women are more likely than men to cut back on time at work in the
face of family contingencies, this fact reflects differences in the opportunities and constraints they face. The organization of economic and family life
leaves women with greater pressures, and more options, to pull back from
work. Although the gender gap in earnings has declined and a rising proportion of wives earn as much as or more than their husbands, most couples do not fit this pattern. (Just one dual-earner household in five has a
wife who earns more than her husband, and some of these cases may represent temporary fluctuations in earnings rather than an enduring role reversal.)[7] The more common situation, in which a husband earns more than
the wife, encourages mothers to reduce their time at work and fathers to
maximize their earnings by working more. Cultural pressures also continue to stress the caregiving obligations of mothers and the breadwinning
responsibilities of fathers. Gender differences in the time spent at work and
in parenting thus reflect the persistence of unequal opportunities even as
the "aspiration gap" between women and men diminishes.[8]

While the problems workers face take different forms, most share the
same desire to integrate gratifying work with family involvement. Beyond
economic security and opportunity, women and men alike wish some
measure of flexibility in how they choose to integrate the many obligations
they shoulder. In a world where both mothers and fathers must work, no
group should have to sacrifice opportunity and economic welfare in order
to make time for their families.

Since the problem of work-family conflict has institutional roots, the
resolutions depend on institutional transformations. To provide genuine
opportunities for committed workers to be involved parents, we need to
focus on workplace organization and the structure of opportunities that
parents (and those who wish to become parents) face. If we fail to see the
social sources of personal dilemmas, we are left blaming ordinary women
and men for conditions they did not create and cannot control. A social
and institutional focus, in contrast, makes it clear that social policy needs
to uphold two important and inextricable principles: equal opportunity
for women and penalty-free support for involved parents, regardless of sex.

Work, Family,
and Social Policy

6

American Workers in Cross-National Perspective

With Janet C. Gornick

Although the growth of time pressures between paid work and domestic life has dramatically altered the lives of American workers, many of these trends are not unique to the United States. The rise of employed women, for example, is a worldwide phenomenon that can be found in all economically advanced societies. Yet the United States appears atypical in its response to these basic economic and social transformations, lagging behind most countries in the social support it provides for families, children, and employed parents.

Comparing the circumstances of U.S. workers to those in other countries who share America's level of economic and social development provides a yardstick by which to measure national changes. By pinpointing the ways in which American workers are similar to, and different from, workers in other countries, a comparative perspective expands the picture provided by historical analysis of work and family change. Cross-national comparisons also provide some clues to the range of policy interventions that might make a difference in the lives of workers. If some aspects of change are shared by all, there is good reason to believe that these trends represent deeply rooted social and economic trends that are not subject to substantial alteration. If, however, the United States looks vastly different from other countries—especially in terms of how it responds to basic economic transformations, there is good reason to conclude that policies can be developed to help Americans better cope with the challenges spawned by change. A comparative perspective allows us to untangle what is endemic to postindustrial development and what is amenable to change. It also provides some hints about how well or poorly policy approaches in other countries can help Americans resolve the dilemmas they confront.

This chapter thus focuses on comparisons between the United States, Canada, and eight European countries using information from the mid-1990s from the Luxembourg Income Study (De Tombeur 1995). We focus on these countries and this time period not only because the information is readily available, but also because these countries share a similar cultural heritage and level of economic development. We compare the average hours of paid work put in jointly by couples as well as the proportion of couples working very long weekly hours. We also assess gender differences in working time within families.

Our analysis is distinctive in several ways. First, while several cross-national studies (OECD 1998; Rubery, Smith, and Fagan 1998) have documented that American workers spend long days, on both an annual and a weekly basis, engaging in paid work, few studies have focused on the joint working hours of dual-earner couples. Second, in addition to the average length of the workweek, we focus on cross-national variation in the dispersion of individuals' and couples' hours. Finally, we integrate concerns about gender equality into our analysis of working time.[1]

A Global Convergence in Time Use?

Although it is difficult to measure and compare time use across countries, Jonathan Gershuny (2000) argues that the relative balance of time between work, family, and leisure is converging by gender, class, and nation. Providing a plethora of details on how time is spent in twenty countries, Gershuny presents a global picture in which women and men are moving toward a similar balance of paid work, family work, and substantial leisure time.[2] He reports, for example, that the time spent in most forms of housework, such as cleaning and laundry, is down, even though time spent cooking has not changed to the same degree, perhaps because it holds more "expressive" significance (De Vault 1991). In contrast, time spent caring for children is up, especially for more educated men and women, and despite the decline in the number of children (Bianchi 2000). And in a remarkable historical reversal, "being busy" appears to have replaced leisure as a sign of social status. If leisure was an indisputable mark of social status a century ago, people with the most education now tend to put in more hours on the job than those with less education.[3]

Gershuny presents some interesting country-specific comparisons, reporting for example that the French watch television for 75 minutes per day on average while Americans average over two hours. His focus, however, is on common historical trends and cross-national similarities, over-looking the telling differences among nations as well as the nuances of time use in specific countries. As a result, it skirts some important questions. Have advanced industrial countries reached or neared a state of balance, and, if not, what obstacles remain and why? And, beyond a picture of convergence, what are the differences among nations, and what do these differences imply about the future prospects for equal opportunity and work-family balance? While Gershuny demonstrates a substantial trend toward equality and balance, convergence—whether across nations or genders—is a strong claim to make for goals that typically remain out of reach.

A closer look at Gershuny's findings reveals both convergence and divergence between countries. He reports, for example, that both employment status and gender explain more variation in time use than does the country in which a person lives. "As a consequence," he notes, "we might say a Dutch woman's daily pattern of life has, arguably, more in common with that of a North American woman than of a Dutch man; an employed Norwegian's time use is more similar to an employed Hungarian's than to a non-employed Norwegian's" (Gershuny 2000, p. 159). Yet this conclusion is based on an analysis that lumps all employed and all nonemployed people in a given country together. If, however, the analysis had focused on differences among countries in paid working time among the employed, plenty of variation would have emerged (as we will show in this chapter).[4]

The picture of a cross-national convergence in time use also relies on homogenized national averages. Yet, as Chapter 1 makes clear, the focus on average experience can be quite misleading, especially when actual reports lean toward a bimodal distribution. Gershuny reports that the average person in his twenty countries spends 297 minutes, or just about five hours, in paid work on the average day; in fact, almost no one works a five-hour day (Gershuny 2000, Table 7.1). In this case, there is no "average" day: some days are workdays while other days are weekend or vacation days. Some workers typically work eight to ten hours per day, while others do not work at all. Reporting averages thus makes it difficult to focus on those sub-groups—such as dual-earner couples, single mothers, and young adults wrestling with decisions about work and parenting—who are at the center of debates over working time. Some people may indeed be overworked and squeezed for time even as early retirement or widespread unemployment combine to produce a growth in "leisure" for others. Imagine a climatologist concluding that the average level of rainfall in the western United States stabilized at a desirable midpoint after averaging the parched Southwest with the soggy Northwest. Residents in neither region would be convinced; nor would they want to base their water policies on this conclusion. Calculating a national average for a country's work experiences can be equally misleading. It ignores the wide variety of ways that nations can reach the same average level and overlooks the differences among workers within each national context.[5] Paying attention to the variety of patterns that emerge as people attempt to reconcile paid work, unpaid work, and leisure will reveal differences between countries that may remain hidden in national averages.

The apparent convergence between men and women provides a telling example of how important differences underlie national averages. While men in Gershuny's study show a clear decline in paid working time, for some countries this trend reflects a rise in early retirement and growing vacations, while in others it reflects changes in the workweek. Educational groups also show divergent trends, with growing workweeks for the educated and reduced workweeks for the less educated. Indeed, even Gershuny shows that, despite an overall decline among men, working times for some educated men have grown along with the length of the workweek (Gershuny 2000, chap. 8).

Although it is no surprise to find that women are spending more time engaged in paid work, the extent and shape of this increase differs markedly across countries. In Sweden, for example, part-time work among mothers is nearly ubiquitous, while in Finland full-time work for women is the norm.[6] In the Netherlands, women's employment rates remain low, and part-time work remains typical for those who do work. Thus, we may say both that women's working patterns vary across countries, and that important differences remain between employed women and their male counterparts.

When the focus turns to unpaid work, similar complexities arise. Gershuny finds that women's housework time has declined, while men's has increased. (This may be said at least for the countries with longitudinal data.) There is still, however, a considerable gap between women and men, and reaching a genuine convergence would require much greater change than those currently reached in any country. The increased housework contributions for men, for example, are real, but they represent an average of twenty to thirty minutes per day, and that includes time spent driving to the grocery or hardware store.

As we pointed out in Chapter 1, the decline in women's involvement in housework reflects a number of demographic shifts that have emerged to a greater or lesser extent in all economically developed countries. Increased age at marriage, delayed childbearing, and smaller families all make for less housework. Indeed, the time squeezes and other obstacles that confront working parents, especially employed mothers, are likely to be contributing to the low fertility rates of many industrial countries.[7]

Focusing on homogenized national averages runs the risk of overlooking or underestimating the time squeezes that are especially problematic for key social groups.[8] Gershuny's cross-national perspective provides an important corrective to the oversimplified conclusion that everyone is busier than ever, but it does not sufficiently address an equally important trend: the rising time pressures facing dual-earner couples, single mothers, employed parents, and those in jobs and occupations that have become increasingly demanding in terms of both time and energy.

The European Social and Political Context

While working time appears to have risen in the United States over the last several decades, it appears to have fallen throughout Europe. In the years between 1979 and 1997, while average annual working time was increasing among American workers, average annual hours fell in Japan and in all of the large economies of Europe, including France, Germany, and the United Kingdom.[9] The European decline was generally greater during the 1980s than during the 1990s, but renewed efforts to reduce the workweek in recent years may result in another round of change.

During the past several decades, the issue of working time has been high on the policy agenda in many European countries. Labor unions, policymakers, and scholars have focused on paid working time from at least three perspectives. First, reducing the number of working hours for individuals is often viewed as a tool for lowering unemployment and distributing the demand for labor more equitably. Since the late 1970s, many European countries have been plagued by persistently high unemployment, and the move to reduce working hours has become a common theme and major focal point for political discussion—even though we have found that reductions in working time may do more to increase productivity than to solve the problem of unemployment (see Chapters 4 and 8).

A second concern is that, in Europe as in the United States, the labor force participation of women, especially of mothers with young children, has steadily increased. European families thus also grapple with time pressures, as both women and men seek to integrate time on the job with responsibilities at home. Concerns have grown that the time demands of employment are affecting the quality of family life as well as the civic involvement of workers.

Europeans concerned with issues of gender equality, like their American counterparts, also continue to wrestle with concerns that working time is linked to persistent gender inequality in the paid labor force. Across all the advanced, postindustrial societies, women continue to face substantial gender differentials in labor participation rates, working hours, and income that grow even larger among parents (Gornick 1999). These inequalities, which are to some extent rooted in women's disproportionate responsibilities for caregiving and family work, have enduring consequences that contribute to longer-term inequalities in earnings and reinforce patterns of gender segregation in jobs and occupations (Padavic and Reskin 2002; Gornick and Jacobs 1998; Blau, Ferber, and Winkler 1998; Rubery, Smith, and Fagan 1998). For women in couples, these inequalities in paid working hours contribute to a power imbalance in the home and to wives' economic vulnerability should they lose access to their husbands' earnings (Hobson 1990; Bianchi, Casper, and Peltola 1999).

For all of these reasons, European countries have grappled with time dilemmas that are similar in many ways to the ones American workers face. Their responses, however, diverge substantially. Several European countries, especially those in Northern Europe, have made sustained, highly publicized, and well-organized efforts to reduce working time as a strategy for reducing unemployment, increasing family time, and reducing gender equalities in the market and at home (ILO 1995; OECD 1998; 32 Hours 2000). Efforts to reduce working time have invoked a wide variety of approaches, including collective bargaining (at the industry, branch, or enterprise level) and diverse public policy approaches.

In Denmark, for example, reducing working time remains an active issue, even though Danish workers currently have among the lowest average annual working hours in Europe. Focusing on restructuring working time to meet the needs of families, the government announced in June 1998 that it would initiate talks with business and labor to make working time more "family friendly." In Sweden, which also has relatively low annual work hours, work time reduction remains at the top of the public policy and collective bargaining agendas. As in Denmark, the goal is not job creation; instead, "shorter work time is seen mainly as a way to improve the well-being of workers and increase equality between men and women" (32 Hours 2000). In Finland, two major labor federations recently called on the government to cut the workweek to 35 hours, although in this case the cuts were intended largely as a job growth effort (32 Hours 2000).

Active efforts to reduce the workweek are gaining strength throughout continental Europe, although these efforts have focused more on the reduction of unemployment than on the promotion of gender equality. In France, the 35-hour workweek recently became law for firms with more than twenty employees, with smaller firms to follow in 2002. In Belgium, similarly, prominent labor and academic leaders called in 1997 for a shift to a 35-hour workweek, and the main trade unions and the Socialist Party endorsed a four-day, 32-hour week. In Germany, while the legislated standard week has remained at 48 hours since the 1930s, collective bargaining has reduced the average workweek, in the western Lander, to 37.5 hours. In Italy, legislation enacted in 2001 (and financial incentives to guide collective bargaining) have reduced the workweek from 40 to 35 hours. And in the Netherlands, a long government-business-labor negotiation dating to the early 1980s has reduced the workweek to 36 hours for half of the workforce (32 Hours 2000).

The United States has also experienced calls for reducing working time, but efforts have hardly gained the momentum—nor sparked the public debate—that has occurred in Europe. Although reducing work time has become a rallying cry for many who are concerned with work-family strains (Gornick and Meyers 2000), insufficient leisure (Schor 1991), persistent gender inequality (Crittenden 2001), and declining civic engagement (Putnam 2000; Skocpol 1999, 2000), calls for reducing work hours to combat unemployment have never received the substantial support in the United States that they have in Europe (ILO 1995). Canada, in contrast, has a more active and highly visible movement to limit working time, with several labor unions and national organizations taking the lead. As in the United States, concerns about working time in Canada are eclectic, with considerable attention paid to work-family pressures and constraints on leisure (32 Hours 2000).

Thus, despite the economic and social similarities among European and North American countries, there are notable differences among countries in how the "problem" of working time is conceived and approached. Comparisons among these countries have much to tell us about the prospects for change in United States.

Differences in Yearly Working Time

If accurate measures of working time for American workers are difficult to ascertain, the complexities are magnified for cross-national comparisons. Such comparisons are typically based on annual hours of paid work, an approach that multiplies hours worked per week by weeks worked per year to get a yearly measure for individuals. Although not an ideal measure, annual hours are readily available for a wide range of countries and, consequently, form the starting point for most cross-national comparisons.

We can see from Table 6.1 that, when working time is measured by annual working hours, American workers stand out.[10] The first column shows that the average American worker puts in 1,976 hours per year, roughly equivalent to a 40-hour week for 50 weeks per year and clearly the greatest number of working hours among all the countries. At the other

Table 6.1 Average annual hours worked for selected countries, by gender

Country	A Actual, per person, 1999	B Full-time workers, 1993	C Men, 1994	D Women, 1994
United States	1,976			
Canada	1,777[a]			
Finland	1,765		1,801.5	1,660.6
United Kingdom	1,720	1,952.7	1,973.8	1,469.2
Italy	1,648[b]	1,709.7	1,766.1	1,600.8
Belgium	1,635[b]	1,711.2	1,728.5	1,512.1
Sweden	1,634		1,906.2	1,748.8
France	1,604[b]	1,790.0	1,792.2	1,595.4
Germany	1,556	1,738.7	1,728.5	1,512.1
Netherlands	1,368[b]	1,788.4	1,679.4	1,233.4

Sources: A, OECD 2000 *Employment Outlook;* B, Eurostat 1995, as cited in Lehndorff 2000; C and D, ILO Key Indicators of the Labour Market, 1999.

Note: Countries are listed in order of the figures in Column A.

a. 1997.

b. 1998.

end of the spectrum, the average German worker puts in 1,556 hours per year, or the equivalent of 35 hours per week for less than 45 weeks, while the average Dutch worker shows only 1,368 annual hours, or the equivalent of 35 hours per week for 39 weeks a year. The most recent OECD data indicate that U.S. workers' hours surpass those of even the notoriously hardworking Japanese.

From the perspective of average annual hours, American workers appear to be harried and overworked compared to the more leisurely work schedules of Europeans. It is not surprising that comparisons of this sort provide fuel for the belief that Americans possess a distinct and unique taste for "workaholism." Commenting on the latest ILO report, which appeared just before Labor Day 2001, the *New York Times* speculated that "the American psyche" and "American culture" explained a national penchant for "overwork" (Greenhouse 2001).

A closer look, however, suggests that the discrepancy between Americans and Europeans, while real, may not be as great as these numbers seem to indicate. The averages in column A of Table 6.1 include all workers and thus mask some differences among different types of workers, including those on part-time and full-time schedules.[11] In Column B, which includes full-time workers only, the differences between countries become much smaller, with the typical full-time European worker putting in about 1,700–1,800 hours per year (or about 40 hours per week for 45 weeks). The United Kingdom leads, with 1,953 hours for full-time workers, while Belgium and Italy are nearly tied for the least full-time hours, at just over 1,700. The Netherlands is often noted as the country with the fewest working hours, but this largely stems from the prevalence of part-time employment and does not reflect especially short workweeks among full-time workers. Full-time Dutch workers put in about the same annual hours as those in France, Germany, and a number of other European countries. Although the United States is not included in this ILO series on full-time workers, the fact remains that the average American worker—including both part-timers and full-timers—puts in more hours per year on the job than the typical full-time worker in Europe.[12]

In columns C and D of Table 6.1, the average annual hours are separated for men and women. From this perspective, the work schedules of European men appear much less leisurely, while European women in different countries appear to have a wide range of average annual hours. German men, for example, put in 1,972 hours per year, or about 42 hours per week for 47 weeks. (In contrast, the *New York Times* reported that the average American worked 499 hours more than their European counterparts.) In all of the European countries except the Netherlands, men work on average between 1,700 and 2,000 hours, while women range from a notable low of 1,233 in the Netherlands to a high of 1,749 in Sweden.[13] Again, it helps to look beyond averages to make sense of differences not only among individual workers but also among countries.

Weekly Working Time

However measured, the annual working time among American workers stands out. One main culprit, of course, is the relative paucity of vacation time. European workers enjoy substantially more time off during the year than Americans do, so their annual working time is proportionately lower even when the length of their workweek is not. But beyond the difference in vacation time over the course of the year, do American workers tend to work longer weekly hours than their European counterparts?[14]

To answer this question, we analyzed data on ten countries from the Luxembourg Income Study (LIS), an international archive of micro-datasets, in order to study patterns of working time.[15] For men, the average workweek in most countries ranges between 40 and 44 hours per week, with only Sweden having a particularly short workweek (results not shown). While average weekly hours in the United States fall at the high end of the range, the average length of the American workweek is not especially distinctive. Where the United States does stand out is in the dispersion among workers in the number of hours worked, especially in the percentage of workers who report working very long workweeks. Over one quarter of American men (26.8 percent) put in more than 50 hours per week on the job, compared with 25.8 percent in Belgium, 17.0 percent in France, 10.6 percent in Finland, and 2.8 percent in Sweden. The United States is at the top of a cluster of several countries having high proportions of men working 50 hours per week or more. Thus, the long workweeks that we have considered throughout this study in the context of the United States continues to be a useful focal point for international comparisons. The proportion of U.S. citizens who work long weeks, rather than those having a long average workweek, most clearly sets the United States apart from other countries.

Several countries have experienced increases in the dispersion of working hours since the early 1990s, including Belgium, Germany, the Netherlands, and the United Kingdom. When we conducted this same analysis for an earlier period, around 1990, the United States stood out even more sharply than it did when we focused on more recent years.

The standard workweek has given way to a wider array of formats (OECD 1998; Mutari and Figart 2000). A growth in part-time work, which has swelled the ranks of those working fewer hours, is a large part of this trend. At the other end of the working-time continuum, European employers have also pushed for greater flexibility in work arrangements among full-time workers, contributing to a growth in the proportion working many hours. (In the U.S. context, "flexible" work arrangements refer to schemes designed to help workers respond to family concerns; in Europe, however, the term "flexibilization" refers to employers' desire to bend regulations such as maximum-hours rules to enhance productivity and cut labor costs.)

Despite these European trends, the proportion of men and women working long weeks is highest in the United States, where there is far less regulation of wages and hours. The OECD findings (1998) show the United States leading all countries in the proportion of those working long weeks, with the exception of men in the United Kingdom.[16]

More dramatic differences emerge in women's weekly hours. American women report among the longest workweeks in the nine countries—an average of 37.4 hours per week, compared with 34.0 in Germany, 31.6 in Sweden, and 30.4 in the United Kingdom. The Netherlands shows the shortest workweek, with the average Dutch woman working 25.5 hours per week. The United States has the highest percentage of women who work 50 hours per week or more. At 11 percent, those women who work very long weeks are not as numerous as their male counterparts, but they surpass the level in Germany (6.8 percent), the United Kingdom (4.2 percent), the Netherlands (0.2 percent), and Sweden (0.4 percent).

These comparisons suggest that the United States stands out more in terms of the percentage of workers who put in very long weeks than it does in terms of the average workweek. Again, we find that a growing dispersion in working time for women and men emerges as a major feature of the American context.

Part-time jobs have more protections in Europe than they do in the United States, especially since the adoption of the 1997 policy designed to eliminate discrimination against part-time work and to afford job protections to part-time workers (European Union Council Directive 1997; for a detailed discussion of European protections for part-time workers, see Gornick and Meyers 2003). In the United States, part-time jobs tend to be concentrated in occupations that typically offer low wages, few benefits, and little or no job security. The disparity in attractiveness between part-time and full-time jobs is greater in the United States than in many other countries (Gornick and Jacobs 1996; Bardasi and Gornick 2002).

Couples' Joint Working Time

We have seen how the time conflicts facing American workers can be better understood from the perspective of families and households. To place these dynamics in a cross-national perspective, we again need to shift from looking at individuals to looking at the time pressures on entire families. A cross-national focus can tell us how the joint working time of American couples compares with that of couples in other countries.

There are good reasons to believe that dual-earner couples face differing conditions across countries. First, there are considerable differences in the kinds of jobs available, including part-time and flexible work. As important, family-support policies, such as universal day care or paid parental leave, vary widely across countries. Differences in the dynamics of gender equality may also shape the options of couples in different national contexts. Since differences in working time between husbands and wives—especially in families with children—contribute to gender disparities in earnings and career opportunities, it is important to see if some countries have reduced time pressures on couples in a way that promotes, or at least does not undermine, the prospects for gender equality. Understanding how couples apportion paid working time also provides a valuable starting point for identifying social policies that can alleviate domestic time squeezes while supporting egalitarian gender arrangements.

To explore these issues, we focus again on weekly working hours. The week is the best unit of time to use when considering family life, since it corresponds most closely to families' needs to supervise and care for their children. Annual vacation time, for example, may be helpful in providing a respite from work and caregiving pressures, but annual vacations will not alleviate much of the pressure that families experience on a regular basis.[17]

Weekly hours also provide a more accurate way to make cross-national comparisons, since several factors make it difficult to compare yearly work experiences across countries. Because annual working hours are sensitive to variations in the number of weeks worked, which in turn reflects labor market entrances and exits, countries with relatively low women's labor force participation (or high rates of part-time work) tend to have large numbers of women entering and leaving the labor force and thus produce relatively few annual working hours for women. High or growing levels of unemployment would also tend to reduce annual working hours, as those losing their jobs (or just regaining employment) leave (or enter) the workforce.

In addition to comparing differences in average weekly hours, we also explore cross-national differences in the variability of couples' working time. We have seen how a time divide has emerged among American workers between those putting in very long workweeks and those who work less. Is this division of working time emerging elsewhere, or is it a peculiarly American development?

To find out how American couples compare to those in other countries, we explore four aspects of couples' working time. First, we examine both average hours and the percentage working very long weeks to see how the paid working time of dual-earner couples in the United States compares to that of their counterparts in Canada and Europe. Second, we see how the relationship between working time and educational level varies across countries. Third, we examine couples with and without children in a given country to see how the difference in working time varies across countries. And, finally, we study the countries that report the most gender-egalitarian patterns of working time. We explore whether the length of a couple's workweek and the presence of children influence gender equality in different ways across countries. Since we have shown in Chapters 1 and 2 that factors such as education, family situation, and combined working time influence the conflicts facing American couples, it will be useful to know if these circumstances influence couples in other countries in a similar way.

Couples' Working Time

Because both men and women work slightly more hours in the United States than in other industrialized countries, American couples are likely to put in the most combined time at work as well. Similarly, the proportion of couples who work very long weeks—more than 80, or even 100, hours per week—are likely to be higher in the United States than elsewhere (see Figures 6.1 and 6.2).

Figure 6.1 presents the joint hours of paid work of husbands and wives for all couples in which at least one partner was employed and for dual-earner couples.[18] American couples report the most joint hours of all ten countries included in this analysis. The typical American couple with at least one employed spouse puts in just over 70 (72.3) hours per week.

This high average reflects the fact that, first, the United States has a high percentage of dual-earner couples and, second, the length of the workweek among these couples is relatively long. In terms of the percentage of couples in which both partners work for pay, the United States trails only two Nordic countries—Finland and Sweden—where special efforts have been made to facilitate women's labor force participation. (For additional details on the workweeks of dual-earner couples in these countries, see Table A.7 in the Appendix.)

In half of the countries (Belgium, Canada, France, Germany, and Sweden), the average married couple spends between 60 and 65 hours a week in paid employment. Even though the majority of couples in these countries have two earners, most work just under 80 hours per week. How cou-

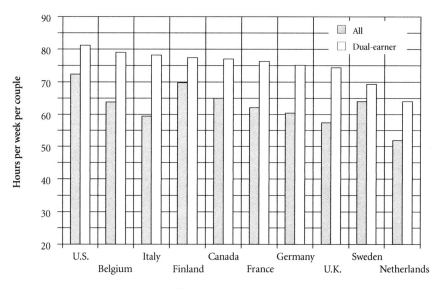

Figure 6.1 Average joint hours of paid employment for married couples, by country (*Source:* Luxembourg Income Study)

ples work this many hours, however, varies from country to country. In Sweden, for example, large numbers of married women work relatively few hours, while in Belgium, fewer employed married women put in longer workweeks (see Table A.7 in the Appendix for the specifics).

The Netherlands and the United Kingdom report the shortest average workweeks, with the typical British couple working 57.4 hours per week (or 14.9 fewer hours per week than U.S. couples do). Indeed, the United Kingdom has the third lowest rate of married women's labor force participation (54.6 percent) and the second shortest workweek among dual-earner couples (74.3 hours per week). The truly exceptional case, however, is found in the Netherlands, where only a bare majority of married women work for pay (52.3 percent) and the average workweek among dual-earner couples is 64.0 hours, more than 17 fewer hours per week than in the United States. Despite the similar level of economic development in these countries, the time pressures families face are markedly different in each.

The open bars on Figure 6.1 present the distribution of working hours among dual-earner couples. U.S. couples put in the longest workweeks, with the average dual-earner couple putting in 81.2 hours per week. In most of the other countries, the figures range from 74 to 79 hours per week, except Sweden and the Netherlands, where dual-earner couples work a combined total of fewer than 70 hours per week.

Figure 6.2 displays the proportion of couples jointly working many hours for pay. Here again, we see that not only is the average American workweek slightly longer than that of any of the other countries, but the United States also ranks first in the percentage of couples working more than 80 hours per week (68.2 percent) and in the percentage of couples working 100 or more hours per week (12.0 percent). The difference between the United States and the other countries when it comes to the percentage of couples working many hours is even more marked than the comparison of average number of weekly working hours.

Finland, Sweden, and the Netherlands are places where very long workweeks are quite rare. Finland presents an especially interesting comparison, since the average Finnish couple logs nearly as many hours per week as the typical American couple (77.4 for Finland, versus 81.2 for the United States). Yet the Finnish distribution is more tightly clustered, and far fewer Finnish couples put in more than 80 hours per week (25.1 percent), with even fewer working 100 hours per week or more (4.0 percent).

Figures 6.1 and 6.2 make it clear that American dual-earner couples, like

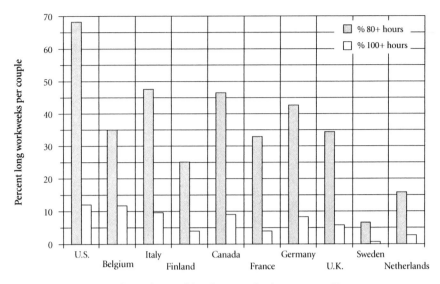

Figure 6.2 Percent of couples working long weeks, by country (*Source:* Luxembourg Income Study)

individual workers, spend more time at the workplace than do their counterparts in other countries. The difference may seem small compared to some countries, such as Finland, but it is substantial compared to others, such as the United Kingdom and the Netherlands. Indeed, dual-earner couples in the United Kingdom put in nearly one fewer person-days per week (6.9 fewer hours) than their American counterparts. Thus, the time demands on dual-earner families vary across countries, and the pressures appear greatest for American couples.

Educational Influences across Nations

We have seen that American workers with higher educational credentials tend to have longer workweeks than those with less. Can this pattern be found in other national contexts as well? Standard economic theories of labor supply suggest that the higher earning potential of more educated workers would lead them to work more in all societies. Since the United States has comparatively high levels of wage inequality, however, the effect might be larger in this country than elsewhere (Freeman and Bell 1995).

In contrast, sociological and institutional analysis suggests that educational differences in working time will vary in ways that reflect local institutional arrangements, such as legislative measures that affect employment choices (Mutari and Figart 2000). From this perspective, the opportunity as well as the incentive to work many hours may vary in ways that favor the more educated in some places and the less educated in others. It is thus not clear whether the effect of education in America will be the same in other countries.

The structure and organization of educational institutions differ across nations, so it is difficult to compare educational levels across countries. In an attempt to do so, Figure 6.3 compares the working time of couples in which at least one partner has a college degree or higher with that of couples in which neither partner has a college degree.[19] Countries in the figure are ranked in terms of the size of the educational difference in mean hours worked.

Education in the United States is positively associated with the length of the workweek. More highly educated couples in the United States tend to put in more hours working for pay than do their less educated counterparts (82.4 hours versus 80.3 hours). The difference is clearest at the extremes, where the proportion of dual-earner couples working 100 hours

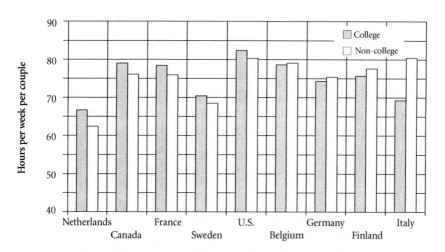

Figure 6.3 Average joint hours of paid employment of dual-earner couples, by educational level and country (*Source:* Luxembourg Income Study)

per week or more is substantially higher (15.2 percent) than for less educated workers (9.6 percent).

Although college-educated couples are more likely to have the longest workweeks in the United States, the education differential, in percentage terms, is larger in four other countries—the Netherlands, Canada, France, and Sweden. Since these countries have lower wage disparities across the workforce than does the United States, a higher level of income inequality cannot explain the education differential in work hours.

The other countries show a different relationship between education and working time. In Italy and Finland, more educated couples put in substantially *shorter* workweeks than do their less educated peers; and, while not shown here, we find that both husbands and wives in the more educated group report shorter workweeks. In Germany and Belgium, the average workweek does not differ by education level, but the more educated are more likely to put in the largest share of the longest workweeks.

It is tempting to attribute the lengthy working time of highly educated couples to the higher economic rewards they can command, and this is surely part of the story. The United States's surprising rank compared to other countries, however, suggests that other processes are also at work. We must consider noneconomic incentives and local institutional conditions to fully understand why people work the hours they do.

Gender Differences in Working Time

Patterns of working time matter because they have consequences for gender equality as well as for the quality of family life. Very long workdays are certainly not family-friendly, and they are also likely to hinder the opportunities for creating egalitarian time allocations within families. If this is so, the relationship between couples' working time and gender equality is likely to be linked in a curvilinear way. Dual-earner couples with relatively fewer combined working hours will probably depend on small contributions from wives, especially compared to husbands' hours. Couples with many working hours, perhaps over 100 hours per week, are likely to depend substantially on wives' contributions, but these couples are also likely to have husbands putting in the most hours and thus contributing even less to the domestic work of the household. Couples with an intermediate amount of time devoted to paid employment are more likely to have a more equal balance between wives' and husbands' economic contributions.

Do short, intermediate, or long workweeks tend to promote more gen-der-egalitarian participation in paid work? Again, it is important to note the distribution of working time as well as the average. For married men, the workweek clusters between 41 and 45 hours in all countries except Sweden, which trails at 38.1 hours per week. The United States has the second longest workweek for married men (at 44.8 hours per week, just behind Belgium at 44.9), but it clearly surpasses all of the others in the proportion working 50 hours per week or more. At just under one-third (30.3 percent), the percentage of married men working over 50 hours per week in the United States is nearly triple that in Finland (10.4 percent) and more than ten times as high as in Sweden (2.8 percent).

Married American women (36.4 hours) rank second only to Finnish women (37.2 hours) in the length of their average workweek, while married women in the United Kingdom (30.8 hours per week) and especially the Netherlands (22.4 hours per week) have the shortest average workweeks. And while the United States ties Belgium and Italy for having the highest percentage of married women working over 50 hours per week (10 percent), such long weeks are nearly unknown for married women in Sweden (0.4 percent) and the Netherlands (1.7 percent).

What about cross-national differences in the gender balance of working hours? Table 6.2 displays this in the ratio of wives' to husbands' average weekly hours. Not surprisingly, gender equality in working hours is high in the United States—absolutely and relatively—among couples without parenting responsibilities (.86), tying with Sweden for second place. Among couples with children under 18, however, American women fare less well. Among parents, the ratio of wives' to husbands' hours falls to .78, and here the United States lags behind Sweden (.79), Italy (.80), France (.81), and especially Finland (.92) (not shown in table).

What about the link between gender equality and the length of families' working hours? Table 6.2 shows that in seven of the ten countries, couples with an intermediate number of working hours also have the most equal gender balance in paid working time. In three countries, however, husbands' and wives' contributions are most equal in the families with the most combined hours.

In the United States, the most gender-balanced contributions occur in couples who put in more than 80, but fewer than 100, hours per week. Among couples working fewer than 60 joint hours, wives contribute less than half the time (.37) their husbands do. This ratio rises to .67 among couples working 60–79 hours per week, peaks among couples working

Table 6.2 Ratio of wives' to husbands' hours of paid work among dual-earner couples, aged 25–59, by total hours of joint paid employment

Country		Total hours of joint paid employment			
	Total	< 60	60–79	80–99	100+
Finland	.93	.54	.96	.91	.83
Sweden	.82	.58	.87	.83	.65
France	.82	.50	.86	.83	.86
Italy	.81	.64	.79	.83	.92
United States	.81	.37	.67	.91	.84
Canada	.79	.43	.78	.87	.85
Belgium	.76	.53	.81	.82	.83
Germany	.71	.41	.67	.87	.77
United Kingdom	.68	.39	.70	.79	.72
Netherlands	.53	.36	.60	.73	.59

Source: Luxembourg Income Study.

Note: Countries are listed in order of the first-column figures.

80–99 hours per week (.91) and falls again among those working 100 or more hours per week (.84).

This general pattern also holds for Canada, Germany, the United Kingdom, and the Netherlands. Sweden and Finland show a similar curvilinear pattern, although the gender balance peaks between 60 and 79 hours per week. Indeed, Finnish couples working 60–79 hours have the most gender balance, with wives contributing 96 percent as much time to paid work as their husbands.

In Belgium and France, however, the balance between wives and husbands plateaus after couples reach 60 joint hours of paid work per week, and in Italy, the most equal balance in working time is found among the couples with the most time at the workplace, where the gender ratio increases as total working time rises. Clearly, there is a relationship between gender equality in working time within couples and the length of the joint workweek. And for most counties, the most equal relationships emerge somewhere in the middle, where both husband and wives have found work that takes a moderate amount of time. In most countries, moderation and balance, rather than very long or very short workweeks, appear to promote gender equality as well as to best fit the ideals of most workers, although the balance point at present involves more working time in some countries (the Netherlands, the United Kingdom, the United States, and Germany) than in others (Finland and Sweden).

The Link between Gender and Parenthood

How does parental status shape couples' working time? Are the effects of parenthood stronger in the United States than elsewhere? And does parenthood have different consequences for women and men? Across countries, parenting is far more likely to influence women's participation than men's (Gornick 1999). Yet it is likely that parenting has an even greater influence among women in the United States, where mothers are less likely to enjoy key institutional supports (such as paid family leave and publicly provided day care) that help parents, especially mothers, integrate work and family than they are in other countries. Scandinavian countries, by contrast, provide paid parental leave for both mothers and fathers, and French families enjoy universally available day care (Henneck 2003).

By comparing the working hours of dual-earner couples with and without children, Figure 6.4 shows the effect of parental status on working time across countries. When the countries are ranked by the length of the workweek, the United States leads all other countries, whether the measure is the length of the average workweek (for both working parents and childless dual-earner couples) or the percentage working very long workweeks. Among childless couples, weekly hours worked in Belgium and Italy approach those in the United States—exceeding 80 hours in both cases—but American parents report a substantially longer workweek than do their peers in all other countries.

The effect of parenting on couples' total working time varies markedly across the countries. In the United States, working parents put in 2.9 fewer hours per week than do their childless counterparts. In percentage terms, that difference (−3.5 percent) is similar to the Canadian (−3.3 percent) and Swedish (−3.7 percent) patterns. In five countries (Italy, Belgium, Germany, the United Kingdom, and the Netherlands), employed parents put in at least 5 percent fewer hours on the job than do their childless counterparts. In the two other countries, Finland and France, there is hardly any difference between parents and other couples.

We also found that the parenting effect is much larger for mothers than for fathers. (These results can be seen in more detail in Jacobs and Gornick

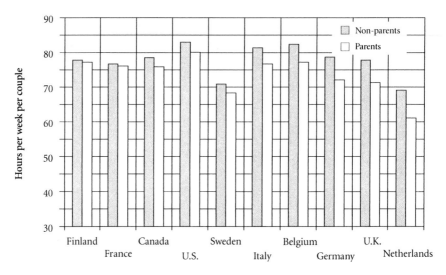

Figure 6.4 Average joint hours of paid employment for dual-earner couples, by parental status and country (*Source:* Luxembourg Income Study)

2002.) Mothers put in less time on the job than other married women in all ten countries. The magnitude of the difference ranges from 3.0 percent or less in France and Finland, to 8.6 percent in the United States, to 20 percent or more in Germany, the United Kingdom, and the Netherlands. For husbands, the effects are much smaller and typically in the other direction. Thus, with the exception of Belgium, France, and Italy, fathers put in more hours on the job than other men, but the increase tends to be quite small. (The 1.8 percent increase in Germany is the largest.) Everywhere, the consequences of having children at home are greater for mothers than fathers.

A parenting effect thus exists cross-nationally and applies largely to mothers. Yet there is considerable variation across countries in the degree to which becoming a parent pulls women away from the workplace. The parenting effect among American wives is substantially larger than it is among their peers in Finland and France (where publicly provided cay care is widely available), but smaller than in the United Kingdom and three continental European countries (Belgium, Germany, and the Netherlands). These differences suggest, again, that national contexts—especially the structure of public policies and work institutions—can either facilitate or inhibit women's ability to combine parenting and paid work.

Policies and Institutional Forces Influencing American Working Time

When viewed in cross-national perspective, American dual-earner couples appear to put in the longest workweeks. American husbands have the second highest average number of hours per week (44.8 hours) and, even more distinctively, the greatest percentage working 50 hours or more (30.3 percent). American wives in dual-earner couples also work relatively long weeks (36.4 hours on average) and are most likely to work 50 or more hours per week (10.2 percent). And while American dual-earner couples without children have achieved relative equality in paid working time, the gender balance falls substantially among parents.

What accounts for these differences in working time and, especially, for the distinctive situation of American couples? Our research suggests that cross-national differences in work institutions and public policies may help explain the unusual patterns in the United States. European countries, for example, have more readily adopted collective agreements and state legislation that regulate working time and set maximum limits by legal statute. The demand for part-time work also varies across countries. And, equally important, the supports available to employed parents—especially in the form of publicly provided child care—though they vary widely, are generally more prevalent in European countries than they are in the United States. Each of these institutional forces is likely to influence the working time of couples as well as how it is apportioned between wives and husbands.

The Regulation of Working Time

Although the United States is an exception, most industrialized countries regulate the standard as well as the maximum working time for a large proportion of the workforce. In most European countries, collective bargaining agreements establish standard working hours for the majority of workers. Jill Rubery, Mark Smith, and Colette Fagan argue that "national systems of regulation {collective and statutory} can be seen to have a major impact on usual working time" (1998, p. 75). And by setting legal limits on normal weekly hours, weekly overtime hours, and/or total weekly hours, government statutes regulate maximum hours as well. Indeed, of all of the countries we examine in this chapter, only the United States and the

United Kingdom have no statutory maximum working time (ILO 1995; OECD 1998).[20] While these direct controls over working time are likely to influence all workers, they are especially important for men, who are more likely to work the maximum possible and less likely to work part-time or pull back from employment to care for children. In most of the countries in our study, collective bargaining agreements covering most of the economy set the standard workweek at between 34 and 40 hours per week. In the United States, however, only 9.0 percent of private-sector workers are unionized (although 37.5 percent of U.S. public sector employees are unionized) (U.S. Bureau of Labor Statistics 2001). In the United States, the regulation of working time falls to the Fair Labor Standards Act, which in 1938 established the 40-hour workweek as the national standard. (We discuss the limitations of this legislation in more detail in Chapter 8.)

As we have seen, the average workweek for men in most European countries in recent years has ranged between 40 and 45 hours per week. European policies thus do more to reduce the prevalence of very long workweeks than they do to reduce the average. The adoption of a 35-hour policy, such as occurred in France, would significantly reduce the average workweek for men in all countries, with the possible exception of the Netherlands. European policies have also succeeded in promoting longer vacations. However, the effort to promote "flexibilization" is eroding the influence of working time regulations in Europe.

Part-Time Work

While government and union regulation of full-time work is likely to place limits on long workweeks, both institutional and labor-supply factors influence the extent of part-time work. A large body of literature shows that rates of part-time work vary markedly across industrialized countries and that part-time work remains predominantly women's work everywhere (OECD 1994, 1999; Rubery, Smith, and Fagan 1998; Gornick 1999).

In theory, the extent to which women prefer part-time work could be ascertained by analyzing rates of "voluntary" part-time work—that is, the percentage of part-time workers who report that they sought part-time hours. In reality, many women who do not "prefer" part-time work in any fundamental way in fact seek part-time work because of substantial constraints on the supply side—for example, a lack of affordable child care of acceptable quality. These part-time workers are counted as "voluntary," strongly suggesting that measured rates of "voluntary part-time work" actually reveal very little about women's preferences (Bardasi and Gornick 2002).

It may be difficult to distinguish the demand-side and supply-side factors that shape levels of part-time work (Hakim 1997; Fagan and O'Reilly 1998; Bardasi and Gornick 2003). We nevertheless agree with Tindara Addabbo's view that "demand-side constraints seem to be the overriding determinants of the level of part-time work" (1997, p. 129). The level of demand for part-time work is in turn shaped by institutional factors, such as the structure of social insurance rules, taxes, and subsidies that reward or penalize the creation of part-time jobs, and the preferences and power of unions.

Many employed wives, especially mothers with young children, seek part-time jobs as a way to balance work and family. In some countries—such as Italy and Finland and, to some extent, the United States—a substantial share of these women may be unable to find suitable part-time work and will work full-time hours instead. Their high rates of full-time employment contribute in turn to the relatively long workweeks of dual-earning couples. In contrast, their counterparts in the United Kingdom, Sweden, and especially the Netherlands face much greater demand for part-time workers and can more easily find part-time jobs; this contributes to shorter average weekly hours for wives and couples alike in those countries.

A prevalence of part-time work, however, constrains the ambitions of women who would prefer to work full-time but cannot find full-time jobs. In countries with a high proportion of part-time women workers, many women are effectively pushed into part-time work. Brendan Burchell, Angela Dale, and Heather Joshi note, for example, that in response to labor shortages in the 1960s, the United Kingdom enacted an official policy of developing part-time work and recruiting married women to fill the jobs. They conclude that the "ramifications of this are still being experienced today" (1997, p. 211). Since the balance of part-time to full-time jobs is much higher in some countries than in others, wives in countries with limited full-time opportunities are likely to be confined to part-time jobs despite wishes to the contrary. In these cases, the working time of wives is likely to be constrained regardless of the needs or desires of women or their families.

Countries that limit women's chances of finding full-time work thus create an institutional context that dampens women's chances of achieving equality in earnings and career mobility as well as working time. In this instance, at least, American women fare better than many of their European peers.

Child-Care Support

While the preponderance of part-time (over full-time) jobs limits gender egalitarian arrangements, publicly provided child care and educational supports are likely to support mothers' employment and encourage more equality in how couples apportion their working time. Table 6.3 shows that this is the case. When countries are ranked according to the ratio of married mothers' to married fathers' working time and compared in terms of their child-care provisions for children below primary school age, the United States lags behind most European countries, both in total public slots and in the hours that care is available. Even more striking, all of the countries with more gender egalitarian allocations of working time among parents—Finland, France, Italy, and Sweden—have also made more extensive public investments in child care for young children.

Table 6.3 Availability of early childhood education and care (ECEC), mid-1990s

Country (ratio of mothers' to fathers' hours)		Share of children served in publicly financed care		Typical schedule of primary form of care for children ages 3, 4, 5
		Ages 0, 1, 2	Ages 3, 4, 5	
Finland	(.92)	21%	53%	Full day
France	(.81)	23%	99%	Full day
Italy	(.80)	6%	91%	Full day
Sweden	(.79)	33%	72%	Full day
United States	(.78)	5%	54%	Part day
Canada	(.76)	5%	53%	Part day
Belgium	(.73)	30%	95%	Full day
Germany	(.63)	2%	78%	Part day
United Kingdom	(.60)	5%	60%	Mixed
Netherlands	(.46)	8%	71%	Mixed

Source: Meyers and Gornick 2003.

Note: The ordering of the countries corresponds to one indicator of gender equality in working time: the ratio of mothers' to fathers' hours of paid employment.

American families face limited access to public care for children below aged 3, with only 5 percent of infants and toddlers in publicly provided or publicly financed care. Public provisions for preschoolers (children aged 3–5) are more extensive, with 54 percent of children in some form of public care (including 5-year-olds in kindergarten), but much of this care is available only part of the day. The relatively low levels of publicly provided child care in the United States clearly work against gender egalitarian divisions of working time. Since women continue to perform the lion's share of caregiving, the paucity of child-care supports drives a wedge between husbands' and wives' hours.[21]

Lessons from Abroad

A cross-national perspective enriches our understanding of the situation of American workers and also provides some lessons about the possibilities for achieving greater work-family integration as well as more gender equality. In the search for a model country, however, these twin goals seem elusive; indeed, they also seem to be in conflict.

The Netherlands, for example, has gone furthest in lessening work-family conflict by reducing couples' combined working time, but only at the price of gender equality in how working time is apportioned. Dutch women typically work part-time and put in shorter weeks than in any other country. In the end, the Dutch supports for family life promote the high degree of economic dependence of Dutch wives. Sweden has created a similar, if less extreme, compromise. Relatively short workweeks for Swedish men and plentiful part-time work for women have helped to reduce work-family conflict, but the gender disparity in working time, especially among working parents, remains substantial. In both cases, family supports have been purchased at the expense of equity, a pattern that in fundamental ways recreates gender inequality even as women enter the world of paid work.

In contrast, Finland has achieved the highest levels of equality in paid working time. Finnish married women work 93 percent as many hours as their husbands, and even working mothers put in 92 percent as many hours on the job as do their husbands. Yet the typical Finnish couple works nearly 80 hours per week. The price of gender equality thus appears to be substantial time pressures in dual-earner families.

Compared to other countries, the United States stands out in terms of both the many hours couples spend at work and the moderate levels of inequality in how they apportion working time. The American labor force has a high proportion of dual-earner couples; relatively long average work-weeks, especially among women; and a high proportion of couples who work very long weeks. It ranks above average in paid working time among dual-earner couples with no children, but its relative position drops among working parents.

The prospects for gender equality in the United States appear mixed. Certainly, the very long workweeks that are faced by so many American couples create not only time pressures on families but also inequality in how domestic time is shared. It is not surprising that in the United States, as in most countries, the gender gap in working time peaks among those couples working 100 or more hours per week. More moderate work sched-ules, in contrast, are more likely to promote greater equality in the working time of husbands and wives while also helping to ease the conflicts be-tween work and private life. And, as we found in Chapter 3, having a mod-erate number of working hours per week appears to be the shared cultural ideal for most workers.

There is also reason to believe that the institutional conditions of work help account for the distinctive position of American workers and espe-cially for the long workweeks and moderate levels of gender equality found in the United States. The reluctance of American employers and legislators to enact policies that regulate and control working time surely contributes to the many hours Americans put in at the workplace. The relatively high demand for full-time rather than part-time work also contributes to long workweeks, especially among employed women. And, finally, the relative paucity of child-care support for employed parents adds to the pressures and conflicts confronting American families.

Yet these same institutional forces have ambiguous implications for gen-der arrangements. Long workweeks among men and the lack of child care pose significant obstacles to achieving equality in how couples apportion their time between home and the workplace. Yet the low level of part-time work, especially among American women, enhances egalitarian work com-mitments—even if it also contributes to time squeezes.

The lessons from abroad appear to be that institutional arrangements and policies matter, but no single policy can suffice. Indeed, institutional constraints and opportunities may work at cross-purposes—especially if the goal is to achieve work-family balance *and* gender equity. Yet this com-parative perspective also makes it clear that the squeezes American workers face are not inevitable or inherent in the nature of modern, and particularly professional, work. Like all advanced industrial economies, the United States faces policy choices. Our decisions shape the degree and nature of the dilemmas American workers face.

The comparative perspective provided in this chapter also illumines why time pressures have become such a focal point for public debate in the United States. Americans work the longest weeks yet have adopted few policies to alleviate the pressures that inevitably ensue. Other countries have chosen to reduce these pressures in a variety of ways, from limiting the amount of paid work in which people engage to providing for the needs of children while their parents are at the workplace. Whether the choice is to limit working time or to provide support for children, the ultimate goal should be to offer options that will allow families to achieve an equitable and satisfying balance between home and work. In the next chapter, we consider a range of policies that would enable American workers to achieve both gender equity and a greater integration between the worlds of home and work.

7

Bridging the Time Divide

"There aren't enough hours in the day" is a refrain that has never had more resonance. Parents lament lack of time and lack of sleep. Workers worry that putting in long days at the office is the only way to prove their worth and safeguard their future prospects. Journalists and politicians routinely cite mounting concerns about a harried, hurried citizenry. Scholars and policy analysts have created a wide-ranging interdisciplinary field focused on explaining how, why, and to what extent time, like money, has come to be seen as a scarce social resource.[1]

The concerns about growing time squeezes are not misplaced, although we have argued that they are frequently misdiagnosed. Since policies can only be as sound as the analysis on which they are based, before making our own policy recommendations we first review the variety of perspectives that have been used to define the work-family "problem" and the kinds of policy prescriptions that stem from these approaches. Placing our own findings within this context, we offer a multifaceted framework for understanding work-family tensions—one that includes some aspects of prevailing arguments but extends beyond them. We then develop a set of policy principles that flow from our analysis and point to the goals we believe work and family policies should attempt to promote. Only then, in our concluding chapter, do we propose a set of specific policies that we believe can promote a better fit between the work needs and the family needs of American households. Throughout, we try to remain sensitive to the variety of challenges faced by people living in diverse situations, from professional couples to working-class and poorer parents to families anchored by single mothers and fathers.

Diverse Diagnoses, Diverse Solutions

Diverse and at times conflicting analyses have been offered to explain the causes and potential cures for the time squeezes of contemporary Americans. At one extreme can be found those that emphasize the ability of individuals to exercise personal control over their use of time. These "individualist," or "self-help," approaches exhort people to manage their time better, but they do not offer strategies for changing the basic conditions of daily life. At the other extreme are approaches that emphasize the all-encompassing grip of technology. In contrast to the self-help perspective, the "technological imperative" argument stresses the need to adjust to conditions that are fundamentally beyond our control. Despite their obvious differences, both of these approaches imply that personal adjustments, not collective responses, are the most workable way to cope with time squeezes.

Cultural approaches, in contrast to both individual and technological arguments, point to the role of values—especially the ethos of consumption, materialism, and overwork. Solutions based on these approaches exhort us to choose a different path by changing our values, habits, and aspirations. Finally, approaches emphasizing the culture of work point to both the lure and the constraints of the workplace.

All of these approaches offers a kernel of truth, but each is too narrowly focused to account for the full range of time divides Americans now face. Instead, we offer a multifaceted approach that recognizes the need for new work and community structures that speak to the growing diversity of needs, aspirations, and time constraints facing American workers and their families. We argue that time squeezes are neither purely personal problems nor inherent processes beyond our control, but arise instead from social structural arrangements. Resolving contemporary time dilemmas will thus require making fundamental changes in the ways modern work is organized.

The Individual Approach: Self-Help and Time Management

In a society that stresses the importance of personal control and the private nature of even socially structured problems, it is no surprise that one of the most prevalent perspectives emphasizes that individuals can and should exert control by using time more efficiently. While rare among scholarly analyses, the self-help perspective has flourished in popular culture. Even a superficial review of bookstores and Internet sites offers a wide array of books and other materials with advice to worried readers about how to use time more effectively. A recent check of listings at Amazon.com, for example, yielded 1,164 books on time management: Alan Axelrod provides *201 Ways to Manage Your Time Better;* Brian Harris offers *471 Time Savers for Busy People;* and Stephanie Culp suggests *611 Ways to Do More in a Day.* In keeping with the spirit of saving time, however, Donna Smallin is most efficient, suggesting only *7 Simple Steps to Unclutter Your Life.*

While these books promise efficiency, others have more ambitious goals. There are, for example, Robert Bly's *101 Ways to Make Every Second Count,* which promises that maximum efficiency will be accompanied by less stress, and Hyrum W. Smith's *10 Natural Laws of Successful Time and Life Management,* which offers inner peace along with increased productivity.

The plethora of self-help books provides compelling evidence that a concern about time is becoming part of a larger cultural preoccupation—one that has clearly created a market for authors and booksellers. It is less clear, however, that they offer much in the way of effective help. Indeed, to the extent that reading them takes time and places the responsibility squarely on the shoulders of each individual, these manuals may contribute to the problems they are ostensibly aimed at solving.

Self-help books are built on an assumption that the problem of shrinking time is a private matter. Yet the time pressures confronting most Americans are rooted in social arrangements that go much deeper than the idiosyncratic inefficiencies of individuals. While time management has its place, it is no substitute for sensible public policies, reasonable corporate practices, and effective institutional supports that offer a range of ways to achieve a reasonable integration of work and family. A focus on purely individual solutions not only siphons needed energy from the job of creating collective responses; it also runs the risk of heightening the difficulties people face by encouraging them to feel responsible for problems over which they actually have limited personal control.

The Technological Imperative

Others emphasize the role of technological change in creating an appetite for fast living. Noted science writer James Gleick suggests that a parade of advances since the advent of the telegraph have made time consciousness nearly unavoidable. From trains and cars to jets, personal computers, and the Internet, technological innovation has steadily increased the pace of life. In his book *Faster* (1999), Gleick notes that time, once measured in days and seasons, is now measured in milliseconds and even nanoseconds (that is, billionths of a second). We are now far more conscious of every minute and even every second that passes. Every moment not used productively is potentially "lost." Companies are eager to produce, and consumers are happy to buy, a wide array of devices, such as speed-dialing telephones, television remote controls, and multitasking computers, that save a few seconds here and there. With the Internet, we can now access news faster, trade stocks faster, correspond faster, and search faster for airline tickets, cars, and loans. And if speedy machines first arose at the workplace, they now follow us home. Whether at home, at work, or just walking down the street, we increasingly "multitask," engaging in several activities at once and comparing ourselves to computers as we do.

In this context of increasing speed, the bottlenecks of modern life—sitting in traffic jams, waiting in airport security screening lines, getting a busy signal, or being put on hold—seem increasingly incongruous and annoying. We want computers that boot up instantly and are attached to printers that generate pages in seconds. We grow impatient when an elevator does not arrive quickly or an Internet browser fails to deliver us promptly to the site we seek. We turn to cell phones when confronted with down time, whether we are stuck in traffic or waiting for a restaurant table. Amid this dizzying pace and growing time consciousness, we paradoxically seek seemingly exotic remedies, such as yoga and meditation, to try to slow things down.[2]

Gleick sees the speed of contemporary life as a challenge to our biological capacities and points out that ostensibly time-saving technologies often take more time. He argues, for example, that multitasking can actually lower productivity by reducing our attention span. He also believes that the consequences of technological change are beyond human control. If there is an inescapable technological imperative at work, Gleick argues, we must simply adjust to the faster speed of life. The drawbacks and ironies of technological change do not make a case against new technology, but rather highlight our inexperience in using them optimally. In its essence, this perspective on our time pressures sees technology as an irresistible, universal force: "It may as well be a law of modern life," writes Gleick.

"Once it was true of machines, as they began infiltrating the fabric of our existence, and now it is particularly true of the technologies of computing and communication. First we disdain them and despise them; then we depend on them. In between, we hardly notice a transition" (Gleick 2001, p. 66).

Certainly, technology is a major component of the process of change. It opens new possibilities even as it closes off earlier options, poses new risks, creates new challenges, and makes some paths hard to resist. A broader view nevertheless makes clear that technology need not determine the way we live our lives. We have seen that the pressures of modern life vary across countries that have access to exactly the same technologies. Cell phones, for example, are even more commonplace in the Netherlands than they are in the United States. Yet the Dutch have made choices, as a country, to maintain the boundaries around work and keep it from dominating social life. The pace of life in Amsterdam is, consequently, quite different from that in New York City.

Theories of a technological imperative, whether Gleick's version or another's, cannot account for the varied ways in which societies and citizens use technology and incorporate it into their lives. A technologically determinist argument assumes that technology outpaces and supercedes our ability to control it. While there is little doubt that technological innovation creates new options even as it sets limits on what is possible, human societies and social actors ultimately give meaning, purpose, and shape to these technological tools. While technology may set the terms within which change can occur, human actors, both individually and collectively, must make choices about when, how, and under what circumstances technological innovations will be used. We have more ability—and more responsibility—to control the use of these tools of modern life than is sometimes realized, even if we rarely exercise such control in a coordinated or effective way. If we cede that control to machines, however, we give up our collective and individual chances to create the kind of world in which we wish to live.

If a broad technological approach is unduly pessimistic about our ability to channel, shape, or slow the pace of modern life, it also offers little insight into the myriad of variations in the culture of "busyness." What Gleick takes as common, everyday experience, for example, more typically describes the experiences of relatively affluent urban dwellers. Generalizing from the experience of fast-paced urban professionals to the experiences of workers and their families in other settings is a common problem with this kind of approach. Proposed solutions may be developed for a specific group that are less able to speak to the needs or problems of those facing different circumstances.

Finally, and ironically, a perspective that emphasizes technological determinism, especially when it is cast in pessimistic terms, downplays the many ways that new technologies can potentially help reduce time squeezes and work-family strains. Whatever form our nostalgic visions of the past may take, few of us would want to return to a world without computers any more than we would prefer to live in a world without washing machines, indoor plumbing, electricity, or telephones. Surely all of these technological innovations have not only speeded up the pace of life but also lightened many time-consuming and burdensome tasks.[3] Computers make it possible to work at home, enabling some to get work done while attending to a sick child or waiting for the plumber to repair a leaky faucet. Cell phones make it hard to avoid a boss, but they also enable parents to check on their teenagers after school while the parents are still at work. E-mail may make it easier for employers to invade the home and find workers at any time and any place, but it also gives workers more flexibility about when, where, and how to integrate jobs with private pursuits. When it comes to information and communication technologies, the work-family balance sheet has positive entries as well. Whether the benefits ultimately outweigh the costs will depend on how we make collective choices that emphasize the liberating possibilities of new technologies while limiting their ability to dictate how we live our lives.

Ruth Schwartz Cowan, a leading historian of technology, notes the often unanticipated consequences of technological change. Labor-saving technologies, she argues, often ultimately produce more rather than less work because they allow for dramatic improvements in the quality of the product or service in question. She notes, for example, that when the cast-iron stove replaced the open hearth as the principal tool for cooking in the nineteenth century, meals became more varied and complex because the stoves made it easier to cook several different items at the same time. Diets improved, and the time each cooking and baking task required declined, but the total amount of time spent cooking did not. Contemporary examples abound: copy machines make reproduction of paper easier but increase the amount of duplicate copies we expect; computer printers are faster and easier to use than typewriters, but they result in many more drafts and corrections. Yet, in contrast to Gleick, Cowan insists that technology can be harnessed for social purposes.

The Cultural Approach: Consumerism and the Culture of Overwork

In contrast to both the individualist and the technological perspectives, the cultural approach stresses the role of social values and mores in shaping the use—and misuse—of time. This perspective covers a wide array of arguments, but the most prominent ones focus on the "culture of consumerism" and its counterpart, the "culture of overwork."

In *The Overspent American,* Juliet Schor (1998) emphasizes culture rather than technology as the driving force behind busy lives. She sees a rising desire for ever more expensive and plentiful consumer goods as a major cause of expanding workdays. The ethic of competitive consumption, she argues, propels the middle class to strive for bigger houses, nicer cars, more exotic vacations, and other symbols of material affluence. These aspirations require a Faustian bargain at work, in which big bills and bigger appetites require higher incomes and thus more hours at work.

This critique of consumerism is even more fundamental than the critique of technology, for it implies that material consumption is a trap that cannot satisfy basic human needs and ultimately leads to frustration and dissatisfaction. It extends a long tradition of social critiques of middle- and upper-class striving, including Vance Packard's *The Status Seekers* (1959) and, in a much earlier era, Thorstein Veblen's *The Theory of the Leisure Class* (1994 [1899]), where the term "conspicuous consumption" was coined. These earlier works make it clear that, for better or for worse, the pursuit of material gain has long been with us. Its hold may have intensified during some periods and waned during others, but these ups and downs are not precisely linked to the rise of greater time pressures.[4]

Why, then, should the passion to consume drive contemporary Americans to pursue frenzied work schedules? Since the rich are as visible today as one's neighbors and peers were in earlier periods, Schor answers, it has become harder to resist the urge to emulate them. It is also possible, as Veblen suggests, that countervailing norms prevailed in earlier periods and helped dampen the passion to consume. One such norm, according to Veblen, is "conspicuous leisure," in which economic status is displayed by *not* working.[5] Unlike our current circumstances, the honor once associated with leisure—and its companions, refinement and cultivation—gave a negative connotation to productive labor.[6] Today, with work elevated to a moral imperative, little of this ethic remains.

By the mid-twentieth century, when "keeping up with the Joneses" became a rallying cry for those concerned with the woes of materialism, the cultural influence of the aristocratic lifestyle had long been in decline (Cannadine 1990). Yet vestiges of the status attached to enforced leisure remained, especially in the form of the "stay-at-home" housewife, who rose to prominence as a cultural symbol in the post–World War II era. For a middle-class man of that period, being able to afford a comfortable suburban house and a wife who devoted her time to domesticity were emblems of successful masculinity (Kimmel 1996). Employed wives in the 1950s were thus disproportionately found in poor and minority households, and many working-class husbands felt uneasy about the prospect of depending on the earnings of a wife.

This cultural norm, which was never embraced by everyone, has also declined to the point of near extinction. As women streamed into the labor force in the second half of the twentieth century, breaking a wide range of occupational barriers in the process, the notion of womanly leisure began to erode as firmly as the notion of manly leisure did in an earlier time. While there remains a strong cultural contradiction between women's responsibilities as caretakers and their obligations to "carry their own weight" as family earners, the era of the valorization of the housewife has surely passed.[7] Deep and interwoven social changes, such as the decline of the male-breadwinner wage, the growth of occupational opportunities for women, and the expansion of alternatives to permanent marriage, insure that most women, no less than most men, will continue to pursue strong ties to work outside the home in the coming decades (Bergmann 1986; Cherlin 1992; Spain and Bianchi 1996).

Comparing Veblen, Packard, and Schor makes it clear that, however compelling, cultural explanations leave many unanswered questions. For one thing, status symbols have changed historically. While it is still prestigious to take an exotic vacation or perfect an amateur athletic skill, the allure of a life of leisure has given ground over the course of the twentieth century to the appeal of a fast-paced lifestyle. As the world of paid work has become an important marker of social status for a growing number, "Busy!" is increasingly the most acceptable reply to the age-old question "How are you?" The cultural shift from the honor of leisure to the prestige of busyness does not itself offer an explanation. Instead, the change in how people value and use time is the very thing that needs to be explained.

The cultural argument undeniably taps an important element of the broad social changes now underway, but it offers an incomplete explanation with uncertain policy implications. If the core problems stem from prevailing values, then only a change in values can provide solutions. Yet attempting such a course of action is likely to be unworkable, fraught with perils, and largely ineffective. There may be some who will embrace the opportunity to defy convention and find deep satisfaction in a low-work, low-earning, low-consumption lifestyle, but this option is not likely to be either attractive or available to most. What's more, it does not and cannot speak to the problems of the large number of workers who are barely able to make ends meet. Whatever shape our national problems may take, exhorting individuals to resist the allure of consumerism is unlikely to redress the deep-seated tensions between home and work that are built into our current social arrangements. Now that women as well as men have the right and need to achieve economic autonomy outside the home, it seems impractical and even unjust to argue that the desire to work is the source of the problem.

We argue instead that the growing difficulties integrating time at work with time for the rest of one's life are not rooted in the aspirations of contemporary women and men, but rather in the obstacles they face to achieving their aspirations. Whether families hope to gain more time at home by working less or need a better web of supports in order to work more, they cannot resolve their dilemmas without the support of governments, communities, and employers. Neither personal downsizing nor blaming a culture of consumerism and overwork will provide a national solution to the broad spectrum of work-family challenges. Beyond a change in values or individual strategies, we need to take basic steps as a society to help make family life more manageable for the large mainstream of working families. People should be able to decide how much (or how little) they wish to earn and consume, but they should be able to do so in a context that offers reasonable options and genuine choices.

The Role of the Workplace

A long and venerable theoretical tradition focuses on how the workplace operates as a primary determinant of time commitments and pressures.

One variant of this approach stresses the ways in which the organization of work incentives and demands creates "opportunity structures" that determine the paths workers can (and cannot) take as well as the motivation they develop for pursuing different paths. In her classic study *Men and Women of the Corporation,* Rosabeth Kanter (1977) argued that three consequential aspects of large work organizations—opportunity, power, and numbers—shape work commitment. Those with high levels of opportunity and power who experience acceptance and integration into the organization are more likely to develop strong, committed ties than are those with low opportunity and power, who feel marginalized.[8] Her framework suggests that those who are well positioned at work are more likely to invest more time as well. By distinguishing among managers, wives, and secretaries, she also pointed out the gendered nature of the traditional work organization. High-opportunity jobs not only demand heavy time commitments but also depend on unpaid workers—that is, wives—whose job is to support the work careers of their spouses and relieve them of domestic responsibilities.

The transformation of the American household and the steady, prolonged march of women into the work of paid work has severely challenged the assumptions on which the classic work organization, which Kanter described so incisively, is based. Few families can now look to a wife to provide full-time domestic service, much less remain available to bolster the career of an overworked husband. And women are increasingly discomfited at the prospect of long years of service to an organization that offers little chance of upward mobility or commensurate economic reward. Yet despite these dramatic changes in the lives of women and the economics of families, work organizations have yet to change in similarly dramatic ways. To the contrary, there appears to be a growing expectation that workers in a vast array of jobs should demonstrate their commitment to put work first, regardless of family needs and responsibilities. An ethic of "professionalism," once reserved for a small sliver of jobs, is becoming a social and organizational standard.[9]

Where does this standard come from? Arlie Hochschild suggests that worker preferences, more than employer demands, are fueling this shift across all levels of the workplace. As the office has become more worker-friendly, the workplace has become a powerful magnet for our time and attention. In an age of family uncertainty, the workplace has also taken on the aura of a haven from rising domestic tensions. As a result, Hochschild argues, even harried workers do not make use of the family-friendly policies companies offer. If the modern family was once idealized as a "haven in a heartless world" (Lasch 1977), Hochschild reverses the picture, contending that the workplace has become a haven from the complexities of private life in an age of diverse and shifting family arrangements.

We agree that the workplace is a powerful magnet and that satisfying jobs attract women and men alike. Yet we have found that when flexible options are available, most workers take advantage of them. Among the large proportion who are not given such options, moreover, many would be willing to trade income and other job perquisites for the chance to have them. For most women and men, the major obstacle to using—or even bargaining for—family-supportive workplace policies is the concern that such actions will exact significant long-term costs to their careers and economic welfare. Our analysis suggests that, despite the vast changes that have taken place since Kanter's study, the organization of the workplace remains a powerful explanation of the choices workers make.

There is, nevertheless, little doubt that new generations are looking to paid work for personal satisfaction and financial security. High work aspirations, once confined to a relatively small group of white men with access to the best jobs, now are found across genders, races, and ethnicities. As ever greater numbers of women join men in embracing the long-revered "work ethic," it is becoming increasingly unreasonable to expect them to choose between satisfying, well-rewarded work careers and a viable family life. Whether the worker is a woman or a man, the lure of work should not preclude the rewards of domestic commitment, and domestic responsibilities should not preclude the chances of building satisfying work over the course of a career. We have repeatedly found that what most workers, both women and men, want is neither escape from family nor work, but rather a reasonable and flexible balance between them.

Hochschild rightly calls for a broad, national discussion about the ways in which more room can be created for family life in a world where most adults not only need to work outside the home but strongly wish to do so. This discussion needs to extend beyond a critique of workers' motives to the basic assumptions around which our work institutions are built.[10] It is no longer plausible for employers to assume that good workers are those that put work first at all times and under all conditions. Now that workers no longer routinely earn enough to subsidize an unpaid worker at home, it is time to recognize that good workers are those who can blend their multiple obligations in effective and satisfying ways over the course of their work and family careers. As individuals' life span expands and family size declines, we also need to develop a longer view of work commitment, one that makes room for intensive parenting time during the relatively brief period when young children need concerted care and attention, as well as for the continuing demands of child rearing through late childhood and adolescence, and for the other family care responsibilities that often follow parenting in the life course. Such a framework would help us to enact specific policies that create a more level playing field for families and work organizations alike.

Work-Family Policies as Win-Win Scenarios

More recently, as work and family issues have prompted a new and burgeoning field of study, analysts have begun to explore the advantages to corporations of work-family reform. An allied group of economists, sociologists, and psychologists are demonstrating that family-friendly policies provide a win-win strategy for corporations as well as parents (see, for example, Barnett and Hall 2001; Barnett and Rivers 1996; Kelly 1999; Berg, Kalleberg, and Appelbaum 2003; Friedman and Greenhaus 2000; Rayman 2001). Though such policies may seem costly in the short run, they provide ample benefits in the long run. By making room for the private contingencies of workers through job flexibility and supportive work environments, corporations can reduce turnover and absenteeism even as they relieve the stress on workers (see, for example, Fernandez 1986; Glass and Estes 1997; Thompson, Beauvais, and Lyness 1999). Flexibility and support from an organization increase workers' loyalty and commitment. Jennifer Glass and Lisa Riley (1998), for example, have shown that new mothers who work for companies with more supportive policies are more likely to return within one year than are those working in other firms (see also Glass and Finley 2002).

Organizations' efforts to institute work-family reforms represent an important breakthrough, for they provide a framework in which worker needs and employer interests are not assumed to be inherently at odds. Work organizations, whether large or small, are crucial arenas that shape the options of workers and thus need to be a part of any comprehensive reform.

It is important to educate corporations about the benefits of family-supportive workplace policies, but this is not sufficient. If the only rationale is enlightened self-interest, corporate support will likely wane when corporate benefits cannot be clearly demonstrated. In such a climate, policies are subject to the whims of organizations and the winds of economic cycles. Family-friendly policies are thus likely to look attractive in tight labor markets, but lose their appeal when the labor supply expands and highly qualified workers are not only plentiful but willing to accept less supportive work conditions.

In addition, in an economic climate where neither employers nor workers are likely to remain loyal for a lifetime, employers may not perceive a fair trade-off between the immediate benefits workers enjoy and the ostensible longer-run benefits for the work organization. And workers are likely to continue to fear that employer-sponsored programs will exact real if subtle long-term penalties in the form of lower income and blocked career mobility. These costs fall most heavily on women, who remain more likely to feel torn between home and work when children arrive.

Finally, if the goal of attractive work-family policies is only to retain the most valued workers, large portions of the workforce will inevitably be left to fend for themselves. For better or for worse, many corporations expect, and even depend on, rapid turnover and have little need to take active and potentially expensive steps to stem this tide (Pfeffer and Baron 1988). Large groups of employees are simply viewed as expendable and replaceable. In this context, family-friendly policies face a precarious fate if they are built only on the premise that they are universally beneficial to work organizations. Effective, broad-based policies depend on defining family support as a right of all workers rather than a privilege or a reward reserved for the few.

Many of the proposals that have found a receptive audience in corporate boardrooms involve trade-offs that do not challenge, and may even enhance, corporate control over the time commitment of workers. As we noted in Chapter 5, "mommy tracks," for example, provide a way for companies to appear supportive of families without changing the fundamental structure of the forty-hour-plus workweek. Mothers are allowed to combine parenting with a job, but only at the cost of forgoing career opportunities open to others. Men are left with few options for involved parenthood, while women are forced to choose between parenthood and work advancement. At lower levels of the organizational hierarchy, and especially in female-dominated positions, companies also tend to offer a wide array of part-time job opportunities at low wages and often without bene-fits. Such policies represent the low road to reducing work-family conflict. Not only do they recreate earlier forms of gender inequality in a new guise, but they also discourage a more basic reassessment of the structure of work in an age where children depend economically on mothers as well as fathers and all parents need the option to attend to their families without fear of either immediate or long-term workplace reprisals.[11]

It is crucial to consider the ways in which organizations as well as work-ers benefit from work arrangements that allow a more equal and flexible integration of family and job. Yet this approach, taken alone, can only pro-vide a partial solution to contemporary work-family dilemmas. In addi-tion to showing how corporations may reap some benefits from actions they take to help their workers meet family responsibilities, we must ac-knowledge the need for national family support policies, even when they may involve some cost to corporations. Beyond corporate interests, the high road to promoting the welfare of working families means focusing on the common good that ultimately enables corporations to thrive. The common good, in turn, can only be achieved through national policies that create a level playing field for all and define corporate interests in broad enough terms to encompass the larger social principles of gender justice and the welfare of new generations.

Overlapping Time Divides

All of the prevailing approaches—from individual and cultural perspec-tives to workplace-based analyses—offer insights into the time dilemmas of American workers and their families. Taken alone, however, each leaves one piece or more of the puzzle missing. Because these dilemmas assume many forms, cut through many levels, and have many sources, addressing them effectively requires a multifaceted approach. Indeed, we have discov-ered not one, but five time divides. First, the transformation of the Ameri-can household has produced a *work-family divide,* in which workers face mounting conflicts between the home and the workplace. Second, a grow-ing bifurcation of the labor force has contributed to a growing *occupa-tional divide,* in which some jobs demand very long days and others do not. Third, as workers are increasingly channeled into jobs with either very high or relatively low time demands, we have also found a growing *aspira-tion divide,* in which workers experience a gap between their actual and their preferred working time. Of course, a *parenting divide* also continues to place involved parents in a disadvantaged and precarious position, separating them from and even pitting them against childless workers. And last, but certainly not least, the persistence of unequal opportunities—for balancing parenting and paid work and for finding promising and flexible jobs—underscores a persisting *gender divide,* which leaves women and men facing different options and dilemmas. These multiple, overlapping, and cross-cutting divides require a wide-ranging approach to the interaction of time, work, and family. They force us to take seriously the social-structural roots of these dilemmas.

The Work-Family Divide and the Transformation of the American Home

The workplace and the home are both "greedy institutions" that lack clear boundaries and have the potential to expand without limit.[12] Is it ever possible to know with confidence that "enough" time has been devoted to a family or a job? Even in the best of all possible worlds, a delicate juggling of competing obligations and loyalties prevails. The transformation of the American household has intensified this age-old challenge.

Despite the popular and scholarly focus on expanding time at work, we have found that the transformation of American family life has produced far more fundamental changes in the ways Americans allocate time. Indeed, average working time for individuals has not increased substantially over the last several decades. Yet even if individual time at work had declined slightly, most families would still be coping with severe and probably unprecedented time squeezes. Family life has undergone fundamental changes, and the structure of work has not changed to the same degree.

To be effective, any policy approach must, first and foremost, recognize the widespread and irreversible nature of family change. Most children depend on either two earners or one parent. Most women know they cannot depend on the earnings of men to insure their own or their families' financial welfare in either the short or the long term. And most men recognize that breadwinning is increasingly a shared endeavor and that few women are prepared to forgo the personal and economic rewards of paid work in exchange for full-time domesticity. The gender and family revolutions that have sent unprecedented numbers of women into the workforce have undermined the once unquestioned assumption that the workplace could be "greedy" because the home was being safely tended.

This new family age has long been in the making, can be found in all advanced societies, and shows no signs of reversing its course. Indeed, as new generations grow to adulthood, dual-earner and single-parent families are likely to become more common, not less.[13] Social policies that fail to recognize this irrevocable change—or, worse, try to reverse it—are doomed to failure. Those who decry the decline of traditional marriage cannot stem the tide toward more egalitarian and fluid family forms, but they can prevent movement toward progressive social policies. We need to move beyond hand-wringing over the perils of irreversible change to a more basic discussion of what needs to be done to help families in this new era. If diverse family forms are here to stay, the policy implications are clear. It is time to rethink the structure of work to better fit the needs of mothers, fathers, and children.

The Occupational Divide and the Bifurcation of the Labor Market

Even though the average working time of individuals has increased only slightly, important changes have nevertheless occurred in the American labor force. In lieu of rising hours for everyone, we have found a growing divide between those who are putting in very long days at the workplace and those who are not. An occupational divide is developing between jobs that demand excessive time commitments and jobs that may not offer sufficient time at work to meet workers' needs or preferences.

Since employers may choose a variety of strategies for enhancing profits and forming contractual bonds with workers, we need to understand why employers seek excessive time commitments from some workers while offering jobs with shorter and potentially insufficient working time to others. One avenue for enhancing profits involves asserting entitlement to employees' time and loyalty. Another, however, points in the opposite direction. By relying on part-time and subcontracted jobs, companies are able to reduce costs and lower their commitments and obligations to a sizable segment of workers. Both strategies may look increasingly attractive to employers, even though neither meets most workers' needs.

What factors are promoting the bifurcation of working time? At one end of the spectrum, employers have an incentive to encourage long workweeks from salaried workers, who receive no additional earnings for the extra time they may be persuaded—or required—to work (see Landers, Rebitzer, and Taylor 1996). In addition, the segment of the labor force most at risk for these heavy time demands has grown markedly. When the

Fair Labor Standards Act was passed in 1938, it hardly seemed necessary to protect the one in seven workers (or 14.8 percent of the labor force) who were classified as professionals or managers. By 1995, however, that proportion had doubled, to nearly two in seven (28.3 percent). The labor force now has a substantial number of workers who do not earn extra pay for additional time at work. In addition, the costs of the most expensive "fringe" benefits, such as health care, are fixed for a full-time worker, no matter how many hours he or she works. As the costs of these benefits have risen (especially as proportion of total compensation), employers may find it tempting to push full-time workers toward longer workdays. For all of these reasons, employers face rising incentives to expect salaried workers to put in more than forty hours a week and to use working time as a measure of work commitment and a basis for promotions and raises.

Once long workweeks become the expected norm, informal rules develop that lend a wider meaning to working time. Time comes to represent work commitment, and long hours may persist even if they are not the most efficient way of organizing work. Those who choose to put in fewer hours then run the risk of being branded "deviants" who depart from accepted "time norms" and are thus not worthy of serious consideration for advancement (Epstein et al. 1999).

At the other end of the occupational spectrum are those who are paid by the hour. Especially when additional working time produces a sharp increase in hourly pay (such as time-and-a-half payments for over forty hours a week), employers may be reluctant to authorize overtime.[14] And the rising cost of benefits, which adds to the appeal of extracting long workdays from salaried workers, also makes it attractive to employ part-time workers. Since part-time workers are rarely offered a benefits package, employers' utilizing part-time employment can substantially reduce labor costs. The creation of part-time jobs with low pay and few benefits may in turn induce many workers to take several jobs to stay afloat, ultimately lengthening their workweek. The high cost of benefits thus tends to enhance the likelihood of both long and short workweeks, without reducing the pressures on workers in either situation.

A set of economic and social forces is thus encouraging the growth of jobs built on the premise of both long and short workweeks. While relatively well-educated and highly trained salaried workers may be facing increased pressure to put in long days at the office, those with less secure jobs, such as hourly workers, part-time employees, and contingent workers, may have a difficult time getting the amount of work they desire. Since the early 1980s, downsizing has become a common response to the growing pressures of international competition as well as a speedy way to cut costs and increase profits. Yet rather than producing across-the-board increases in working time, downsizing has had different consequences for different groups on the occupational ladder. At higher levels, the ranks of professionals and managers have often been trimmed, with those left behind expected to pick up the slack and put in more time. At lower levels, however, reducing jobs and outsourcing have taken precedence over extending the workweek. A general increase in the intensity of work thus does not automatically produce across-the-board increases in working time (see, for example, Cappelli 2001; Gordon 1996; Pfeffer and Baron 1988).

Time demands, like other work-related opportunities and pressures, are not distributed equally across the labor force. The growing bifurcation into longer and shorter workweeks reminds us that the labor force consists of a diverse collection of workers. Any policy response needs to take account of the varying pressures, constraints, and contingencies attached to different jobs.

These changes also imply that it is time to reconsider the form and scope of legislative measures adopted decades ago, when hourly wage work predominated. The growth of salaried occupations and the increasing variation in working time point to the need for new forms of protective labor legislation that recognize the changed realities of professional as well as nonprofessional workers. If those at some levels of the occupational structure need some respite from the ever-increasing time demands of their jobs, then those in other occupational niches need jobs that offer enough working time, along with sufficient pay and benefits, to provide for their own and their families' welfare.

The Aspiration Divide and the Gap between Ideals and Options

The increasing diversity of the labor force has also created a gap between the kinds of schedules workers desire and the options available to them. Especially at the extremes of the working time spectrum, the supply of jobs available neither reflects nor fits well with workers' preferences and needs. Many workers express a significant gap between their ideal and actual working conditions. Those putting in very many hours tend to wish to work less, and those putting in relatively few tend to wish to work more.

While the drawbacks of long workweeks may be most obvious in the current climate, the drawbacks of short ones are equally significant. If current trends continue, we are likely to see a widening gap between those who would prefer to work less and those who wish to work more.

Whatever the benefits to work organizations, the personal and social costs of long workweeks are becoming increasingly clear. Certainly they undermine a worker's ability to achieve his or her preferred balance between work and home, public life and private life, earning a living and caring for self and others. Beyond these personal and family dilemmas, however, are social costs as well. Excessively demanding jobs erode the time people have to participate in civil society; and, as we discuss next, they undermine the prospects for gender and parenting equality.[15]

Similarly, personal, familial, and social costs are also linked to overly brief workweeks. Often these jobs signify underemployment, inadequate income, and financial insecurity. They may also lack the benefits that provide a safety net for those who have fuller workweeks. And just as overly long workweeks erode the chances for parenting equality, overly short ones—especially for women—can contribute to gender inequality at home and at work.

Creating opportunities for a more equitable balance between paid work and the rest of life is thus not simply a private issue between employers and employees, but a matter of great public interest. This social need is also reflected in the personal ideals of workers, whose expressed desires belie the argument that the dispersion of working time merely reflects individual preferences. To the contrary, most workers aspire to a balance between home and work that eludes them. The gap between ideal and actual circumstances makes it clear that workers' needs and desires are often out of sync with job structures and options. This suggests that work organizations, left to their own devices, have not produced the mix of jobs that matches the needs and preferences of the American workforce.[16]

In short, the growing divide in working time neither reflects nor supports workers' desires for a balance between paid work and family time. Effective responses to this growing "aspiration divide" need to focus on establishing reasonable expectations and boundaries for how jobs are structured and rewarded. The public good and the welfare of families depend on creating public policies that promote a level playing field, in which employers do not face incentives either to shorten or to extend the workweek unduly.

The Parenting Divide and the Penalties of Involved Parenthood

A parenting divide separates involved parents from other workers. When it comes to parenting, mothers and fathers alike continue to confront work structures that penalize parental involvement and reinforce parenting inequities. These structures do not fit either the needs or the ideals of many families. Many women—and men—would prefer to blend a thirty- to forty-hour-a-week work career with a rich and committed life outside the office. This blend is unlikely to prove workable, however, in jobs and occupations where fifty to sixty hours is the norm and considerable costs accrue to working less. The emerging occupational structure thus allows choices, but for too many these are forced choices between unpalatable alternatives.[17]

While undoubtedly challenging, combining parenting and paid work can also be invigorating.[18] For most current and future parents, it is likely to be the preferred choice. Young women and men tend to agree that a busy life is to be preferred over the potential isolation and economic insecurity of not holding a paid job.[19] In a world where parents and workers confront increasingly diverse circumstances, there can be no "one size fits all" pattern that is right for everyone, and parents need to make the choices they deem best. For the growing proportion who wish to integrate parenthood and work, the challenge is to help lessen the dilemmas and provide needed supports.

The Gender Divide and the Persistence of Work and
Parenting Inequality

The multifaceted time divides between work and family, long and short workweeks, and ideals and aspirations contribute to a gender divide between women and men. This divide takes several forms, all of which promote the recreation of earlier gender inequalities in new and problematic ways.

The time divides of the labor force, for example, are not gender neutral. Women are more likely to hold part-time jobs, which may not meet their families' financial needs or provide long-term opportunities for career development. Women work about six hours less per week than men do, on average, and the proportion of women putting in very long weeks trails the proportion of men by even more. And since the statistics most often cited on the gender gap in wages adjust for these differences, they capture only a portion of the gender gap in earnings that emerges from differences in working time.

On the other side of the occupational time divide, jobs requiring excessive time commitments also subvert gender equality. Certainly these demanding job expectations contribute to the glass ceiling on women's mobility and women's relative absence in the highest echelons of management and the professions. Further, we found that women holding highly demanding jobs with long workweeks are less likely than their male peers to enjoy the flexibility and autonomy to meld heavy work commitments with life outside the workplace.

Despite the gender divide in opportunities, however, there appears to be growing convergence in ideals and aspirations between women and men. We found that both women and men tend to prefer a flexible balance between home and the workplace. While women may wish to work slightly less than men, on average, this small difference is overshadowed by the large diversity within gender categories and the growing agreement on matters that would ease work-family conflicts. Fathers as well as mothers would like more family-supportive workplaces and would trade other work-related benefits to have them.[20] Yet workers across the gender divide continue to worry that any time they take for family pursuits will undermine their credibility as committed workers and exact a heavy price in the long run. It would thus be misleading to equate workers' actions with their preferences.

The principles of justice and fairness are reason enough to remedy the inequities that continue to separate workers by gender and parental status. Beyond its intrinsic merit, however, equal opportunity for integrating work and parenting provides a crucial means to provide for the welfare of new generations and for the common good. In an era of diverse and changing family arrangements, children increasingly depend on the earnings of women and need to be able to count on a wide net of caretakers, including fathers, mothers, and others. Creating equal opportunities—for women as paid workers and for men as family caretakers—is thus an essential ingredient in the formulation of effective and just social policies.

8

Where Do We Go from Here?

Time, like money, is a scarce and unequally distributed resource. Although each day contains twenty-four hours and each week consists of seven days, institutional arrangements and personal responsibilities constrain the ways that time can be "spent." Yet social arrangements pose time constraints and create time dilemmas in different ways for different social groups. In considering the future of family, work, and gender equality, we thus need to look beyond individual choices or values to consider the full range and sources of our time squeezes.

The American economy is producing too much work for some and too little work for others, leaving workers at both ends of the spectrum facing real, but different, difficulties. Neither the structure of work nor the provision of public services has changed sufficiently to accommodate the widespread and deep changes taking place in gender and family relationships. As a consequence, America faces consequential divides not just between family and work, but also between overly demanding and underrewarded jobs, between workers' aspirations and the options they are offered, between parents and other workers, and between men and women. Any debate about the changing contours of time use needs to consider not just worker preferences but also the rights of workers and parents to meet their own and their families' needs. Beyond a focus on individual behavior, resolving our growing time dilemmas requires reconsidering the structure of work and the nature of community responsibility.

Specific policy reforms will work best if they reflect a comprehensive, yet flexible, vision of the goals we seek to achieve. These goals include a more equitable and pliable balance between work and family responsibilities, protection for parents and children and for the opportunities of all workers, and an array of genuine options for overcoming the time divides we face. To reach these goals, we should consider new and broader ways to re-structure the workplace, to affirm the principle of equal opportunity as well as the rights of parents and workers, and to rethink the responsibilities of employers, communities, and public institutions.

There is, however, no "one size fits all" solution to the time dilemmas of contemporary Americans. Beyond any one specific approach, work-family policies need to promote family-supportive working conditions without assuming or imposing a uniform vision on everyone. The new diversity in family arrangements and worker circumstances implies that social poli-cies should be sensitive to the myriad needs facing households with vary-ing structures, incomes, and priorities. This means reducing time for the overworked and providing more work to the underemployed. It means im-parting more flexibility to rigid job structures and creating institutional supports outside the workplace. It means being attentive to the needs of workers contending with different economic resources, family circum-stances, and gender arrangements. It means creating a range of policies that enable people to meet their work and family aspirations, as they define them now and as they change over the course of their lives. Workers need genuine choices and social supports, not moralizing. Indeed, creating a "culture of tolerance" that recognizes the diversity of needs among parents and workers may be the most important contribution a national debate can make.

In addition to discussing the place of work and family in our national culture, we need to consider three types of policy approaches: *work-facili-tating and family-support reforms* that foster a better integration of family and paid work; *equal-opportunity reforms* that insure the rights of all work-ers, regardless of their gender or family circumstances, to combine the pur-suit of work opportunities with parental involvement; and *work-regulating reforms* that provide more equitable and reasonable ways to organize—and limit—working time. Each of these policy approaches is part of a broad ar-ray of needed reforms, including new workplace regulations and worker protections, the provision of social services, and legislative initiatives. Though we discuss on each policy arena, we pay most attention to the pos-sibilities for reorganizing working time. Although it has received far less at-tention than policy approaches stressing family support, changing the way we structure and regulate time at paid employment holds the potential to alter the entire range of options available to workers and their families.

Facilitating Work through Family Support

Many worthwhile proposals to reduce work-family conflict are "work facilitating" because they help to reduce the barriers to participation in paid work, especially in the context of dual-earning and single-parent households. Community-based and on-site child-care supports, for example, make it easier to combine work and family without necessarily reducing work commitments. Supports of this sort, while relatively undeveloped in the United States, are commonly available in other advanced industrial societies.

Caretaking and other supports for employed parents are essential now that even mothers of very young children are expected to support themselves and their families. With two thirds of mothers with infants and preschoolers now in the workforce and strict mandated limits on government support for poor mothers and their children, there is simply no substitute for high-quality, widely available caretaking services for children and their parents. In addition to a well-developed system of child care, there is a growing need for educational reforms, such as longer school days and years and well-developed after-school programs.

Family Support through Child Care and After-School Programs

High-quality child care for young children is a central—indeed, an indispensable—ingredient in any work-facilitating approach to work-family conflict. So, too, are well-developed after-school programs. Without such supports, parents are often forced to choose between providing for their children's economic needs and providing for their children's psychological and emotional development.

Child Care

As we saw in Chapter 6, women in the United States have among the highest labor force participation rates and, among those working, put in the most hours of those in any of the countries in our analysis. Working parents in dual-earner couples in the United States also put in the most hours. These employment patterns, when combined with the paucity of support for child care, create a larger challenge for American parents than for those in other economically developed countries.

Publicly sponsored or subsidized child care for preschoolers (children aged three to five) is not uncommon in the United States, with 54 percent of American children getting some form of public care (including five-year-olds in kindergarten); but much of this care is available only part of the day. In contrast, 91 percent of Italian children, 95 percent of Belgian children, and a remarkable 99 percent of French preschoolers spend either part of the day or, in most cases, all of the day in publicly provided care (see Table 6.3). As the exemplar in this area, France makes available child care and early education to all families. The French child-care system welcomes children from all classes and uses a sliding scale of payments, asking families with differing economic means to pay only what they can afford (Bergmann 1997; Helburn and Bergmann 2002).

When it comes to younger children, the situation for American families is even worse. Below age three, only 5 percent of American infants and toddlers are in publicly provided or publicly financed care. Some European countries provide much more (for example, 23 percent in France, 30 percent in Belgium, and 33 percent in Sweden). Despite the United States's position as a child care "laggard," this is one area where we do not have to reinvent the wheel but rather can draw on the experience of other countries.[1]

The lack of high-quality, affordable child care limits the ability of mothers to maintain their connection to the workplace after the birth of a child and makes working full time more difficult. Studies have found that some women report they would work more if child care were more available (Hayes, Palmer, and Zaslow 1990; Mason and Kuhlthau 1992). Combined with parental leaves (Glass and Riley 1998; Klerman and Leibowitz 1999), high-quality child care addresses the concerns of working mothers, enables more mothers of young children to work, and has the potential to contribute to economic growth.

Yet resistance to child care abounds in the United States, although it is usually based on misleading and inaccurate assumptions. Discussions of child care, like discussions of working time, are typically too sweeping, lumping all kinds of care together and distinguishing all "other care" from "mother care" in overly simple ways (Scarr 1984; Clarke-Stewart 1993). Developing a promising child-care agenda thus requires that we first make a few simple but important distinctions. We need to pay attention to the extent to which families depend on extrafamilial care, the ages of the children being cared for, the quality of the care being provided, and the types of families relying on it.

The European example should make it clear, even to the most skeptical Americans, that well-supported and widely available child-care services can contribute to the welfare of children, or at least certainly do them no harm. Yet having a four-year-old at child care from nine o'clock until five o'clock is quite different from having a three-month-old in the same setting from seven in the morning until seven at night. The long hours that some children spend in child care make many observers uncomfortable, particularly when this involves the very youngest children.[2] Efforts to shorten the working day (which we discuss below) and thus lessen the need for an overreliance on day care would defuse one of the main concerns leveled against it. Paid parental leaves, which would lower the need for child care for the very young, would dampen the other principal concern, that child care is inappropriate for very young children. In this way, the disparate pieces of the work-family puzzle can be put together in ways that make the entire situation more manageable.

Beyond concerns about the extent of care and the ages of the children who receive it, however, the quality of child care matters. Despite the concerns of some that nothing less than parental (read: maternal) care will do, the record shows that high-quality child care is beneficial. For example, the NICHD Early Child Care Research Network reports that children in care offered by well-trained caretakers with smaller groups of children show improved cognitive and social skills.[3] The problem, then, is not with child care *per se,* but with the lack of high-quality child care, especially for the poor and the working class. The sad news is that, by the measures of caregiver training and caregiver-child ratios, most child care (estimated as high as 57 percent) cannot be described as high quality (McCartney 2001). The challenge is to build a system of child-care supports that provides for higher-quality care, including smaller classes, more adults per child, and less turnover from better-trained and remunerated caretakers. Creating such a system requires funding, but the costs of failing to do so are much higher.

The dilemmas created by our collective resistance to creating high-quality child-care options are perhaps best—and most painfully—exemplified by the situation facing poor, single mothers. While welfare policies adopted during the 1930s and expanded in the postwar period were based on the principle that unmarried mothers with no other means of support should receive enough assistance to allow them to care for their young children, current policy reverses that principle. Instead of welfare, poor mothers now face "workfare" and strict time limits on government support.[4] Yet these new and sweeping work requirements have been enacted in a child-care vacuum. Although many states do not exempt even mothers with children under one year of age (and welfare policy is implemented in a decentralized manner), the provision of care for their children continues to fall short.[5]

Even with some form of child-care assistance, many low-income families are unable to afford day care because it absorbs too high a fraction of their income (Scarr 1998). Children in poor families are thus more likely to be cared for in informal settings, which are not regulated, or by family, friends, and neighbors, who may or may not receive some payment (Ross and Paulsell 1998). And for many poor parents working at minimum-wage jobs, even substandard day care is out of reach.

It is ironic that poor mothers with meager child-care supports are being pushed into the less attractive and poorly paid jobs while middle-class mothers with better job prospects face criticism for securing high-quality care for their children. These contradictions in our policies and perceptions surrounding work and family issues reveal more than just a deep ambivalence about the nature of social change; they point to the class and gender inequalities in how this ambivalence is expressed.[6] Child care thus raises one set of issues for poor, single mothers and another for affluent parents. Yet all children, regardless of their economic and family circumstances, need high-quality care, and good social policy would recognize the collective stake we all have in providing it. Whether support is offered in the form of subsidies for kin networks and neighborhood efforts or for the direct provision of care, we need a variety of approaches that speak to the needs of parents and children facing different obstacles and possessing different resources.

After-School Programs

In addition to the lack of child-care supports for preschool children, the United States also lacks supports for after-school programs and older children. Yet the need for such programs is clear. The school day, which starts around 8:30 or 9:00 A.M. and ends around 3:00 or 3:30 P.M., remains out of synch with the workday.[7] Getting children to school in the morning is challenge enough, but the scheduling gap is clearly larger and more consequential in the afternoon, when children leave school well before even those parents with nine-to-five schedules can leave work. For those who return home even later, a yawning gap looms between the end of the school day and the end of the workday.

According to the 1997 National Survey of America's Families, which gives estimates on children's after-school arrangements (Capizzano, Tout, and Adams 2000), 5 percent of children aged six to nine report "self-care" as the primary arrangement; and 10 percent report regularly spending some time alone. Among children aged ten to twelve, 24 percent report self-care as the primary arrangement and 43 percent report regularly spending some time alone.[8]

In response to this gap, after-school programs appear to be on the rise. A 2001 survey finds that two thirds of public elementary schools offered an optional after-school program (National Association of Elementary School Principals 2001), most having been established within the previous five years. Yet the principals of these schools also report serious concerns that lack of funding and staffing will cloud the future of these efforts.

The No Child Left Behind Act of 2001, passed by Congress in January 2002, included $1 billion in federal funds for after-school programs, an 18 percent increase over the previous year. The rapid expansion is from a modest base, however, since as recently as 1997 only 21 percent of children aged six to nine and only 10 percent of those aged ten to twelve were enrolled in after-school programs. Even excluding teenagers, a much more dramatic expansion is needed if after-school programs are to become available to more than a fraction of the children whose parents work outside the home.

Such programs not only help to address the scheduling discrepancy between working parents and their children; they also address other difficulties for parents, children, and the nation. If, for example, some of the myriad of activities—from sports to music lessons—that now take up so much family time in middle-class families were built into after-school programs, a large slice of time for family life could be reclaimed. Even more important, after-school programs hold great educational potential, providing enrichment and support beyond in-school activities and offering edifying alternatives to other, more dangerous uses of the free time between school and dinner. A government report on after-school programs, *Working for Children and Families*, which was released in 2000 and reflected the joint efforts of the U.S. Department of Education and the Justice Department, noted that half of juvenile crime occurs between 2:00 P.M. and 8:00 P.M. (U.S. Department of Education 2000). Enhanced after-school programs thus hold the promise of improving the psychological and physical health of children and potentially alleviating some of the greatest risks facing teenagers and their younger peers.

Whether the goal is to create better and more widely available preschool care or to enhance and expand the opportunities for school-age children, it is time for national policy to back up the oft-stated ideal of "putting children first" with real resources and commitments. Child-centered policies should not replace efforts to bring work into a better balance with family life, but they are part of a comprehensive and equitable approach to alleviating contemporary time squeezes.

A wide array of caretaking services and educational reforms will provide educational benefits as well as support to employed parents. Yet, while needed, they are not sufficient. They will help parents develop and sustain work commitments and provide for their families, but they skirt the issue of structural reform in the nature of jobs. It is not enough to help parents work more; we also need to support and protect the rights of parents to provide care and the rights of children to receive it. "Work facilitating" policies thus span a range of approaches, from public support for child care and other educational initiatives, to income supports for the working poor, to the creation of more flexible jobs and workplaces.

Income Supports for Families

Providing income supports to those in need is one of the most straightforward ways to support working families (Ehrenreich 2002; Sklar, Mykyta, and Wefald 2001). For those holding jobs at the bottom of the economic ladder, just staying afloat may require working two (or more) jobs and overtime. These jobs can be personally as well as economically unrewarding. Like those in high-paying and high-pressure professions, workers with more modest jobs, whether women or men, also generally seek a balance between work time and family time. But they also need to provide for the economic well-being of their families. Work-family policies should thus include efforts to insure that all workers are able to earn a decent standard of living—or at least avoid falling into poverty—at a forty-hour-a-week job. With such income guarantees, some will surely continue to pursue overtime and supplemental jobs, but others will have the option of working less.

The most direct efforts to provide an income floor, or living wage, involve either raising the minimum wage or giving an earned income tax credit for jobs with severely depressed wages. Tax credits are often favored by those who see this approach as a way to increase incomes without reducing the number of jobs for the poor, although those eligible often are unaware of them and do not sign up for these benefits. Minimum-wage increases, in contrast, provide a way to raise incomes without changing the tax structure, leaving employers with the primary responsibility for offering a fair reward for the efforts of their workers. Finding the right level and balance—so that minimum wages do not inhibit job creation and earned income tax credits do not encourage employers to create pay scales that are not economically justifiable—is a challenge, but this should not prevent us from using these policy tools. A mix of measures that support higher wages and tax credits can—and should—be combined to insure a living wage for those who work hard but are poorly paid.

Insuring Equal Opportunity and Protecting Parental Rights

Unless family-friendly and work-facilitating supports are intertwined with equal opportunity policies that insure the rights of workers regardless of gender or parental status, involved parents—who are more likely to be women, but increasingly include men as well—will have to sacrifice career opportunity for the sake of care, and committed workers will have to sacrifice family involvement for the sake of career and even financial security. In an economy that depends on the contributions of women as well as men, mothers as well as fathers, and parents as well as childless workers, we can afford nothing less.

Providing such protections depends on creating legislative measures comparable to the rights gained by workers during the nineteenth and twentieth centuries. Just as the minimum wage and the forty-hour workweek were legislative achievements that once seemed out of reach but are now taken for granted, securing parental rights and gender-equal opportunities at work need to be seen as an integral aspect of the restructuring of work and family in the twenty-first century. And just as earlier movements for workers' rights once seemed overly intrusive but are now deemed essential to a productive and humane economy, insuring the rights of women and parents also promises to enhance our social fabric as well as our private lives.

The costs now attached to taking some time from work to provide domestic care, for example, are not an inherent feature of work, but rather a socially constructed arrangement that is subject to social redefinition. Just as men who served in the military in the Second World War were not penalized for the time they spent serving their country, the time parents, and especially women, take to care for children need not be unduly disadvantaged. As adults live longer and spend more years engaged in paid work, there should be protections for taking time for child care (and other dependent care), especially for the relatively brief period when family responsibilities are at their peak. Without such opportunities for women and involved parents, many will find the price of care too high and those who take time off from work to provide such care will be penalized.[9]

Family Support through Work Flexibility

Even if families could routinely rely on high-quality child care, widely available after-school programs, and income supports for the working poor, another crucial set of reforms would still be needed to give workers greater flexibility at the workplace, so that they have more options in deciding how to weave their public and private commitments. The Family and Medical Leave Act, for example, gives more private time to parents and those with ill or elderly dependents. These reforms increase the flexibility provided to workers and begin to redress the imbalance between work demands and family needs. By legislating the rights of workers across a broad range of work settings, these reforms provide a needed floor of minimal supports for new parents and others with heavy, but temporary, family responsibilities. Studies show that this legislation has created protection for more workers than had previously been the case (Waldfolgel 1999).

Though they are essential, many of the proposals to promote individual flexibility are insufficient to meet the changed circumstances of workers. By limiting the time span and assuring unpaid leave only, the Family and Medical Leave Act leaves the obligations of employers fundamentally unchanged and the basic structure of jobs intact. If long working hours and uninterrupted work patterns remain a requirement for job success, those who choose to cut back from work, however temporarily, will continue to pay a considerable price in both the short term and the long term.

S. Jody Heymann (2000) documents the case for flexibility with great care and attention to detail. She shows, for example, how difficult it is for those with inflexible schedules to attend conferences with teachers and guidance counselors at school, and to make other weekday appointments. She notes, for example, that several million children suffer from chronic conditions such as asthma that routinely require doctors' visits and other parental interventions. Exactly when these family crises will arise is unpredictable, but one can predict with confidence that they will occur from time to time and that, as a matter of protecting the public health, working parents need to have the flexibility to attend to such crises. Economic analyses have suggested that flexible work arrangements, such as flextime, enhance worker productivity by improving attendance and reducing turnover, and even result in higher wages for employees (Gariety and Shaffer 2001).

Work flexibility is important, but it is difficult to legislate and needs to take different forms in different jobs. It is nevertheless possible to begin to consider ways to create more flexible working conditions across the occupational structure. Beyond the minimal parental leave policies that currently exist, tax incentives and other tools can be used to reward employers' efforts to create flexible jobs and persuade reluctant companies to develop innovative job structures.

Although men may take parental leave and other flexible work options, it is no surprise that these arrangements are often dubbed "mommy tracks." Women face greater pressures to spend time with young children, and their generally lower earnings often make this the path of least resistance, even in households preferring another strategy. Mothers and prospective mothers thus face difficult trade-offs between caretaking and career building, while fathers continue to be discouraged from family caretaking. In the absence of basic protections for women and involved parents of both sexes, such policies contribute to a cumulative cycle of lower earnings, increased career interruptions, and blocked mobility for "primary" caretakers. In the long run, gender inequities are reinforced and exacerbated as women disproportionately bear the brunt of these costs. When fathers have flexible jobs, in contrast, they are much more likely to become equal partners in the home (Coltrane 1996; Gerson 1993; Risman 1998).

Flexibility needs to be coupled with equal opportunity protections—including more energetic application of equal opportunity laws and more comprehensive job security for workers. Equal opportunity laws date from the 1960s but have never been rigorously enforced. Enforcing laws on the books and addressing related concerns, such as efforts to provide equal pay

for jobs of comparable worth, are important ingredients in achieving gender equality in the workforce.

American workers in general are among the easiest to fire of any in the
industrial world, and part-time workers generally have even less job security than do full-time workers. In addition to the lower wages and loss of
benefits, working part-time puts employees at risk of abrupt economic dis-
location. Many other countries offer job security to part-time workers on
an equal basis with their full-time counterparts. The European Union policy that prohibits discrimination against part-time work offers one model
of such protections (European Union Council Directive 1997).

The Limits of Work-Facilitating and Family-Friendly Policies

Policies that provide family support and facilitate work involvement are
necessary, but they are destined to fall short because they do not address
the structural sources of the time divide. While individuals need more options and supports, such efforts need to be part of a larger, more integrated
effort to restructure the choices and alternatives that form the context of
choice. Individual choices put the onus on workers to use family-friendly
policies, even when doing so can endanger one's job, career, and financial
security. As long as the culture of the workplace and the message from
bosses and supervisors equate work commitment with overwork, workers
face a "damned if you do and damned if you don't" set of alternatives that
exact considerable costs no matter what the choice. Those who take advantage of family-support policies must bear the costs at work, and many will
understandably forgo such "opportunities" in favor of protecting their
work and career prospects. Indeed, the current structure of incentives leads
many to put in more hours on the job than they would prefer if they faced
genuinely less costly options.

The problem is not that people may make irrational choices, but that the
set of options available leaves them with few winning alternatives. The expansion of "choice," without changing the opportunity structures in which
choices are made, leaves people facing decisions in which most options are
problematic and provide less than a satisfying solution. Working fifty to
sixty hours a week and rarely seeing your family or having time for other
pursuits is an attractive option to few, but many positions require it. The
alternative of a less desirable job or profession, with lower pay, fewer benefits, and limited movement over time, is a heavy price to pay for creating

the time to care for others. A policy model stressing choice alone thus penalizes parents who choose to be involved with their children and undermines the prospects for gender equity at a time when women (and their families) need economic justice.

In principle, "individual choice" approaches assume that taking advantage of family-friendly options is cost free. Certainly, a main objective of greater workplace flexibility is to reduce the penalties attached to choosing "nonstandard" work arrangements. In practice, however, working time has become a proxy for work commitment. Unless strong protections are created, those seeking a more equitable balance between work and private life—even for a brief period of time—are likely to pay a price. Rather than posing a devil's dilemma, the structure of options needs to offer meaningful choices between attractive and feasible alternatives. Creating such options requires policy approaches that include not just more choices but fundamental structural reforms. In addition to expanding choice through work-facilitating and family-friendly measures, we need policies that provide equal opportunities, insure the rights of involved parents, protect workers, and regulate working time.

Regulating Working Time

Equal opportunity alone cannot resolve American workers' time dilemmas unless it is tied to basic changes in the structure and culture of the workplace. Social policy thus needs to address the organization of working time. The current structure induces some people to accept more hours than they would prefer or pay a substantial penalty in the long run. It encourages others to accept part-time jobs with fewer hours than they would prefer and less benefits, job security, and economic resources than they need. Public policy can address the large-scale mismatch between workers' needs and the structure of jobs. In doing so, it can level the playing field on which employers compete, remove the counterproductive incentives built into the current system, and make family-supportive and gender-equal opportunities the standard rather than the exception. Such efforts can do more than expand workers' choices; they can make choices more feasible and fair.

Without reforms that directly address the issue of working time, those who continuously and consistently put in long workweeks—despite their family needs—are likely to garner the lion's share of economic and social rewards, while those who work less than a full-time and even overtime schedule, even temporarily, will face dampened opportunities. The growing time divides can only be bridged by restructuring the organization of working time. We now turn our attention to this overlooked aspect of social policy and consider reforms that would rebalance the economic forces that skew jobs into too-long and too-short workweeks, reduce the time pressures on the overworked, increase the opportunities for the underemployed, and create a new, more gender-equal balance between paid and domestic work.

Working Time in Historical Perspective

The current framework for regulating working time in the United States was put in place in 1938, when the Fair Labor Standards Act (FLSA) established the forty-hour workweek as the standard for much, but not all, of the U.S. labor force and entitled those covered to time and a half overtime pay when they work more than forty hours in a week. This framework represented the culmination of decades of struggle and debate dating back to the late nineteenth century, when the issue of working time became one of the earliest and most visible demands of the labor movement. Workers in Great Britain, the United States, and other industrializing countries fought for a twelve-hour day, then a ten-hour day, and finally an eight-hour day. As late as 1929, over 80 percent of manufacturing workers in the United States were still scheduled to work at least forty-eight hours per week.[10]

Several arguments were put forth to support the demand for a shorter workweek. First, advocates maintained that a fixed amount of work could be more equitably distributed among workers—that is, it would be fairer to have everyone employed for six hours a day than to have two thirds employed at ten hours a day and the other third unemployed. A second theme argued that a shorter workweek would help stimulate demand for the purchase of more goods. If wages were maintained, the increase in employment would raise the purchasing power of workers overall and generate more demand for goods, which in turn would help solve the central economic challenge of the Depression. Some also suggested that a shorter workweek would increase efficiency on the job, which would in turn justify paying workers the same daily rate even though they were working fewer hours.

Over the six decades since the FLSA was adopted, basic changes have occurred in the American occupational structure that warrant rethinking how working time is governed. The increasing prevalence of dual-earner and single-parent families raises questions about the appropriateness of a forty-hour standard, which was adopted when most households did not depend on two earners or one parent. The growth of the professional and managerial workforce, moreover, has created a sizable group of workers not covered by protective legislation. And, finally, the cost of benefits—such as health insurance—as a fraction of total compensation costs has risen precipitously, making it attractive to split jobs into those that provide benefits but require very long workweeks and those that do not provide benefits because they fall below the forty-hour standard (Lettau and Buchmueller 1999).

Today's world provides a different context in which to consider the issue of working time. Beyond the traditional arguments (for example, that shorter workweeks will reduce unemployment and spread the wealth), the case for reforming the regulation of working time rests on new, more modern concerns.[11] Regulating work to create generally shorter workweeks and a more even distribution of working time across jobs provides an important way to reduce the stress on working families and promote gender equity at work and in the home.[12] It also speaks to the needs and preferences of American workers, whose aspirations for striking a balance between family and work are often thwarted by the job options they encounter. Furthermore, it holds the potential to reduce growing class inequalities between the highly paid but overworked and the poorly paid and underemployed.

We propose three policy reforms regarding working time that will promote more family-supportive, gender-equitable, and occupationally inclusive working policies. First, shifts in the occupational structure make it timely and appropriate to extend the Fair Labor Standards Act to professional, managerial, and other salaried workers. Second, it is time to consider mandatory benefits for all workers, accrued in proportion to the amount of time they work. Third, in a world where dual-earning and single-parent households are the clear majority, it is time to consider a thirty-five-hour standard for the workweek. While these proposals may seem out of reach and impractical to those who assume the past must dictate the future, a historical perspective suggests that what may seem impractical and impossible today may be seen as indispensable and inevitable tomorrow.

Expanding Work Protections and the FLSA

When the Fair Labor Standards Act was passed in 1938, about one in seven workers (14.8 percent) was classified as a professional or manager. By 1995, that proportion had doubled to nearly two in seven (28.3 percent).[13] As this segment of the labor force has grown, it has also become the one facing the strongest pressures to work very long weeks. Now that nearly three in ten workers occupy the ranks of professional and managerial employees, this group should be included among those entitled to extra pay for every additional hour worked. Expanding the FLSA to include overtime protection for salaried as well as hourly workers would reduce employers' incentives to push these workers to put in very long weeks and thus to divide workers into overworked and underworked groups.[14]

How can these protections be expanded without creating unappealing or excessive bureaucratic hassles? Certainly, professionals and other salaried workers do not wish to punch a time clock. There are less obtrusive ways to monitor working time, however, and many professionals—especially those who charge by the hour, such as lawyers or accountants—already carefully monitor their time. If personal time monitoring is not possible or acceptable, other methods could be devised, just as a multitude of procedures have developed to measure working time for wage workers.[15] Rather than extending the range of the Fair Labor Standards Act to include more workers, the Labor Department is in the process of promulgating new rules that would narrow FSLA coverage by including additional groups of workers under the rubric of "managers." Congressional efforts to block these changes remain unresolved (Hulse 2003). If, as we suggest, the FSLA were broadened to cover salaried workers, including professionals and managers, workers' protections could not be endangered by changes in how jobs are labeled.

Mandating Proportional Benefits

The "all or nothing" nature of most benefits packages is another problematic consequence of the forty-hour standard. Under our current system, full-time workers receive no increment in benefits if they work more than forty hours, and part-time workers consider themselves lucky to receive any benefits at all. Mandating proportional benefits to all workers would protect those who cannot or do not wish to work full-time and yet who still, after all, need health care and other supports, while providing a fair additional reward to those putting in very long weeks.

If a standard package based on a forty-hour workweek covered the basic benefits, such as health insurance, retirement funds, and disability, those employees who work more hours could receive additional flexible benefit dollars, which they could apportion to retirement contributions, life insurance, or even more income. Similarly, those who work slightly less than the standard workweek would no longer be denied all benefits but would receive a fraction of the standard benefits package proportional to the hours they work. Part-time employees could be provided with flexible benefits packages that can be used in the way most useful to them, including trading those benefits they choose not to use for others they need.

Extending coverage for life's contingencies to all workers would remove another incentive for employers to divide workers into the overworked and the underemployed. Work arrangements would then better reflect the underlying logic of the tasks at hand rather than the costs of employing workers in artificially partitioned ways. When a small number of employees is actually more efficient than a large number, employers could still choose to hire those willing to put in long workweeks. Although this reform would make part-time jobs more expensive and thus might reduce their number, it would also guarantee that part-time jobs would provide workers with basic needs and thus become a more genuinely attractive choice.

Proportional benefits would make long workweeks more costly as well. Additional benefits expenses, like paying more for overtime, would encourage employers to reduce both long and short workweeks and to offer such jobs only when they are the best way to generate a product or provide a service. Thus, having proportional benefits would remove another artificial reason for dividing the labor force.

Toward a Thirty-Five-Hour Workweek

Policies such as expanding the FLSA and providing proportional benefits alter the incentives faced by employers and employees, but they are not a direct or fundamental shift in policy toward working time *per se*. The time has arrived to reconsider our basic assumptions about the length of the workweek as well. The forty-hour workweek was created for the male-breadwinner family and based on the assumption that one income was sufficient for an entire household. This is clearly no longer the case. Since employers no longer routinely subsidize an unpaid (female) partner at home, it is time to reexamine a standard that emerged at a different time to fill different social and personal needs.

In a world where dual-earning families and single parents are the clear majority of workers, a thirty-five-hour workweek not only makes sense but takes on a new urgency. Even this slight reduction in the standard would ease the time crunch on working parents, provide more time for care-taking, create the possibility of more gender equity in parenting and paid work, and allow workers in all types of families to participate more fully in their communities. Just as the forty-hour workweek has never been mandatory for everyone, the thirty-five-hour workweek would not be required of all. It would, however, become an expected standard that would help articulate the ideals, values, and norms of our society.[16] It would set expectations for employers and employees alike, promote coordination and efficiency within and among firms, and foster greater cooperation among workplaces, families, and communities.

The thirty-five-hour workweek may appear to be a radical idea, but the forty-hour week seemed equally revolutionary before collective social action made it the standard. More important, the alternatives are less attractive. The most obvious alternative is to take no action and leave conditions as they are—that is, with the onus of responsibility on individual workers to cope as best they can. This scenario means leaving parents to face continuing and probably mounting pressure and allowing employers to presume fifty- to sixty-hour workweeks for many workers, until they either burn out, retire early, or simply relinquish the hope of having a life outside of work. The next alternative is to emphasize individual flexibility and choice, but to ignore the structure of work in which such choices are made. Such an approach may help some workers find a better balance, but only at the expense of equal opportunity and gender equity.

An approach that focuses on creating a new work standard more in line with the new realities of family life has several advantages for workers, employers, and communities. It creates a level playing field in which genuinely family-supportive employers are not penalized for their efforts. It helps all workers, regardless of gender or family circumstance, to better integrate home and work without sacrificing either financial security or children's well-being. And it reduces at least some of the forces that lead toward gender inequality in jobs and careers.

How can such a seemingly radical approach be achieved? As history has shown, strong collective support from citizens, workers, and the government can bring about fundamental change in how we organize and think about work. More specifically, tax incentives could be used to encourage firms to adopt a shortened workweek. Employers who offer thirty-five-hour schedules, for example, could be allowed to make reduced payments to social security, workers compensation, unemployment insurance rates, and other mandatory employer contribution systems. This would give employers an economic incentive to allow workers fewer hours while reducing their incentive to expect excessive hours and overtime. There are many ways to move toward a shorter standard workweek. The first step is to imagine that it can be done.

Limiting Mandatory Overtime

Mandatory overtime poses time squeezes for wage workers as surely as expectations of fifty- and sixty-hour workweeks put pressure on salaried workers. There are surely some instances in which it may not be possible or desirable to prohibit required overtime. Some employers, such as hospitals with nursing shortages, face labor shortages so severe that they have no alternative to requiring overtime in order to provide essential services or to meet mandated regulations.

Yet mandatory overtime can easily be misused by employers who seek to avoid hiring more workers. In these cases, overtime keeps some workers overworked and others out of jobs. Some face a difficult choice between losing their jobs and having little time for years on end, while others cannot find work. In these cases, it would surely be better to shift from mandatory overtime for some workers to more jobs with reasonable time demands. At the least, we can place sensible limits on the length of mandatory overtime, so that it does not go on for months and even years at a time.

A Shorter Workweek and Economic Productivity

Is it possible to sustain our standard of living with a shorter workweek, or would reducing the workweek diminish economic health and lower the

American standard of living? A comparative perspective provides strong grounds for concluding that the economic costs of shorter weeks are likely to be modest and that, in the final analysis, the social benefits will outweigh them. European countries, for example, routinely offer workers significantly longer vacations and also have relatively few people working more than fifty hours per week. Countries with notably shorter average workweeks, such as the Netherlands, have nevertheless been able to sustain a high standard of living.

In considering the economic consequences of a shortened workweek, it is important to distinguish between total output and efficiency per hour. Would the total supply of labor decline? While the average workweek would be shorter, some women might work more because their husbands would be more available at home. Reduced hours might also stem the decline in older men's labor force participation, which has been dropping steadily since the 1960s.[17] The total decline in working time for the labor force might thus be significantly less than the decline in working time for individuals.

Because American workers take shorter vacations, the total time worked in the United States would continue to rival Europe's even after moving to a thirty-five-hour workweek. And since women's labor force participation is higher in the United States and U.S. working women put in more hours than do their European counterparts, the United States would still lead Europe in working time per capita. The percentage of the American population in the paid labor force has risen gradually since the end of World War II and is currently at an unprecedented high. Over two thirds (67.1 percent) of those age fourteen and older were in the labor force in 1997, up from 59.2 percent in 1950. Reducing the length of the standard workweek is likely to encourage even more citizens to join the workforce.

Would working fewer hours per week undermine efficiency per hour worked? Being available at all times might be efficient when coordination is needed between a client or coworker, but reducing working time for those putting in forty hours or more would probably have few consequences for coordination—certainly no more than instituting a policy regime that emphasizes individual flexibility. And though some may argue that a shorter workweek might increase inefficiency because it takes longer to get back into the flow of work after being away from the job, fewer hours also enable workers to come back to work refreshed and ready to move full steam ahead. Surely, many who work extremely long days reach a point of diminishing effectiveness, and studies of job performance have shown that excessive hours on the job tend to produce fatigue, reduced performance, and more accidents (Rosa 1995; Harrington 1999; Insurance Institute for Highway Safety 2002; International Council of Nurses 2002). A shorter standard workweek thus offers the potential for greater productivity in a more limited time span.

Reducing the workweek might make labor more scarce and consequently more expensive. However, if a scarcity occurred, it would encourage employers to use workers more efficiently, an incentive that hardly exists if workers are poorly paid or putting in many additional hours at no extra cost. If workers' time is at a premium, labor-saving measures that improve efficiency and improve work conditions become more attractive.

How has the thirty-five-hour workweek influenced the French economy? It has remained controversial to both labor and business—to labor because the reduction in hours was accompanied by relaxation of many protective work rules; for business because employers were required to pay the same wages for thirty-five hours as they did for thirty-nine. And it remains to be seen if the French government will continue to implement "le trente-cinq" fully for small employers.

Nonetheless, the initial economic impact looks favorable in a number of important respects. French GDP growth averaged 3 percent per year from 1998 (when the legislation was implemented) through 2001, exceeding the average for Europe. And productivity has increased as well. Unemployment declined, but progress has been stalled by the recent recession. Productivity has risen more than employment. In many cases, employers have been able to improve productivity rather than add new workers, thus verifying Chris Nyland's (1989) view that the real benefit of reduced hours is not more jobs but higher productivity. Despite the speedup at work, the thirty-five-hours policy is apparently viewed favorably by the majority of the French public (Manpower Global 2000; Economist 2002).

Of course, there are many differences between the French and the U.S. situations that would prevent the United States from simply copying this model. For example, the United States would not be able to go directly to thirty-five hours, since this would require a drastic cut in the work times of many workers, especially professionals and managers. The first step would have to be moving these groups toward a forty-hour workweek, which would be a noteworthy accomplishment. But the French experience bears watching. Although they adopted the thirty-five-hour workweek standard

principally to reduce unemployment, the French experiment holds promise for simultaneously advancing family-friendly and gender-equity goals
as well.

On balance, a shorter workweek might reduce overall economic output,
but only to a modest degree. In terms of lifetime working hours, the effect
is likely to be even smaller, as workers find it easier to maintain a steady
commitment to work as their responsibilities elsewhere ebb and flow with
the changing currents of different life stages. Mothers of young children
and older (especially male) workers, for example, would find it easier and
more attractive to remain in the labor force. And since the costs of coordination would likely be counterbalanced by the benefits of having a more
refreshed, alert, attentive, and satisfied workforce and by the eventual addition of technology to enhance productivity, any decline in efficiency per
hour worked would likely be minor as well.[18]

Most important, any loss of economic productivity would be more than
offset by the benefits to families, communities, and even workplace morale.
In the final analysis, economic productivity needs to be weighed against
other social goals. It would be possible, for example, to increase economic
output by increasing the standard workweek from forty to fifty hours, but
the social costs of such a policy would be considered far too high. Any society must ultimately decide the proper balance between those pursuits that
are counted as economically productive and those activities that may not
involve monetary transactions but are equally productive and indeed essential to the health and well-being of its citizens.[19] A shorter workweek
would provide more time for the essential activities—such as spending
time with children, participating in public life, and creating community
bonds—that form the larger fabric of every worker's life. In the long run,
the benefits to the public good, and even to the work organizations that resist such changes, would be incalculable. Employers, who will eventually
depend on the current generation of children as they become the future
generation of workers, have a stake in creating a society in which work and
family life are not at odds.

Of course, regulating working time is just one part of a package of reforms that should be considered. Concerted effort and creative thinking
are required on a variety of fronts to bridge time divides that can no longer
be ignored. If these goals seem utopian, it is important to remember that
most social goals seem out of reach until they are accomplished. The
nineteenth- and twentieth-century struggles for a forty-hour workweek,
safe working conditions, a minimum wage, anti-discrimination legislation,

protection for the unemployed, and even Social Security should serve as reminders of what can be accomplished. The existence of shorter work-weeks and other family-friendly policies in many European countries (as we discussed in Chapter 6) serves as evidence that these policies are realistic options.

Evening, Night, and Weekend Work

As the notion of a nonstop economy that provides goods and (especially) services "24–7" becomes more accepted, the number of jobs scheduled for evening, night, and weekend hours can be expected to expand (Presser 2003). While it would be neither desirable nor possible to try to eliminate such jobs, it is important to recognize the social risks of such work, especially in terms of family disruptions and the personal toll of working for extended periods, particularly at night. The economic rewards of such jobs should be raised to match the social costs. Higher wages for night-shift workers would better compensate those doing such work and potentially reduce their number. For example, supermarkets and other retail outlets are testing self-serve checkout lanes. People may soon be scanning their own soup cans and weighing their own produce. If cashiers' salaries on the graveyard shift were increased, such technologies might become more attractive, especially for the low-volume night shift.

Just as we now provide a 50 percent overtime premium for working more than forty hours per week (at least for workers who are covered by the Fair Labor Standards Act), we could adopt a set of graduated bonuses for working nights and weekends. For example, legislation could specify that workers would be paid an additional 25 percent for working in the evening or on weekends and up to 50 percent extra for working after midnight. At present, relatively few workers receive extra pay for working non-standard shifts (Kostiuk 1990; Schumacher and Hirsch 1997).

Harriet Presser has noted that there is a very high incidence of evening and night shifts among parents of young children. This creates "tag-team" parenting, with one partner watching the children during the day and the other in the evening, to avoid high-cost or low-quality day care. But in doing so, couples may pay a price, including an increased risk of divorce. More, better, and less expensive child care would reduce this pull into night shifts for parents and help families generally.

Finally, parents who work nights and weekends need child care, especially in the context of welfare reform requiring recipients to take paid jobs. Initiatives to require forty hours per week of work from welfare recipients could make this need even more acute.

The Politics of Work and Family Policies

A social policy agenda for gender equity and work-family balance has generated—and will no doubt continue to generate—considerable political opposition. Social changes of this magnitude are bound to create ambivalence and backlash, not only from political conservatives but also from those who feel left behind or otherwise disconcerted as deep-seated social and economic changes take root. In this case, three general, intertwined concerns are apt to fuel resistance. First, economic conservatives draw on the traditional American reluctance to intervene in the "free market," to use government to regulate the private sphere, or to provide public funds for "private" needs. Added to this, cultural conservatives resist the transformation of women's place and related changes in family structure, framing women's move into the workplace as well as the rise of dual-earning and single parent homes as "family decline."[20] As Rebecca Klatch (1987) has pointed out, concerns over free-market intrusion versus concerns over the decline of "family values" distinguish economic and social conservatives. While social conservatives are more likely to oppose women's employment, nonmaternal child rearing, gender equality, and new family forms, economic conservatives are more concerned with limiting government's reach.[21] Starting from these different perspectives, however, both groups are likely to oppose and resist collective efforts to enact work and family policies that support new family forms.

A third, less vocal but growing, group argues that family, and especially parental, support policies are inherently unfair. Though less well known and less organized, these advocates for the childless express concerns that echo the themes of free-market individualism and ambivalence about family change, albeit in a new way that articulates the concerns of many who do not consider themselves conservative, at least in any traditional sense. Each of these sources of resistance raises concerns about work and family policies that are likely to persist. Each deserves a response.

The Free-Market Critique

Political conservatives who espouse free-market principles oppose government solutions to economic and social problems, especially those that place limits on private enterprise, involve taxation, or require substantial government spending. These concerns are not new to the American context. Indeed, the paucity of government-sponsored programs in the United States, especially compared to Europe, is a testament to the continuing political power of this conservative economic philosophy.

Our analysis should make it clear, however, that government regulations and programs do not cripple advanced industrial economies or business enterprises. To the contrary, our European counterparts have built thriving economies using a mix of the same kinds of approaches we propose. We also need to remember that the policy choices we face are not between regulation and the free market; employers currently face many regulations. The challenge is to adapt and develop regulations and programs in a sensible manner that reflects and speaks to the fundamental and enduring changes in American society.

Concerns over government spending are entirely legitimate. High-quality child care, after-school programs, and government-subsidized family and medical leaves depend on funding. Yet surely this is one area in which government should spend generously. High-quality child care and other services for children are as central as education to the current welfare and future prospects of our nation. It is difficult to imagine a more important use of our resources. The rise of high-quality, mass public education in the United States over the past century provides an example of what can be accomplished when government recognizes the importance of children and its responsibility to them. With the proper commitment, we can muster similar broad-based political interest in building and sustaining support for the nation's children.

Opposition to Gender Equality and Family Change

Efforts to achieve gender equality, like policies that call for government regulation or spending, continue to evoke deep ambivalence and considerable opposition. Several decades ago, when women's movement into paid work began to elicit popular notice, criticism often focused on the costs women bore as they moved away from domestically centered lives. Some even argued, in Sylvia Ann Hewlett's words, that these changes meant a "lesser life" for women.[22] Several decades later, this argument appears far less tenable. As women have established themselves across an array of jobs and occupations, most have welcomed their increased economic and social autonomy. Women continue to face obstacles at work and in the home, but the solutions to these problems can be found in creating more equal opportunities, not in confining women to domesticity.

The more common focus of contemporary critiques of women's equality has moved from adults to children. According to this argument, women's workplace commitments may appeal to adults, but they pose dangers for the young. The concern over "neglected" or "latchkey" children has insidious overtones, implying maternal indifference and fueling a moral panic over the transformation in women's lives. While it is appropriate and important to focus on the ways our society is not meeting the needs of children, it is equally important to disentangle these concerns from parental, and especially maternal, blame. The dangers to children rest not with their mothers' work commitments, but rather with the paucity of supports—at the workplace and in our communities—for employed parents and their children.

Rather than causing harm, the paid employment of mothers tends to enhance children's well-being in a number of ways. Most obviously, women's employment provides economic resources to their families; whether they live in a two-income or a single-parent home, children depend on their mothers' earnings. Equal economic opportunity for women thus protects children from poverty and improves their life chances.

Children tend to recognize the benefits of having an employed mother, as well as the challenges posed by long hours and inflexible work settings. Most children support their working parents and believe employed mothers are making crucial contributions to their welfare (Galinsky 1999; Gerson 2001). They report emotional and social benefits as well. Both daughters and sons tend to see employed mothers as uplifting models for women and dual-income partnerships as attractive models for marriage (Barnett and Rivers 1996; Gerson 2002). And when the focus is on direct, "quality" time devoted to children, employed mothers appear to spend almost as much time with their children as do nonemployed mothers (Bianchi 2000).

While children appreciate the resources their parents' jobs provide, they also recognize the toll that long days and unsatisfying work can take on mothers and fathers alike. What children need, then, are flexible, family-friendly workplaces for their parents as well as family-supportive communities for children and adolescents (Glass 2000). Rather than focusing on maternal employment as a social problem, we need to attend to the ways that workplaces and communities can better accommodate this fundamental transformation in family life.

Concerns over replacing full-time maternal care with other forms of child rearing are also based on the dubious, but persisting, belief that biological mothers are uniformly and universally superior to all other caretakers. It is hard to imagine any other form of work for which such a claim could be made or taken seriously. Mothers are an enormously large and varied group, with differing interests, desires, and talents. It makes little sense to assume that they are all equally and uniquely prepared to be their child's only or best caretaker. Instead, children benefit from having a range of committed, concerned caretakers—including fathers, other relatives, and paid professionals. They also benefit from having parents who are satisfied with their choices, whether that means working or staying home.[23]

The expansion of opportunities for professional women in the United States and other countries has fueled a demand for paid caretakers, especially in the absence of widely available, high-quality, publicly sponsored child care. Conservatives, uneasy with women's march into the workplace, have consistently raised concerns about the propriety of relying on paid caretakers to help rear children. Recently, however, some feminists have joined the chorus of critics who worry about this strategy, especially when these caretakers are drawn from the ranks of immigrants from poorer countries. Some worry that the expanded market for paid caretaking encourages working parents—especially full-time employed mothers—to participate in a new form of international colonialism. From this perspective, affluent families in rich countries are extracting caregiving and even love from poorer immigrants, who may leave their own children behind (Ehrenreich and Hochschild 2002).

In a society that fails to accord appropriate social or economic value to the care of children, all child-care workers (like all involved parents) face disadvantage and discrimination. Immigrants and other women who work as caretakers in private households may, indeed, be even more vulnerable than others who care for children in public settings, especially if they do not speak English and can count on few friends or relatives for support. Like their American-born counterparts, immigrant domestic workers may not be paid fairly or regularly and may be physically or emotionally abused; unlike their American peers, they may be threatened with deportation if they complain. And the problems facing private domestic workers, whether or not they are immigrants, are especially prone to invisibility because the isolation of these workers limits their options for organizing as a group or informing others of their plight.

The deficiencies and dangers of an inadequate child-care system should not, however, be laid at the feet of employed mothers, who confront equally perplexing obstacles. Such an approach pits women against each other, making it seem that the economic independence of middle-class women comes at the expense of poor, immigrant women and their children. By framing paid caretaking as the "commodification" of care, this perspective adds to the critique facing all women who hold paid jobs, whether in public workplaces or private homes. As important, the focus on private child care obscures the more widespread trend toward greater reliance on child-care centers, where the conditions of work and the rights of workers are more visible.

The rise of employment among middle-class women does not inevitably create a major infusion of foreign caretakers. Indeed, published statistics on the U.S. labor force suggest that the largest increase in child-care employment has occurred among workers in child-care centers, not among domestic workers in private households. (Since an unknown portion of domestic workers are undocumented, it is difficult to calculate these comparisons precisely.) Most child-care workers are also born in the United States, with immigrants claiming a substantial, yet minority, proportion only among domestic workers in private households.

The number of private household workers is, moreover, a small and declining segment of the U.S. labor force. The number of domestic workers peaked in 1940 at 2.4 million (which represented 4.6 percent of the labor force) and declined sharply during the 1960s. It fell below one million for the first time in 2000 and now represents less than one percent (0.66 percent) of the labor force. Every decade since 1960 has seen steady declines in the number of private household workers.[24]

It appears, then, that the prevalence of private caretakers, or "nannies," declined just as married women entered the labor force in ever-growing numbers. Of those who work in private households, many are not providing child care. In 2000, roughly 275,000 were doing child care in private household settings, while the rest were cooking, cleaning, and doing other domestic service work. All of these workers deserve good pay and working conditions, but they are not all caring for children.

These recent labor-force statistics probably miss some immigrants, but they are also more complete than those of earlier censuses. The level of underreporting would have had to grow at a remarkable rate to offset the marked declines they show. These declines can also be found in other studies. Surveys that examine who is taking care of children reinforce the view that nannies represent a small slice of the child-care pie. According to U.S. Census information, 4.8 percent of preschool children in 1991 were cared for in the child's home by a nonfamily member. The Census Bureau's 1998 statistics show a downward trend over time in this arrangement, from 7.0 percent in 1977 to 5.1 percent in 1994. Hofferth and Phillips (1987) also report a decline in nanny care between 1965 and 1982. Clearly, the growth of mothers' labor-force participation has not depended on a growing pool of nannies, whether they are from the United States or from poorer countries. Child-care centers have absorbed much of the growing demand for child-care services, and these centers principally employ U.S.-born women workers. Our preliminary estimates from the 2000 Census suggest that nearly 90 percent of employees in child-care centers are U.S. born, while about 30 percent of nannies are foreign born.

There are surely heart-wrenching cases of immigrant women leaving their own families to care for other people's children, but these cases are not the norm and do not tell the complete, more complex story of child care. Most child-care workers are not immigrants, and most immigrants come to the United States seeking opportunities they could not find in their native land. They also are likely to be embedded in a process of chain migration, in which they join a spouse or family member who has already established a base and then work to bring other family members to their newly chosen home. Indeed, many immigrant women are married either to an immigrant husband also residing in the United States or to a native-born American. Many either bring their children with them or send for their them once they feel settled and secure. The wages of domestic workers in the United States are certainly not high enough, but even these modest wages typically exceed what these immigrants could have expected to earn in their country of origin. For these reasons, the image of exploitation highlighted by scholars needs to be balanced by a story of opportunity as well.

Child-care workers should receive a living wage as well as fair and just working conditions, whether they are U.S. or foreign-born caregivers. Living wages for paid caretakers benefit children as well as workers. Such wages reduce turnover, create more satisfied employees, and promote durable relationships, which are key to high-quality care. In seeking these objectives, we join those scholars who critique the current child-care system. Yet we also find that the contours of the child-care puzzle are far broader and more complicated than what is captured by the image of exploited foreign workers.

Women in the United States are coping as best they can within the confines of a system that provides few supports for employed mothers, whether they work in an office, a child-care center, or a home. All child-care workers deserve high-quality working conditions and a reasonable level of compensation, but American society, much more than other employed mothers, is responsible for the failure to make that happen on a wide scale. Certainly, all carework cannot and need not be done by employed parents, and there is nothing inherently wrong with hiring domestic help. If those workers are well paid and respected, they and their families can benefit from the job opportunities afforded by the rise of paid employment for all women.

However ambivalent or opposed some may be, the social and economic forces that have sent women into the workplace are both irreversible and, on balance, beneficial. If the purported dangers of women's employment are illusory, the dangers of turning a blind eye to the need they create for workplace flexibility, child-care support, and equal opportunity are real. Resistance to policies that recognize these new contingencies cannot prevent changes in gender arrangements, but they can make daily life in contemporary America more difficult for women and their families.

"Life-Choice" Interest Groups and Childless Adults

Opposition to family-friendly policies has emerged from another, less likely, source. Some childless (or "child free") adults argue that parents should not receive "special" benefits that are not available to those without children. In *The Baby Boon* (2000), for example, Elinor Burkett argues that parenthood is a personal choice and its consequences should be borne only by those who choose it. High-income parents, in particular, should not expect others to absorb the costs of their lifestyle.[25]

At the workplace, Burkett argues that work is shifted from parents to non-parents on a daily basis, with mothers leaving work early to attend their children's soccer games or insisting on the most convenient assignments and schedules. Worse, she claims, is maternity leave, where the work of the expectant mother is heaped upon coworkers, who are unlikely to receive reciprocal or offsetting benefits. In addition, companies are encouraged to spend substantial funds for targeted benefits, such as on-site daycare centers, without investing in comparable supports for childless workers.

Despite these complaints, it appears that family-friendly policies have actually generated very little backlash. To the contrary, according to Jody Heymann, national surveys show that large majorities, including childless workers as well as parents, support policies that offer workers time off to meet a variety of family needs, such as responding to a family illness, attending routine doctors appointments, or meeting with children's teachers (Heyman 2000, p. 164). Once we recognize that most of us, including the currently and even permanently childless, are members of families, with brothers and sisters, nieces and nephews, fathers and mothers, the widespread support for family-support policies seems less surprising. Most Americans, whether or not they are parents, acknowledge a national interest in supporting children, whether in traditional forms, such as the public provision of elementary and secondary schooling, or in the newer forms provided by work-family support policies.

As important, the policy approaches we have suggested recognize diversity among workers and unpredictable changes in the lives of individuals. The childless deserve support as well, but their interests need not be opposed to those of other groups. Indeed, many of the currently childless may become the parents of tomorrow, especially with rise of delayed childbearing and step-parenthood.

Our approach stresses providing a variety of supports for the differing needs of different social groups. Medical and family leave benefits, for example, can be made available not just to parents but to anyone with caretaking responsibilities, whether they be for elderly parents, friends in need, or other relatives. Leave options could even be expanded to include community service for those with few family obligations.

In a similar way, employers could avoid shifting work from parents to non-parents when an employee takes a family leave by hiring a temporary replacement. This strategy might add some costs, but it would reduce resentment and enhance goodwill.[26] To the extent that coworkers are asked to absorb the work of those on leave, the ensuing resentment is created not by the existence of family-friendly policies, but by how employers choose to implement them. Of course, regulating staffing levels may be beyond the scope of national policy, but an incentive system could discourage employers from refusing to make arrangements to cover for a worker on temporary leave. The government could subsidize family and medical leaves to individuals, for example, on the condition that employers responded in kind by hiring temporary replacements.

The ostensible problem of providing special benefits to parents can also be easily addressed. Many companies already offer a menu of benefits, in which employees allocate "flexdollars" as they choose. Those with spouses and children can purchase more expensive family medical coverage, for example, while single, childless workers can select individual coverage, making it possible for the latter group to choose additional benefits. Some organizations offer benefits that target some groups more than others and are not part of a flexible-benefit menu, but they could include such items in the menu of flexible benefits and expand it to include options more attractive to those without children.[27] In principle, then, employee benefit plans need not pose a fundamental divide between parents and non-parents, and flexible programs can reduce, if not eliminate, inequities between employees with and without children.

Responding to the Critiques

The ongoing critique of family-friendly policies—whether from politically organized groups or from ordinary Americans perplexed about social change—should remind us that these policies need to be designed as flexibly and fairly as possible, not only to limit interference with private-market prerogatives but also to lessen potential cleavage and create political support among women and men, professionals and wage earners, parents and other workers. Work and family policies can and should be designed to speak to the needs of people at diverse life stages who have made various life choices.

Taken as a whole, our proposals have the potential to help all workers. A shorter workweek, for example, would benefit women and men, rich and poor, those with and without children. Changes to help parents who wish to put in long workweeks, such as a longer school year, would help to reduce absenteeism and any spillover to other workers that this might produce.

Policies that can command broad and enduring support need to recognize the diversity of life stages and life choices. Yet, in the end, children are a collective resource, and their needs should take precedence in our national agenda. Not all workers have children, but nearly all children have working parents. Parenting is a time-intensive job that is difficult to reconcile with long days at the workplace, no matter how satisfying and well-rewarded the job may be. Women, moreover, bear most of the costs of parenting and caregiving in the form of forgone work and career opportunities. To assert that such costs are "a (woman's) choice" is to ignore the social arrangements that create this dilemma, to accept the myriad costs of gender inequality, and to fail to provide for children, who are our collective future.

Integrating Family and Work in the Twenty-First Century

Amid the voices of opposition, strong social and political forces support—indeed, require—change. The underlying demographic shifts that have created our time squeezes have left few Americans untouched. As these demographic changes continue to make work and family issues more pressing, they are bound to gain political momentum. Some political observers, including Theda Skocpol, Stanley Greenberg, and Mona Harrington, have thus proposed to make support for "working families" the compelling rubric for advancing a progressive political agenda. Not simply a disparate collection of fanciful ideas, family-supportive policies are becoming increasingly central to the needs of families and to the nation's political agenda. What ordinary Americans need and increasingly want is not utopia, but rather a reasonable set of supports and options for managing work and family conflicts.

The policies we suggest represent only a few of the myriad of possible approaches to address the dilemmas created by work and family change. Effective policies, whatever their form, can only emerge from a national debate that extends beyond cultural critiques and a framework of parental blame to reconsider workplace organization, community support, and the structure of opportunities confronting workers and their families.

The time balance people are able to strike in their lives matters, but the picture is not a simple one of overwork. For the "overworked Americans," job flexibility and genuine formal and informal support for family life matter as much as, and possibly more than, actual hours. For the underworked, who are concentrated in the less rewarded jobs, security and opportunity are paramount for their own welfare and that of their children.

One facet of change, however, spans occupation and class: the emergence of women as a large and committed group of workers. They need and have a right to expect the same opportunities afforded men, and their families depend on their ability to gain these opportunities. There are significant points of convergence between women and men in their commitment to work and their desire for family supports. However, women workers, especially those putting in long days at the workplace, do not enjoy the same level of support as do their male counterparts. Principles of justice as well as the new realities of families suggest that gender equity needs to be integral to any policy initiatives aimed at easing the conflicts between family and work.

At the broadest level, our discovery of multiple and intertwined time divides suggests that reform efforts should uphold two important principles: equality of opportunity for women and men, and generous support for all involved parents regardless of gender or class position. We cannot afford to build work-family policies on old, outdated stereotypes, in which women are seen as less committed to work than men. Yet we can also not afford to build our policies on new stereotypes, in which working mothers and, to a lesser extent, fathers are depicted as avoiding their families and neglecting their children.

These images place all too many workers in a difficult bind, in which work commitment is defined as family neglect and family involvement is defined as a lack of work commitment. These are inaccurate images that result in untenable choices. If our findings are a guide, what workers need most is flexible, satisfying, and economically rewarding work in a supportive setting that offers them a way to integrate work and family life. With these supports, contemporary workers and the generations to follow will be able to bridge the time divides they face.

APPENDIX
NOTES
REFERENCES
INDEX

Appendix: Supplementary Tables

Table A.1 Pooled regression analysis of joint paid working time of couples, 1970 and 2000

	Model 1		Model 2	
Variable	Parameter estimate	Standard error	Parameter estimate	Standard error
Intercept	78.30***	0.19	63.23***	1.84
Year (2000)	2.97***	0.25	1.20***	0.28
No. of children under 18			−1.28***	0.11
Husband				
Age			0.55***	0.15
Age squared*10			−0.06***	0.02
Education:				
College graduate			−1.93***	0.51
Some college			−1.55***	0.45
H.S. grad.			−0.34	0.38
< H.S. grad.			—	—
Occupation:				
Managerial			4.73***	0.35
Professional			0.29	0.40
Sales			3.80***	0.44
All others			—	—
Wife				
Age			0.29	0.15
Age squared*10			−0.04*	0.02
Education:				
College graduate			2.43***	0.56
Some college			−0.34	0.48
H.S. grad.			−0.27	0.40
< H.S. grad.			—	—
Occupation:				
Managerial			6.36***	0.42
Professional			1.17***	0.37
Sales			0.30	0.43
All others			—	—
R^2			0.01	0.05

* $p < .05$; *** $p < .001$.

Table A.2 Work-family stress measures, by gender and parental status

Stress measure	Total, both sexes	Men			Women		
		Total	W/children < 18	W/out children < 18	Total	W/children < 18	W/out children < 18
Interference between job and family (% "a lot" or "some")	44.6	47.1*	55.6**	37.1	42.0	49.4**	33.4
Interference between job and free time (% "a lot" or "some")	45.6	47.2	52.4**	42.8	44.1	47.8**	40.8
Conflict in balancing work, personal life, and family life (% "quite a lot," "a lot," or "some")	57.6	59.8	70.3**	50.6	55.5	66.9**	46.3
Not enough time for self because of job (% "very often" or "often")	31.6	31.5	37.9**	26.1	31.7	40.2**	24.5
Not enough time for family or important people because of job (% "very often" or "often")	27.4	28.7	33.9**	24.4	26.0	31.7**	21.1
Not enough energy for family or important people because of job (% "very often" or "often")	28.8	27.2*	30.7**	24.3	30.4	33.3**	27.9
Not able to get everything done at home because of job (% "very often" or "often")	35.8	33.5**	39.3**	28.8	38.2	42.7**	34.4
Not in good mood at home because of job (% "very often" or "often")	25.3	24.2	25.9*	22.8	26.5	30.4**	23.1
Family or personal life prevented concentration on job (% "very often" or "often")	6.2	6.4	6.1	6.5	5.9	7.3**	4.7

% missing days in the past three months to care for sick child	9.4	6.1**	13.4**	0.0	13.0	28.4**	0.0
% missing days in the past three months due to child-care breakdown	2.0	1.4**	3.3**	0.0	2.7	6.4**	0.0
% missing days in the past three months for other family reasons	12.0	10.8	17.1**	5.6	13.3	15.5**	11.4
% missing partial days in the past three months due to family responsibilities	18.3	16.1**	24.4**	9.1	20.7	34.0**	9.6
Emotionally drained from work (% "very often" or "often")	26.0	23.0**	25.1*	21.2	29.2	29.4	29.1
Feel used up at end of workday (% "very often" or "often")	36.2	34.7**	36.4	33.4	37.9	38.0	37.8
Feel tired when waking and having to face another day on the job (% "very often" or "often")	36.0	36.5	37.6	35.7	35.3	38.2**	32.8
Feel burned out or stressed by work (% "very often" or "often")	26.3	23.7**	24.5	23.2	28.9	28.4	29.2
Feel nervous and stressed (% "very often" or "often")	22.8	17.0**	15.3	18.4	29.0	30.0*	28.2
Cannot cope with responsibilities (% "very often" or "often")	13.4	11.1**	10.3	11.8	15.9	18.7**	13.6

Source: National Study of the Changing Workforce, 1997.

* $p < .05$; ** $p < .01$.

Table A.3 Regression analysis of negative spillover from job to home

	Women (n = 1,258) b (Std. error)	Men (n = 1,122) b (Std. error)
Demographics		
Married	0.111	0.079
	(0.226)	(0.300)
Working spouse	0.041	−0.084
	(0.654)	(0.181)
Children < 18	0.295***	0.218***
	(0.000)	(0.000)
Age	−0.003	−0.003
	(0.150)	(0.200)
Education	0.005	0.021
	(0.700)	(0.084)
Work time and intensity[a]		
Weekly hours	0.014***	0.012***
	(0.000)	(0.000)
Nonstandard shift	0.160***	0.194***
	(0.004)	(0.000)
Pressure on job	0.346***	0.290***
	(0.000)	(0.000)
Bring work home	0.075***	0.076***
	(0.000)	(0.000)
Flexibility[b]		
Schedule control	−0.023	−0.067**
	(0.229)	(0.022)
Autonomy	−0.106***	−0.071
	(0.003)	(0.095)
Family-friendly supervisor[c]	−0.129***	−0.175***
	(0.001)	(0.000)
Family-friendly workplace	−0.054***	−0.046***
	(0.000)	(0.004)
Job satisfaction	−0.175***	−0.214***
	(0.000)	(0.000)
R^2	0.300	0.282

Source: National Study of the Changing Workforce, 1992.
** $p < .01$; *** $p < .001$.

Table A.3 *(continued)*

Note: Negative spillover (from job to home) is a composite measure constructed from five items (reversed): (1) In the past three months, how often have you not had enough time for yourself because of your job? Would you say very often, often, sometimes, rarely, or never? (2) In the past three months, how often have you not had enough time for your family or other important people in your life because of your job? Would you say very often, often, sometimes, rarely, or never? (3) In the past three months, how often have you not had the energy to do things with your family or other important people in your life because of your job? Would you say very often, often, sometimes, rarely, or never? (4) In the past three months, how often have you not been able to get everything done at home each day because of your job? Would you say very often, often, sometimes, rarely, or never? (5) In the past three months, how often have you not been in as good a mood as you would like to be at home because of your job? Would you say very often, often, sometimes, rarely, or never?

a. Includes hours worked per week, if the worker worked a nonstandard schedule, if he or she brings work home, and if he or she works under pressure.

b. Includes a composite measure of autonomy, the worker's sense of control over his or her schedule, whether he or she has a family-friendly supervisor, and whether the workplace culture is supportive of families.

c. Comprised of questions that ask about a supervisor's willingness to accommodate an employee's need to take care of personal/family issues, a supervisor's level of understanding when an employee talks about personal or family issues affecting his or her work, the respondent's level of comfort in bringing up personal or family issues with his or her supervisor, and the supervisor's degree of concern about the effects that work demands have on the respondent's personal/family life.

Table A.4 Determinants of workplace flexibility

	Men		Women	
	b	Std. err.	b	Std. err.
Intercept	0.585*	(.389)	0.482	(.356)
Demographic variables				
Age	−0.003	(.004)	−0.007+	(.004)
Education	0.075*	(.030)	−0.008	(.030)
Children under age 18	−0.191*	(.097)	−0.117	(.081)
Married	0.006	(.124)	0.126	(.146)
Spouse works	−0.188+	(.103)	−0.185	(.179)
Occupation				
Professional/technical worker	0.131	(.145)	0.382**	(.151)
Manager	0.141	(.124)	0.717**	(.179)
Clerical	0.377+	(.207)	0.582**	(.143)
Sales	0.272*	(.119)	0.590**	(.143)
Other	—	—	—	—
Workplace environment				
Autonomy	0.540**	(.070)	0.647**	(.064)
Workplace culture	0.126+	(.062)	0.173*	(.071)
Supervisor support	0.119	(.086)	0.066	(.074)
Job attributes				
Hours worked	0.001	(.004)	−0.013**	(.003)
Eligible for overtime	−0.203*	(.098)	0.159+	(.084)
Time spent commuting	−0.026*	(.012)	0.006	(.014)
Supervisor	0.042	(.095)	0.233**	(.089)
Union	−0.368**	(.108)	−0.475**	(.105)
Public sector	−0.298+	(.162)	−0.421*	(.191)
R^2	0.18		0.19	

Source: National Study of the Changing Workforce, 1992.

+ $p < .10$; * $p < .05$; ** $p < .01$.

Table A.5 Availability and use of flexible schedules (% saying yes)

Benefit	Total sample	All women	All men	Prof./tech. workers	Nonprof. workers	Prof. women	Prof. men	Prof. women w/chldn. under 6	Prof. men w/chldn. under 6
Availability of flexible schedules									
Set hours	29.4	28.3	30.5	36.2	24.5	32.1	40.1	25.9	39.6
Change hours daily	40.2	44.5	36.3	36.4	55.7	44.7	30.3	37.6	23.1
Change hours as needed	85.8	89.4	83.0	87.3	83.9	88.0	86.9	84.6	74.2
Extended lunch/break	46.9	43.8	50.0	54.5	41.2	54.1	62.6	56.9	62.4
Work more one day, less next	43.9	45.0	42.7	48.1	40.7	53.4	50.4	49.2	54.3
Work at home									
Allowed to regularly	23.6	23.1	24.1	38.5	12.7	38.1	38.9	35.5	33.5
Allowed to occasionally	12.5	12.1	13.0	21.4	7.9	17.9	24.7	16.9	23.2
Part time									
Allowed	45.4	52.8	38.2	45.8	45.1	53.8	38.3	59.0	45.3
Job sharing	1.2	1.4	1.0	0.9	1.5	1.5	0.3	0.7	0.0
Both	10.1	11.4	8.8	12.9	8.0	13.9	12.0	13.8	7.1
Utilization of flexible schedules, when available									
Extended lunch/break	69.2	69.3	69.1	73.3	65.1	73.1	73.5	69.2	63.9
Work more one day, less next	74.8	75.7	74.0	74.4	75.2	75.3	73.6	81.2	74.2
Work at home occasionally	78.9	80.6	77.5	82.4	74.1	86.6	79.5	88.0	83.5
Sample size	3,381	1,588	1,793	1,511	1,870	795	716	149	143

Source: National Study of the Changing Workforce, 1992.

Table A.6 Availability of, use of, and demand for family-supportive benefits (% saying yes)

Benefit	Total sample	All women	All men	Prof./ tech. workers	Nonprof. workers	Prof. women	Prof. men	Prof. women w/chldn. under 6	Prof. men w/chldn. under 6
Availability of benefit									
Child care/parental leave	88.4	92.6	84.4	92.2	85.6	94.6	90.0	95.5	89.6
Employee assistance plan (EAP)	54.8	50.1	59.2	63.6	48.2	57.0	69.7	62.8	69.1
Family sick leave	90.2	91.0	89.3	94.5	86.9	94.0	95.0	94.8	93.0
Child-care resource and referral	20.3	18.4	22.2	25.9	16.1	23.9	28.0	23.5	26.2
Employer-sponsored child care	10.4	10.9	9.8	15.0	6.9	15.6	14.5	18.7	13.7
Vouchers for child care	4.1	3.6	4.5	4.9	3.4	3.9	5.8	3.4	7.2
Elder-care resource and referral	10.7	10.6	10.8	14.5	7.9	13.9	15.0	8.5	9.6
Utilization of benefit, when available									
Child-care resource and referral	10.8	12.0	9.8	12.5	8.7	15.0	10.5	30.7	38.4
Employer-sponsored child care	11.7	12.1	11.3	12.7	10.1	11.9	13.6	42.4	46.8
Vouchers for child care	8.3	15.1	3.1	9.8	6.6	18.3	4.4	40.2	15.9
Elder-care resource and referral	6.4	9.8	3.1	6.6	6.1	10.2	3.3	0.0	22.1

Would trade other benefits to obtain (when not available)

Flexible schedule	27.8	31.2	24.1	28.4	27.4	30.8	25.5	48.8	11.9
Work at home	21.3	24.8	17.8	19.4	22.2	22.0	16.7	47.8	18.3
Part time	16.1	23.6	9.3	18.6	14.2	28.2	9.3	32.0	4.6
Child-care resource and referral	17.4	18.5	16.3	16.4	18.0	18.7	13.6	18.2	18.2
Employer-sponsored child care	23.5	26.6	20.5	22.5	24.1	25.3	19.2	49.4	30.7
Vouchers for child care	23.4	25.7	21.0	22.6	23.9	24.3	20.8	39.9	34.5
Elder-care resource and referral	14.6	15.7	13.4	13.9	15.0	16.2	11.3	17.2	7.9

Would change jobs to obtain benefit (when not available)

Flexible schedule	26.1	29.6	22.4	25.1	26.7	27.2	22.7	32.1	29.0
Work at home	22.4	24.2	20.7	19.9	23.7	19.5	20.3	31.5	23.5
Part time	11.3	15.6	7.3	11.7	10.9	15.3	8.3	14.6	4.6
Sample size	3,381	1,588	1,793	1,511	1,870	795	716	149	143

Source: National Study of the Changing Workforce, 1992.

Table A.7 Joint hours of paid work of married couples aged 25–59

Country	All couples, mean hours per week	% dual-earner	Dual-earner couples		
			Mean hours per week	% 80 + hours	% 100 + hours
United States	72.3	75.5	81.2	68.2	12.0
Finland	69.8	80.6	77.4	25.1	4.0
Canada	65.0	65.6	77.0	45.6	9.0
Sweden	64.0	85.1	69.3	6.6	0.7
Belgium	63.8	57.5	79.0	35.0	11.7
France	62.1	61.3	76.3	32.9	4.0
Germany	60.4	55.9	75.1	42.7	8.3
Italy	59.4	45.7	78.2	47.6	9.6
United Kingdom	57.4	54.6	74.3	34.4	5.8
Netherlands	51.9	52.3	64.0	15.8	2.7

Source: Authors' analysis of fourth-wave LIS data.

Note: Countries are listead in order of first-column figures.

Notes

Introduction

1. Although a multitude of family tasks and activities constitute genuine forms of "work," we generally use the term to refer to paid market work in order to distinguish it from the unpaid work that takes place in the domestic sphere.
2. A related theme in a number of recent articles and books is the issue of care and carework (Heymann 2000; Harrington 1999; Folbre 2001). These works highlight the gaps in the provision of care by families and by institutions and underscore the low pay and recognition given to carework. A focus on time is a necessary complement to the concern with the provision of care, since time spent working sets the boundaries on individuals' ability to care for their families and to participate in their communities.
3. In thinking about work and family connections, some scholars, such as Anita Garey (1999), argue that the term "balance" should be avoided in favor of other metaphors, such as "weaving." While we agree that other terms can also be useful and that no one word can capture the full range of ways that work and family interact, we use "balance" to point to the inescapable fact that time is a finite resource that must be divided among competing activities. Like acrobats who must find their balance as they move through changing positions or juggle many objects at once, ordinary Americans seek ways to strike a balance among the multiple and often competing demands on their time. Many seek to combine or integrate their disparate roles and time commitments, and we use these terms interchangeably. We thus join other scholars (e.g., Spain and Bianchi 1996) who rely on this metaphor to capture some of the complexity of modern lives.
4. Here we use the *National Study of the Changing Workforce* (Bond, Galinsky, and Swanberg 1998), which was conducted by the Families and Work Institute, and we also draw on supporting information from an earlier 1992 survey of the same name (Galinsky, Bond, and Friedman 1993).

5. The costs of choosing to work less than exceedingly long hours can be particularly acute for professional workers. For a further discussion of this issue, see Epstein et al. 1999, Drago and Colbeck 2003, and Chapters 4 and 5 below.

6. We use the term "career" or "work career" interchangeably to refer to a series of jobs held over the course of one's life. A work career, broadly conceived, includes both white-collar and blue-collar jobs and is not confined to the linear upward trajectory found in some professional contexts. As Phyllis Moen (2003) has shown, the sequence of jobs that many people, especially women, hold over time does not fit this narrower sense of the term "career." Moen also breaks new ground in studying the careers of couples rather than just individuals.

7. We use the terms "postindustrial," "advanced industrial," and "affluent" interchangeably to refer to societies with a large white-collar and service-oriented workforce and a high degree of technological development. For a classic discussion of the meaning and social implications of the rise of "postindustrial" societies, see Bell 1976.

1. Overworked Americans or the Growth of Leisure?

1. Also known as the "experience sampling method," or ESM, beeper studies were developed by psychologists interested in creating an "experience monitoring system" to track respondents' state of mind as well as their activities (Csikszentmihalyi 1991). A recent example of this approach can be found in Schneider and Waite (2003). For a discussion of different methods of measuring time use, see Juster and Stafford (1985).

2. When time diaries are administered over the phone, as was done during the 1990s (Robinson and Godbey 1999), the interviewer is able to encourage more detailed responses and to prompt for omitted events.

3. Schor obtained this figure from the March *Current Population Survey* by multiplying the usual number of weeks worked during the previous calendar year by the number of hours usually worked per week during that same period.

4. This analysis draws on data from the *Current Population Survey (CPS)*. A large and reliable data series, the *CPS* has been quite consistent in design and administration since the 1960s and thus is arguably the best source for examining historical trends in the length of the workweek. There were small changes in the wording of labor-force questions in 1993, but these had little effect on the issues explored here. Trends over the period 1970–1990 display much the same pattern as those documented between 1970 and 2000. We may therefore conclude that the wording of the questions had little effect. For further details about the *CPS*, see U.S. Bureau of Labor Statistics 2002a.

5. Annual hours are commonly employed in international comparisons, which are discussed in Chapter 6.

6. The National Study of the Changing Workforce (NSCW) was administered in 1992 and again in 1997 (Galinsky, Bond, and Friedman 1993; Bond, Galinsky, and Swanberg 1998). Both surveys are useful, although many questions were changed in the 1997 version. For example, the "vacation time used" question was not included in 1997. Although its goal is to be representative of the U.S. labor force, the NSCW overstates the average workweek by about five hours for both men and women compared with findings from the *CPS* for the same years. This is an unfortunate weakness for use in a study such as ours that focuses on the use of time. Nonetheless, we do make use of this survey with the caveat that the sample includes too many individuals with long workweeks and too few of those with short workweeks.

7. U.S. Bureau of the Census, *Statistical Abstract of the United States* (1998), Table 644.

8. Robinson and Godbey's second edition of *Time for Life* (1999) includes a chapter that updates trends through 1995. The 1995 findings are largely in line with those presented by Sayer (2001), who drew on 1998 data.

9. While some might scoff at the idea that shopping should count as work, Gershuny (2000) points out that shopping is a necessary unpaid complement to such paid jobs as retail sales. Moreover, he reports that grocery shopping and other routine purchases (which may feel more like a chore) comprise the great majority of shopping time in most countries.

10. In *Time for Life* (1999), Robinson and Godbey report findings on how people evaluate their activities. In general, recreational trips are ranked as pleasurable, while doing the laundry is ranked as unpleasurable. Yet these general rankings are not linked to the particulars of the time diary, so that we cannot know if a particular set of multitasked activities would be characterized as leisurely or rushed.

11. See Robinson and Godbey (1999, p. 104) for a brief mention of single mothers.

12. Gershuny (2000) mentions some exceptions for European countries. S. Jody Heymann (2000) reports results from a different type of weekly time diary, which asks about respondents' needs as well as how they spent their time.

13. The first U.S. time diaries to cover all the members of a family for an entire week are currently being collected. See Bianchi, Robinson, and Milkie (forthcoming).

14. Jerry A. Jacobs (1998) notes that there is less dispersion in an annual, compared to a weekly, measure of working time. Unfortunately, a measure of hours typically worked at the respondent's job in the previous year is not available in the 1970 *Current Population Survey*. We reestimated the results over the period 1976–1997 with information about the longest job held in the past year and obtained results similar to those reported here.

15. While Juliet Schor (1991) and Barry Bluestone and Stephen Rose (1997) have

pointed to a growing bifurcation in working time, they have focused on the average worker rather than those at each end of the distribution and on annual
hours rather than on the average workweek.

16. These statistics are based on the 1997 *Current Population Survey* and were generously provided by Harriet Presser.

17. In the early 1960s, concern that automation would cause widespread unemployment led some social analysts to contemplate how best to make life meaningful in a leisure society (see, for example, Faunce 1963). In a volume that
focused on the "problem" of the growth of leisure (Smigel 1963), Harold
Wilensky sounded a note of caution. Although he did not directly juxtapose
the busy elite of 1960 with Thorstein Veblen's leisure class of 1900 (Veblen
1994 [1899]), he pointed out that leisure was not growing among professionals
(Wilensky 1963).

18. Interesting and important differences by race, marital status, and other factors
are too numerous to discuss in detail. For example, the longer workweeks of
black women are not simply a matter of their lower marriage rate, since married black women work about three hours longer per week than do married
white women.

2. Working Time from the Perspective of Families

1. Phyllis Moen and her colleagues not only focus on couples but also explore the
way work and family issues unfold over the course of the careers of husbands
and wives. See Moen (2003), Clarkberg and Moen (2001), and Moen and
Sweet (2002).

2. Hariet Presser (2003, 1994) has examined the distribution of shift work among
dual-earner couples, but she does not focus on the length of the workweek *per
se*. Steven Nock and Paul William Kingston (1988) found that long workweeks
take away time that parents could otherwise spend with children, but they also
found that this primarily resulted in reducing activities in which children were
peripherally involved rather than activities in which children were the center
of attention. Moreover, Nock and Kingston did not explore historical trends in
the length of the workweek for employed spouses.

3. Comparing the March Annual Demographic Files, we created files organized
by household rather than by individual working time and sorted individuals
by household. We then sorted families within households. Finally, we matched
married individuals within families. In 99.5 percent of the households, there
were no more than two married individuals in the family—the householder
and the householder's spouse. In 0.5 percent of households, however, there were
two additional married individuals. In these cases, we sorted individuals by

family within the household and then matched husbands and wives within each.

4. This procedure produced a sample of 24,125 married couples in 2000 and 27,494 married couples in 1970. We weighted the data using the March supplement person-weight so that the weighted sample would reflect the characteristics of married couples in the United States at these two points in time.

5. The education measures for 1970 and 2000 are not strictly comparable. In 1970, the CPS solicited information on the number of years of schooling completed, but in 2000, respondents were asked to report the highest degree attained. To make these measures more comparable, we grouped the 1970 measure into four categories: (1) less than high school; (2) high school graduate (i.e., twelve years of schooling completed); (3) some college (thirteen to fifteen years of schooling completed); and (4) college graduate (sixteen or more years of schooling). To see how much difference resulted from the change in the educational measure, we replicated our analysis with data from the 1990 CPS, which coded education in the same manner as in 1970. This produced results entirely consistent with those reported in this chapter.

6. This finding is consistent with those of Mary Coleman and John Pencavel (1993a, 1993b) on educational differentials in working time.

7. When changes over time are displayed by husbands' education, the changes are similar.

8. Pooling data from 1970 and 2000, we sought to account for the three-hour increase that occurred during this period by estimating a series of regression equations predicting the total number of hours in paid employment of husbands and wives in dual-earner couples. To measure the influence of demographic changes, we included four individual measures for both husbands and wives. These include age, age squared, education (including three dummy measures of degree attainment, with college graduates serving as the reference group), occupation (again with three dummy measures—managerial, professional, and sales—all others as a reference group), and one family measure, the number of children under eighteen.

9. These results can be seen in Table A.1 by comparing Model 1, which documents the three-hour increase in working time between 1970 and 2000, with Model 2, where the trend coefficient shrinks from three hours to one hour after controls are included in the analysis.

10. Calculated from the March 2001 Current Population Survey.

11. Over the last twenty years, a range of studies have consistently demonstrated that a child's social or academic competence does not depend on whether a mother is employed (see, for example, Hoffman and Youngblade 1999; Galinsky 1999; and Parcel and Menaghan 1994). Suzanne Bianchi (2000) has

also found that mothers today spend as much, if not more, time with their children than they did in 1965, even though the percentage of mothers who work for pay rose from 35 percent to 71 percent. Employed mothers may be getting less sleep, but they are not shortchanging their children.

3. Do Americans Feel Overworked?

1. For earlier analyses (including our own) on the ways that the structure of work organizations shape workers' choices and perceptions, see Kanter (1977), Gerson (1985, 1993), and Jacobs (1989).
2. We rely on survey information collected in 1997 by the Families and Work Institute. Telephone interviews of 3,551 employed individuals aged eighteen years or older were conducted. For more details about the survey, see Bond, Galinsky, and Swanberg (1998).
3. Ann Swidler (2001, 1986) considers culture as a tool kit for action. Kathleen Gerson (2002) shows how new generations of women and men are responding to ambiguous and contradictory values that stress both achieving autonomy and caring for others.
4. Rosabeth Kanter's book *Men and Women of the Corporation* (1977; see also Cancian 1987) shows how the structure of work organizations actually shapes worker preferences in ways that remain hidden to the workers who develop them.
5. Cynthia Epstein and her colleagues (1999), among others, make it clear that work organizations create cultures that stigmatize and penalize those who choose to pull back from work even briefly or intermittently to attend to the needs of their families.
6. See John Robinson and Geoffrey Godbey (1999) for an exception, especially their discussion of "time deepening," a term they use to discuss a variety of related aspects of time pressures.
7. Here we are considering total hours worked on all jobs. In Jacobs and Gerson (1997), we compared dual job holders to the majority of workers, who hold only one job. Dual job holders are more likely to express a preference for fewer hours. Yet only 8 percent of the sample reported holding more than one job. Thus, most of the sense of being overworked cannot be attributed to the experiences of people who work at two jobs. In other words, the total sample of workers feels only a bit more overworked than do single job holders.
8. Juliet Schor (1991) anticipated this point when she noted that an increasing number of workers would like to work more than they actually do. Her main focus, however, is on the general increase in working hours rather than on the increasing bifurcation of the labor market.

9. The difference between single and married men in their ideal working hours is not statistically significant.

10. This 8.9 percent is slightly higher than the 7.5 percent who volunteered the same answer in a supplement to the *Current Population Survey* in 1985; see Shank (1986) for details. Shank reports that the desire to work less is concentrated among those with the longest workweeks and, conversely, that the desire to work more is concentrated among those with the shortest workweeks. The key question here is whether the group expressing interest in working less is a substantial minority of the labor force or a small minority.

11. Another item to note is that the "day's free time for a day's pay" question breaks down somewhat differently than does the "ideal time" question. Those working the most hours were more likely to want to trade pay for time than were those working forty-hour weeks. This was true for both men and women, and, along with the ideal-hours data, suggests that very long workweeks are not caused by a taste for unending work in the American labor force. However, there was also higher interest in this trade-off among those working the fewest hours, which differed from the pattern found in the "ideal hours" question.

12. The finding that Americans tend to share ideals has also been reported by researchers examining cultural trends in American society. See, for, example, DiMaggio, Evans, and Bryson (1996) and Wolfe (1998).

4. How Work Spills Over into Life

1. Jean Yeung (2001) reports, for example, that contemporary fathers put in more hours on all aspects of child care than did their counterparts a generation ago, even if they still lag behind contemporary mothers (see also Coltrane 1996; Furstenberg 1995; Gerson 1993).

2. This term, while perhaps not quite as well known as the "glass ceiling" or the "second shift," nonetheless nicely captures the experience of adults caught between the needs of their children and elderly parents (Miller 1981; Brody 1985; for imporant qualifications, see Soldo 1996). Many Web sites use this phrase, and a number of self-help books have employed it in their titles (*www.the sandwichgeneration.com*; Zal 2001).

3. The results are presented in more detail, along with tests of statistical significance, in Table A.2 in the Appendix. The NSCW surveys provide much more detail on the nature of jobs and the workplace experiences of employees than does the much larger *Current Population Survey*. The NSCW was designed to replicate many of the questions utilized in the 1977 Quality of Employment Survey. The NSCW surveys were also designed so that they could

be readministered on a regular basis and provide a comparable source of information about workplace practices and the experiences of American workers.

4. Sylvia Hewlett (2002) reports that a high percentage of professional women are remaining childless and concludes that occupationally successful women risk forgoing motherhood. In a critique of Hewlett's analysis, however, Garance Franke-Ruta (2002) shows that professional women are as likely to marry and to have children by age forty as women in other jobs. Franke-Ruta also points out that by postponing childbearing until they have established both a stable work life and a committed relationship, well-employed women are significantly better off than their poorer counterparts, who are more likely to bear children early and outside the context of a strong and enduring relationship. Professional women may still lack the opportunities available to professional men, but they nevertheless have more options than women who lack their economic resources.

5. The findings in this section are drawn from the 1992 Changing Workforce survey (Galinsky, Bond, and Friedman 1993), which unfortunately asked only a third of respondents about their ideal balance between family, self, and work or career. The percentages for actual and ideal time allocations are thus not strictly comparable. Since the smaller group is a random subset of the entire sample, however, there is good reason to have confidence in the comparisons.

6. While it is possible that those with family needs select more supportive work environments, our research, along with a number of other studies, suggests that those with the most need for flexibility are often unable to secure jobs that feature such flexibility (Heymann 2000).

5. The Structure and Culture of Work

1. The voluminous literature on comparisons between employed mothers and mothers who do not have a paid job has shown that working, by itself, has no effect on the well-being of children. What matters are the mother's level of satisfaction with her choices, the involvement of the father, and the quality and degree of satisfaction with child-care arrangements. See, for example, Hoffman et al. (1999); Nye and Hoffman (1963).

2. For men, the correlation between working hours at one's main job and control over scheduling is .05, and the correlation between total hours worked and control over one's schedule is .04. Neither correlation is significant. For women, the respective correlations are −.13 and −.10.

3. Although the Changing Workforce survey lacks specific information on men's

and women's structural positions at work, other studies make it clear that male managers and professionals are more likely than their female counterparts to occupy high-level positions in organizational and occupational hierarchies.

4. The correlation between flexibility and being married is $r = .00$ for women, $-.02$ for men; with having children under 6, $r = .02$ for women, $r = -.02$ for men; and with having children under 18, $r = -.04$ for men, $-.02$ for women. None of these relationships is statistically significant.

5. Having a supportive workplace culture increases the chances of having control over one's schedule for both men and women. The effect of having a supportive supervisor is not statistically significant in Table A.4 because this relationship is closely connected with having a supportive workplace culture. When these effects are examined individually, both are statistically significant.

6. Peter Meiksins and Peter Whalley (2002) examine the lives of engineers, computer professionals, and technical writers who choose to "put work in its place" by "customizing" or reducing their time on the job. Although they find many advantages to this arrangement, they also report that those who choose it must sacrifice career opportunities and upward mobility, especially in the form of management positions.

7. We base this figure on information from the 1997 National Study of the Changing Workplace.

8. For analyses of the ways in which gender can be considered an institution that structures options and life chances, see Lorber (1994), Jackson (1998), and Risman (1998).

6. American Workers in Cross-National Perspective

1. We focus here on the issue of working time. For more general discussions of European social policies, see Wilensky (2002) and Gornick and Meyers (2003).

2. In his book *Changing Times: Work and Leisure in Postindustrial Society* (2000), Gershuny presents findings from the Multinational Time Use Surveys (MTUS), a study of thirty-five time-diary micro-datasets covering twenty countries. For nine countries, information is available for at least two time periods.

3. Harold Wilensky (1963) reported that male professionals and managers put in more hours on the job than did their blue-collar counterparts. For Thorstein Veblen (1994 [1899]), leisure actually signified social status.

4. Combining the employed and nonemployed population in the same analysis introduces a substantial amount of variance, which can then be explained by employment status. Because Gershuny puts the contribution of other variables

in terms of the proportion of variance explained, having a great deal of variance that can be attributed to employment status (and secondarily to gender differences) makes all other effects seem tepid in comparison. It is partly a matter of perspective: Earth, viewed from Mars, appears to be round; but when it is viewed from the earth's surface, tall mountains and deep valleys cannot be ignored. Gershuny takes a more distant view and sees congruence among postindustrial societies; but when each country is viewed up close, the distinctiveness of each is unmistakable.

5. Gershuny's own evidence reveals a telling contradiction. His conclusion that there is a trend toward convergence in time use across countries is supported by the finding that the dummy variables by country explain little of the variation among individuals in time use (which, as we mentioned earlier, stems from lumping the employed and nonemployed into one group). In Chapter 6 of *Changing Times,* however, he argues that neither the "period" (time) variable nor the level of economic development explains much of the variance. If country effects are downplayed because of their small explanatory power, then should not the period and economic development effects be discounted as well? It is not clear which data in Gershuny's book should carry more weight—the graphs that point to convergence (in Chapter 5) or the statistics that show paltry time-trend effects (in Chapter 6). To resolve this apparent contradiction, it helps to distinguish between explanatory power and effect size. The time trends are revealing, but the "proportion of variance explained"—the measure Gershuny uses in Chapter 6—understates the impact of these time trends as well as the remaining differences between countries. The trend toward convergence may be sizable, but important differences nevertheless remain between countries.

6. These differences have deep historical roots. While Sweden implemented an explicit strategy aimed at increasing female labor force participation through the growth of a large public service sector—with many part-time jobs—Finland pursued a strategy of promoting full-time employment for women (Blossfeld and Hakim 1997; O'Reilly and Fagan 1998).

7. Sylvia Hewlett's (2002) finding that highly successful employed women are the most likely group to forgo childbearing provides support for this view. Yet Gershuny nearly ignores demographic changes and presents no data on single parents, preferring to focus on economic development. Economic changes are key ingredients to postindustrial transformations, but they are also intertwined with major demographic and social shifts.

8. Indeed, the few tables in Gershuny's book that divide respondents by education (see Gershuny 2000, chap. 7) indicate that educated men have increased their working time and housework contributions in many countries, while educated women (to whom these men are often married) have sharply increased

their paid-work time. The limited information on social class differences in Gershuny's data seems to point to growing class divisions in time use rather than to a convergence of time use.

9. Steffen Lehndorff (1998) reports these findings in a study of average annual hours based on OECD data between 1979 and 1997. He also reports that average annual hours per U.S. employee increased from 1,884 to 1,966 hours—an increase of almost two full-time weeks of work per year.

10. We rank the countries in descending order in all tables to highlight the relative position of the United States and how this position changes depending on the measure.

11. For example, there are probably few Dutch workers who actually work only 35 hours per week for 39 weeks. Annual hours in the Netherlands include the hours of some full-time workers who contribute 1,800 hours and those of part-time workers (mostly women) who may work 1,100 or 1,200 hours.

12. The falling hours throughout Europe reflect—to varying degrees in different countries—declines in the hours of both full-time and part-time workers as well as the rising rates of part-time work (OECD 1998). Unfortunately, available data on trends in annual hours do not readily allow a analysis of the factors underlying these changes over time.

13. Another way to compare countries is to focus on a single industrial sector to remove the potentially conflating effect of varying industrial mixes across countries. Two reports that compare hours in a single sector—manufacturing—conclude that U.S. workers report the most hours (ILO 1995; Tagliabue 1997).

14. As we demonstrated in Chapter 1, most of the increase in annual working hours in the United States reflects an increase in the weeks worked per year rather than a rising number of hours worked per week. The increase in the number of weeks worked per year largely reflects changes in women's labor force participation rather than changes in the nature of employment or a decline in the length of vacations.

15. The Luxembourg Income Study (LIS) datasets, based principally on household surveys, contain detailed data at the individual and household level on a range of demographic, labor market, and income variables. There are several advantages to using the LIS data to study working time. The fact that the study uses micro-data allows a range of flexible analyses that cannot be conducted using aggregate data, such as the hours series regularly published by OECD (e.g., 1998), Eurostat (e.g., 1984), and the ILO (e.g., 1995). Furthermore, compared to other cross-national micro-datasets, the LIS sample sizes are relatively large (De Tombeur 1995). Our selected sample comprises all civilian nonagricultural workers, including both self-employed and wage and salary workers. Persons are coded as "working" if they report working at least one hour in the sur-

vey reference week. We restricted the age range to 25–59 in order to maximize comparability by focusing on prime-aged workers. The lower-end cutoff of age 25 allows us to avoid most of the variation across countries in educational enrollments, which might affect the working hours of younger workers. The upper-end cutoff of age 59 enables us to avoid the potentially confounding issue of early retirement, which again varies markedly across countries.

16. The OECD results show the United Kingdom ahead of the United States on long workweeks by men, whereas we found the reverse (Jacobs and Gerson 1998). The difference between the two may be due to the different cutoff points (45 hours for the OECD report versus 50 hours for our own analysis) and also to differences in data sources.

17. John Robinson and Geoffrey Godbey (1999) suggest that additional vacation time is the best way to provide for additional leisure, since adding small increments of free time during normal weeks will simply promote television viewing. We, however, believe that giving parents more time during the week would relieve some of the pressures on both parents and children. Vacation time is important, but it does not alleviate the pressures of daily and weekly routines.

18. Results are presented for couples where both the husband and wife are between the ages of twenty-five and fifty-nine. The definition of marriage varies somewhat across datasets, with cohabiting couples included in six of the countries, but not in Belgium, France, the Netherlands, and the United States.

19. College completion or higher was coded as follows: Belgium: higher nonuniversity (4 years) or university; Canada: university degree; Finland: 16 years, or postgraduate education; France: university degree or higher; Germany: technical college, university, or foreign university; Italy: bachelors degree or postgraduate qualification; Netherlands: tertiary lower, postgraduate or old masters, or postdoctorate; Sweden: university, or research; United States: bachelor's degree, master's degree, or doctorate. The U.K. data do not include usable educational measures. When we restricted educated couples to those where both husband and wife had a college degree, the results were substantively similar to those presented here. The "either spouse" definition produces a larger sample size in countries with small datasets, such as Belgium, or with relatively few college graduates, such as Italy.

20. We considered the possibility that self-employed workers, who are not covered by government policies that regulate working time but are included in our study, put in substantially more hours than wage and salary employees (Rubery, Smith, and Fagan 1998). After repeating the analyses presented here on wage and salary workers alone, we found that the proportion of workers putting in more than 50 hours per week is somewhat lower for most countries, but the proportion for the United States changes only slightly.

21. It is important to note, however, that we cannot easily sort out the effect of the level of demand for part-time work from the effects of child care since there is considerable co-variation. In Italy, for example, the long workweeks of employed wives are likely shaped by both the very restricted part-time work options as well as the availability of nearly universal, full-day, preschool coverage for children starting at the third birthday.

7. Bridging the Time Divide

1. Several decades ago, Claire Vickery (1977) pointed to the emergence of dual-earning and other households that should be considered "time poor" in much the same way that many families are poor in economic resources.
2. Gleick (1999) helps us see the familiar in a new light. He points out, for example, that being able to see things in slow motion, by using techniques such as freeze-frame photography, helps heighten our sensitivity to speed. Eviatar Zerubavel (1981, 1997) demonstrates vividly and convincingly how experiences of time, like other apparently natural phenomena, are powerfully shaped by social and cultural forces.
3. Some argue that "time-saving" devices only raise the standards without actually saving time, though even this argument concedes that such innovations offer choices that were heretofore unavailable. See, for example, Ruth Cowan's *More Work for Mother* (1983). The fact is, however, that time spent on housework has declined in the two decades since Cowan's book was published, as we saw in Chapter 1.
4. Schor, for example, is never able to correlate the spending patterns of individuals with their decisions about working time. This may be because big-ticket items, such as a house, car, or college tuition, challenge the financial resources of all but the most affluent families.
5. For Veblen, a gentlemanly life of leisure did not necessarily mean one of idleness. His critique encompassed all manner of cultivations and refinements that were not strictly utilitarian. Leisure time was one of the most conspicuous displays, for those with inherited wealth were the most likely to be able to afford it and thus "spend" time extravagantly. For Veblen, leisure meant avoiding profitable endeavors, but leisurely pursuits could include civic participation in government, war, sports, and devout observances. The allure of the lifestyle of leisure thus derives from the fact that, as Veblen put it, "In itself and in its consequences the life of leisure is beautiful and enobling in all civilised men's eyes" (1994 [1899], p. 38).
6. Veblen thus states, "Abstention from labour is not only a honorific or meritorious act, but it presently comes to be a requisite of decency" (1994 [1899], p. 41). For Veblen, the more removed from practical significance an activity is

(for example, learning an ancient language that is no longer spoken, or racing horses), the greater its allure.

7. There is, perhaps, no better symbol of the devaluation of the nonemployed mother than the government's decision to replace "welfare" with "workfare," thus requiring single mothers to seek paid employment. For an insightful analysis of the "cultural contradictions of motherhood," see Sharon Hays's book of the same name (1997).

8. The term "numbers" refers to the size of the group in which a worker is considered a member. Kanter (1977) thus makes distinctions among "dominants," "majorities," "minorities," and "tokens."

9. Several decades ago, Wilensky (1964) predicted the diffusion of the term "profession" from a small set of high-status occupations to a broad swath of jobs requiring at least some college education. In describing professional commitment as "a calling," Max Weber used language once reserved for the religious sphere to describe changes in the secular world of work that accompanied the rise of modern societies. In doing so, he suggested that professional commitments involve more than just financial or personal incentives; they often take on a moral dimension as well. Mary Blair-Loy (2003) shows how this moral aspect of professional obligation characterizes many jobs today. She finds, for example, that women finance professionals describe a "devotion to work" that echoes Weber's quasi-religious conception. Surely such devotion can be found among many contemporary workers across a varied range of jobs.

10. There is a "damned if you do and damned if you don't" quality to the persisting critiques of employed parents, especially mothers, who are expected to uphold a strong work ethic even as they are chastised for leaving their children in pursuit of paid work.

11. In a revealing study of workers on Wall Street, Louise Roth (2000) found that high-powered investment firms supported antidiscrimination policies that allowed dedicated women to compete more equitably with dedicated men as long as these policies did not call into question the basic assumption that the job should be a worker's first priority. In other words, these firms were reluctant to support family-friendly policies that undermined their ability to enforce the view that work success requires long days at the office.

12. This term was coined by Lewis Coser and Rose Laub Coser, who describe the family as a greedy institution that places unlimited demands on the time of housewives and especially mothers. The modern workplace, they suggest, is not as greedy because "the amount of time that an individual legitimately owes to his employer is normatively and even legally established" (1974, p. 2). Only a few occupations, such as the priesthood and live-in personal service, qualify as "greedy" in their analysis.

13. Figures from the 2000 census confirm the extent of family change: less than

one quarter of all households now conform to the married, two-parent model so prevalent in the mid-twentieth century (Queenan 2001). And, as pointed out earlier, even in married, two-parent families, most wives are likely to be employed. In 2002, 66.6 percent of married mothers with children under eighteen were employed, including 57.9 percent of mothers with children under six. (Thanks to Barbara Bergmann for this calculation from CPS data.) Contrary to the occasional report purporting to show that more mothers are staying home, all indications are that families with mothers in the workplace are here to stay.

14. Some situations, however, may lead employers to prefer to retain a smaller number of workers who often work overtime despite the added costs. In cyclical industries, for example, where expected downturns mean periodic layoffs and union contracts may require employers to assist those who are laid off, firms may prefer a smaller workforce. And despite the increase in hourly pay, there are no additional benefits costs associated with requiring a smaller pool of workers to put in overtime. Nonetheless, analysis of national survey data indicates that those eligible for overtime tend to work fewer hours than those who are not eligible (Jacobs and Gerson 1997).

15. Robert Putnam (1996, 2000) has called attention to the declining engagement in volunteer groups, civic associations, and other forms of involvement in public life. Participation in community clubs and activities is no doubt undermined by long workweeks, especially for those trying to balance jobs and child rearing. See also Skocpol (1999) for a discussion of the complexities of the issue of civic participation.

16. One strand of economic theory suggests that an efficient labor market should produce just the type of jobs that workers want. In other words, if employers offered jobs that were too far out of line from what workers want, they would be forced to pay an extra "compensating differential" to attract an adequate staff. The evidence presented thus far, as well as findings on shift differentials for evening and night work discussed in our next chapter, suggest that the labor market does not operate in this way. For a more detailed discussion of this issue, see Jacobs and Steinberg (1990) and Wax (2002).

17. Marcia Meyers and Janet Gornick (2002, p. 22) point out that "the meaningful question is neither 'What do women and men want?' nor 'What do families want?' but, instead: 'In a much changed world—one where women are fully valued as earners and men as carers, where employment arrangements enable workers to combine employment and parenting, where public policies provide critical supports and incentives for both women and men—would women and men choose differentiated engagements in earning and caring, up through and including their children's teenage years?' In our view, the answer to that question constitutes a classic counterfactual; in today's socially constructed and

highly constrained world, it simply cannot be answered. If public policies that support and facilitate a gender egalitarian earner/carer society were adopted, implemented, and sustained for a long period of time, we might be able to uncover what it is that women and men—and families—'really want' in relation to earning and caring."

18. Faye Crosby (1987) shows that coordinating and carrying out the many activities associated with being a spouse, parent, and worker can be both stressful and rewarding.

19. In another study, Jacobs (2002) found that 93 percent of college seniors of both sexes consider balancing work and family a top job priority, second only to having interesting work. Gerson (2002) finds a similar desire to combine work with parenthood in a study of the generation that has come of age during the recent period of work and family change.

20. The precipitous rise of single-parent families headed by fathers, which now account for over 10 percent of all single-parent families, points to men's growing desire and need for jobs that do not penalize parental involvement (see Chapter 2; see also Fritsch 2001).

8. Where Do We Go from Here?

1. Harold Wilensky (1974) uses the terms welfare state "leaders" and "laggards," but his underlying premise that welfare states inevitably expand over time to follow the leaders has been questioned over the past two decades.

2. In her book *Unbending Gender,* Joan Williams cites the long workweeks of some professional parents as a major reason for resistance to day care as a solution to the work-family dilemma (2000, p. 50).

3. It is probably no coincidence that these are the same factors that make a difference in school outcomes for children as well. See NICHD Early Child Care Research Network (2002, p. 199–206).

4. Current policy, based on 1996 reform legislation, expects 50 percent of welfare recipients to work, and President George W. Bush hopes to raise that level to 70 percent.

5. Although $7.4 billion in federal funds was allocated to child care through the Child Care Development Fund and TANF (Temporary Aid to Needy Families) in FY 2000, surveys find that this sum leaves many eligible women without subsidies, because of inadequate information and lack of space. See Adams and Rohacek (2002) and R. Schumacher and Greenberg (1999).

6. In another irony of the debate over child care, affluent families, including those with nonworking mothers, routinely rely on nursery schools and "early childhood education programs" to give their children an educational head

start. Yet "early education" becomes "child care" when the focus turns to critiques of employed mothers.

7. The yearly calendar, with three months of summer vacation for schoolchildren and two weeks for their parents, poses another set of challenges. See Heymann (2000) for a good discussion of summer school in the context of work-family concerns.

8. This information is the basis for the often-cited statistic that 4 to 8 million children are unsupervised after school. The lower figure represents 4.5 million children aged twelve and under whose primary arrangement is unsupervised care, while the higher figure represents 8.3 million who report regularly spending any unsupervised time at home.

9. For economic analyses of the benefits of equality in parenting and work, see Folbre (2001) and Gornick and Meyers (2003). Ann Crittenden (2001) offers a critique of the myriad economic penalties attached to caring for children, as we also noted in Chapter 5.

10. Amid the widespread unemployment of the Great Depression and calls for a shorter workweek, Alabama senator Hugo Black (later a Supreme Court Justice) introduced legislation in the spring of 1933 that established a thirty-hour workweek for the nation. The bill passed the U.S. Senate by a vote of 56 to 21, but was bottled up in the House of Representatives. President Roosevelt argued against the Black bill and in favor of the National Industrial Recovery Act (NIRA), which created councils that had the authority to set wages and hours in specific industries. The councils established by the NIRA established a forty-hour workweek for about half of U.S. workers, but in 1936 the NIRA was declared unconstitutional by the U.S. Supreme Court. Hours of work immediately jumped back to their earlier levels, and remained there until 1938, when the Fair Labor Standards Act established a national minimum wage and a forty-hour standard for working time (Roediger and Foner 1989).

11. Advocates of shorter workweeks, especially in Europe, continue to return to traditional themes in making the case for a shorter workweek. The calls for reductions in working time are loudest during periods of economic stagnation and high unemployment. During the economic doldrums in Europe during the 1980s and 1990s, for example, calls for a shorter workweek were common. The logic of distributing a fixed amount of work among a larger group of people seems to be a compelling point in favor of a shorter workweek, whether those debates take place in England, Italy, or France, where it was the main argument promoting the thirty-five-hour workweek in the 1990s.

12. This case has been made in recent years by the Nordic countries and the Netherlands.

13. These figures were drawn from the 1940 U.S. Census and the 1995 Current Population Survey, as reported in *Historical Statistics of the United States* (U.S.

Bureau of the Census 1975), and the *Statistical Abstract of the United States* (U.S. Bureau of the Census 1996).

14. For additional discussion of this exemption, see Rakoff (2002), who also endorses the extension of FLSA to many professional and managerial positions.

15. For example, rather than requiring that each employee's time be monitored, standards could be established for the average working time of employees in a workplace. In lieu of clumsy, legalistic enforcement procedures, moreover, tax incentives could be established to reward companies that can show that they have reduced the workweek for their employees.

16. As Cynthia Epstein and her colleagues (1999) point out, the current normative standard for professional workers now extends well beyond the forty-hour week, which is defined as "part-time" in law and other high-pressure occupations. These writers call for a fundamental restructuring of the "time norms" that equate work success with all-consuming commitment.

17. The labor force participation rate of men aged 55–64 declined from 83.0 percent in 1970 to 65.5 percent in 1997. These data are drawn from *Employment and Earnings* (U.S. Bureau of Labor Statistics 1971, 1998).

18. As we noted in Chapter 4, there is substantial historical experience with reductions in working time, and the result has repeatedly been marked improvements in efficiency. Over the last one hundred or so years, the workweek has declined sharply while living standards have improved. This could only happen through improved technology and worker efficiency. It may seem unrealistic and even utopian to expect more work in less time in the short run, but in the long run this has repeatedly occurred.

19. This socially valuable but economically unrewarded work is exactly the work that women have been expected to perform since the rise of industrialism.

20. Some examples of the "family decline" perspective, which generally laments the rise of single-parent and dual-earning households, can found in Blankenhorn 1994; Poponoe 1989; and Poponoe, Elshtain, and Blankenhorn 1996. Lina Guzman, Laura Lippman, and Kristin Moore (2003) found that the American public generally overestimates the social and economic problems of children. For rebuttals to the "family decline" argument, see Acock and Demo 1994; Barnett and Rivers 1996; Coontz 1997; Skolnick and Rosencrantz 1994; and Stacey 1996.

21. The opposition to abortion rights and the move to encourage marriage through welfare policy serve as reminders that all conservatives are not alike. While economic conservatives argue that economic life should be free of government intrusion, cultural conservatives argue that government should indeed intrude by enforcing a specific moral standard on our most private decisions concerning sexuality, childbearing, and child rearing.

22. See Hewlett 1986. Sylvia Hewlett's recent book, *Creating a Life* (2002), focuses on the relatively high rates of childlessness among highly accomplished profes-

sional women, using this development as a cautionary tale about the costs of success for women. The real story here, however, is not women's ticking biological clock, but rather the lack of change in the time demands and "career clocks" of highly rewarded jobs to accommodate the needs of working women.

23. Recent research shows that the absolute amount of time spent with children is less important than the amount of support and sensitivity parents provide. A. C. Crouter and colleagues (1999), for example, report that children's willingness to share information with their parents matters more than parental monitoring of their time. These researchers also find that when mothers work, fathers become more knowledgeable about, and involved in, their children's care.

24. We created a time series for each census year from 1900 through 2000, drawing on census data of *Current Population Survey* data as available.

25. Burkett's book rages against the perceived injustices inflicted on non-parents in the name of family friendliness—from the focus of politicians on children to the invisibility of the childless to the way deductions and credits for children shift the tax burden onto childless adults. It is worth looking past this histrionic style to examine the substance of her opposition to family-friendly policies.

26. Since employers are not required to pay for family leaves, a replacement can be paid from employer savings, although it would be a positive step forward to begin to provide paid parental leaves, as do several European countries.

27. Private universities, for example, often offer (limited) tuition benefits to the children of employees, but these institutions also offer tuition assistance to employees themselves, many of whom are childless.

References

Acock, Alan C., and David H. Demo. 1994. *Family Diversity and Well-Being.* Thousand Oaks, Calif.: Sage Publications.

Adams, Gina, and Monica Rohacek. 2002. *Child Care and Welfare Reform.* Brookings Institution Policy Brief No. 14. Washington, D.C.: Brookings Institution.

Addabbo, Tindara. 1997. "Part-Time Work in Italy," pp. 113–132 in Hans-Peter Blossfeld and Catherine Hakim, eds., *Between Equalization and Marginalization: Women Working Part-Time in Europe and the United States of America.* Oxford: Oxford University Press.

Bardasi, Elena, and Janet C. Gornick. 2002. "Explaining Cross-National Variation in Part-Time/Full-Time Wage Differentials among Women." Paper presented at conference, Comparative Political Economy of Inequality in OECD Countries, Cornell University, Ithaca, N.Y., April 5–7.

———. 2003. "Women's Part-Time Employment across Countries: Workers' 'Choices' and Wage Penalties," pp. 209–243 in Brigida Garcia, Richard Anker, and Antonella Pinnelli, eds., *Women in the Labour Market in Changing Economies: Demographic Issues.* Oxford: Oxford University Press.

Barnett, Rosalind C., and Douglas T. Hall. 2001. "How to Use Reduced Hours to Win the War for Talent." *Organizational Dynamics* 29 (3): 192–210.

Barnett, Rosalind C., and Caryl Rivers. 1996. *She Works/He Works: How Two-Income Families Are Happier, Healthier, and Better-Off.* San Francisco: HarperCollins.

Becker, Gary S. 1981. *A Treatise on the Family.* Cambridge, Mass.: Harvard University Press.

Beers, Thomas M. 2000. "Flexible Schedules and Shift Work: Replacing the '9-to-5' Workday?" *Monthly Labor Review* 123 (6): 33–40.

Bell, Daniel. 1976. *The Coming of Postindustrial Society.* New York: Basic Books.

Berg, Peter, Arne L. Kalleberg, and Eileen Appelbaum. 2003. "Balancing Work and

Family: The Role of High-Commitment Environments." *Industrial Relations* 42 (2): 168–188.

Bergmann, Barbara. 1986. *The Economic Emergence of Women.* New York: Basic Books.

———. 1997. *Saving Our Children from Poverty: What the United States Can Learn from France.* New York: Russell Sage Foundation.

Bianchi, Suzanne M. 2000. "Maternal Employment and Time with Children: Dramatic Change or Surprising Continuity?" *Demography* 37 (4): 401–414.

Bianchi, Suzanne M., Lynne M. Casper, and Pia K. Peltola. 1999. "A Cross-National Look at Married Women's Economic Dependency." *Gender Issues* 17 (Summer): 3–33.

Bianchi, Suzanne M., Melissa A. Milkie, Liana Sayer, and John P. Robinson. 2000. "Is Anyone Doing the Housework? Trends in the Gender Division of Household Labor." *Social Forces* 79 (1): 191–228.

Bianchi, Suzanne, John Robinson, and Melissa Milkie. Forthcoming. *Changing Rhythms of American Family Life.* New York: Russell Sage Foundation.

Blair-Loy, Mary. 2003. *Competing Devotions: Career and Family among Women Executives.* Cambridge, Mass.: Harvard University Press.

Blankenhorn, David. 1994. *Fatherless America: Confronting Our Most Urgent Social Problem.* New York: Basic Books.

Blau, Francine, Marianne Ferber, and Anne Winkler. 1998. *The Economics of Men, Women, and Work.* Upper Saddle River, N.J.: Prentice Hall.

Blossfeld, Hans-Peter and Catherine Hakim, eds. 1997. *Between Equalization and Marginalization: Women Working Part-Time in Europe and the United States of America.* New York: Oxford University Press.

Bluestone, Barry, and Stephen Rose. 1997. "Overworked and Underemployed: Unraveling an Economic Enigma." *American Prospect* 31 (March–April): 58–69.

Bond, James T., Ellen Galinsky, and Jennifer E. Swanberg. 1998. *The 1997 National Study of the Changing Workforce.* New York: Families and Work Institute.

Brody, Elaine M. 1985. "Parent Care as Normative Stress." *Gerontologist* 25: 19–29.

Budig, Michelle J., and Paula England. 2001. "The Wage Penalty for Motherhood." *American Sociological Review* 66: 204–225.

Burchell, Brendan, Angela Dale, and Heather Joshi. 1997. "Part-Time Work among British Women," pp. 210–246 in Hans-Peter Blossfeld and Catherine Hakim, eds., *Between Equalization and Marginalization: Women Working Part-Time in Europe and the United States of America.* Oxford: Oxford University Press.

Burkett, Elinor. 2000. *The Baby Boon: How Family-Friendly America Cheats the Childless.* New York: Free Press.

Cancian, Francesca M. 1987. *Love in America: Gender and Self-Development.* Cambridge: Cambridge University Press.

Cannadine, David. 1990. *The Decline and Fall of the British Aristocracy.* New Haven: Yale University Press.

Capizzano, Jeffrey, Kathryn Tout, and Gina Adams. 2000. "Child Care Patterns of School-Age Children with Employed Mothers." Occasional Paper 41. Washington, D.C.: The Urban Institute.

Cappelli, Peter. 2001. "Assessing the Decline of Internal Labor Markets," pp. 207–245 in Ivar Berg and Arne Kalleberg, eds., *Sourcebook of Labor Markets: Evolving Structures and Processes.* New York: Kluwer Plenum.

Cherlin, Andrew J. 1992. *Marriage, Divorce, Remarriage,* 2d ed. Cambridge, Mass.: Harvard University Press.

Clarkberg, Marin, and Phyllis Moen. 2001. "Understanding the Time-Squeeze: Married Couples' Preferred and Actual Work-Hour Strategies." *American Behavioral Scientist* 44 (7): 1115–1136.

Clarke-Stewart, Alison. 1993. *Daycare.* Cambridge, Mass.: Harvard University Press.

Coleman, Mary T., and John Pencavel. 1993a. "Changes in Work Hours of Male Employees, 1940–1988." *Industrial and Labor Relations Review* 46 (2): 262–283.

———. 1993b. "Trends in Market Work Behavior of Women since 1940." *Industrial and Labor Relations Review* 46 (4): 653–676.

Coltrane, Scott. 1996. *Family Man: Fatherhood, Housework, and Gender Equity.* New York: Oxford University Press.

Coontz, Stephanie. 1997. *The Way We Really Are: Coming to Terms with America's Changing Families.* New York: Basic Books.

Coser, Lewis A., and Rose Laub Coser. 1974. "The Housewife and Her Greedy Family," pp. 89–100 in Lewis A. Coser, *Greedy Institutions: Patterns of Undivided Commitment.* New York: Free Press.

Cowan, Ruth Schwartz. 1983. *More Work for Mother: The Ironies of Household Technology from the Open Hearth to the Microwave.* New York: Basic Books.

Crittenden, Ann. 2001. *The Price of Motherhood: Why the Most Important Job in the World is Still the Least Valued.* New York: Metropolitan Books.

Crosby, Faye J., ed. 1987. *Spouse, Parent, Worker: On Gender and Multiple Roles.* New Haven: Yale University Press.

Crouter, A. C., H. Helms-Erikson, K. Updegraff, and S. M. McHale. 1999. "Conditions Underlying Parents' Knowledge about Children's Daily Lives: Between- and Within-Family Comparisons." *Child Development* 70: 246–259.

Csikszentmihalyi, Mihaly. 1991. *Flow: The Psychology of Optimal Experience.* New York: Harper Collins.

Current Population Survey. *See* U.S. Bureau of Labor Statistics 2002a.

De Tombeur, Caroline, ed. 1995. *LIS/LES Information Guide,* rev. ed. Luxembourg Income Study, Working Paper Number 7. Luxembourg: Centre d'Etudes de Populations, de Pauvrete et de Politiques Socio-Economiques (CEPS).

De Vault, Marjorie. 1991. *Feeding the Family: The Social Organization of Caring as Gendered Work*. Chicago: University of Chicago Press.

DiMaggio, Paul, John Evans, and Bethany Bryson. 1996. "Have Americans' Social Attitudes Become More Polarized?" *American Journal of Sociology* 102 (3): 690–755.

Dobrzynski, Judith H. 1996. "Somber News for Women on Corporate Ladder." *New York Times*, November 6.

Drago, Robert, and Carol Colbeck. 2003. "The Avoidance of Bias against Caregiving: The Case of Academic Faculty." Manuscript, Pennsylvania State University.

Economist. 2002. "France's 35-Hour Work-Week Is Fine, So Long as It Is Voluntary." June 15.

Ehenreich, Barbara. 2002. *Nickel and Dimed: On (Not) Getting By in America*. New York: Owl Books.

Ehrenreich, Barbara, and Arlie R. Hochschild, eds. 2002. *Global Woman: Nannies, Maids, and Sex Workers in the New Economy*. New York: Metropolitan Books.

Epstein, Cynthia Fuchs, and Arne Kalleberg. Forthcoming. *Rethinking Time at Work*. New York: Russell Sage Foundation.

Epstein, Cynthia Fuchs, Carroll Seron, Bonnie Oglensky, and Robert Sauté. 1999. *The Part-Time Paradox: Time Norms, Professional Lives, Family, and Gender*. New York: Routledge.

Estes, Richard J., and Harold L. Wilensky. 1978. "Life-Cycle Squeeze and Morale Curve." *Social Problems* 25 (3): 277–292.

European Union Council Directive. 1997. *1997 Directive on Part-Time Work*. Council Directive 97/81/EC. December 15. Brussels.

Eurostat. 1984. *Working Time Statistics: Methods and Measurement in the European Community*. Luxembourg: Office for Official Publications of the European Community.

Fagan, Colette, and Jacqueline O'Reilly. 1998. "Conceptualizing Part-Time Work," pp. 1–31 in Jacqueline O'Reilly and Colette Fagan, eds., *Part-Time Prospects: An International Comparison of Part-Time Work in Europe, North America and the Pacific Rim*. London: Routledge.

Faunce, William A. 1963. "Automation and Leisure," pp. 85–96 in Erwin O. Smigel, ed., *Work and Leisure*. New Haven, Conn.: College and University Press.

Fernandez, John P. 1986. *Child Care and Corporate Productivity*. Lexington, Mass.: D.C. Heath.

Figart, Deborah M., and Ellen Mutari. 1998. "Degendering Work Time in Comparative Perspective." *Review of Social Economy* 56 (4): 460–480.

Folbre, Nancy. 2001. *The Invisible Heart: Economics and Family Values*. New York: New Press.

Frank, Robert H. 1995. *The Winner-Take-All Society.* New York: Free Press.

Franke-Ruta, Garance. 2002. "Creating a Lie: Sylvia Ann Hewlett and the Myth of the Baby Bust." *American Prospect* 13 (12) (July 1): 30–33.

Freeman, Richard B., and Linda Bell. 1995. "Why Do American and Germans Work Different Hours?" pp. 101–131 in Friecdrich Buttler, Wolfgang Franz, Ronald Schettkat, and David Soskice, eds., *Institutional Frameworks and Labor Market Performance.* London: Routledge.

Freidson, Eliot. 1986. *Professional Powers: A Study of the Institutionalization of Formal Knowledge.* Chicago: University of Chicago Press.

Friedman, Stewart D., and Jeffrey H. Greenhaus. 2000. *Work and Family—Allies or Enemies?* Oxford: Oxford University Press.

Fritsch, Jane. 2001. "A Rise in Single Dads." *New York Times,* May 20.

Furstenberg, Frank F. 1995. "Fathering in the Inner City: Paternal Participation and Public Policy," pp. 119–147 in William Marsiglio, ed., *Fatherhood: Contemporary Theory, Research, and Social Policy.* Thousand Oaks, Calif.: Sage Publications.

Galinsky, Ellen. 1999. *Ask the Children.* New York: Quill–Harper Collins.

Galinsky, Ellen, James T. Bond, and Dana E. Friedman. 1993. *The Changing Workforce: Highlights of the National Study.* New York: Families and Work Institute.

Galinsky, Ellen, Stacy S. Kim, and James T. Bond. 2001. *Feeling Overworked: When Work Becomes Too Much.* New York: Families and Work Institute.

Garey, Anita I. 1999. *Weaving Work and Motherhood.* Philadelphia: Temple University Press.

Gariety, Bonnie Sue, and Sherrill Shaffer. 2001. "Wage Differentials Associated with Flextime." *Monthly Labor Review* 124 (3): 68–75.

Gershuny, Jonathan. 2000. *Changing Times: Work and Leisure in Postindustrial Society.* Oxford: Oxford University Press.

Gerson, Kathleen. 1985. *Hard Choices: How Women Decide about Work, Career, and Motherhood.* Berkeley: University of California Press.

———. 1993. *No Man's Land: Men's Changing Commitments to Family and Work.* New York: Basic Books.

———. 2001. "Children of the Gender Revolution: Some Theoretical Questions and Findings from the Field," pp. 446–461 in Victor W. Marshall, Walter R. Heinz, Helga Krueger, and Anil Verma, eds., *Restructuring Work and the Life Course.* Toronto: University of Toronto Press.

———. 2002. "Moral Dilemmas, Moral Strategies, and the Transformation of Gender: Lessons from Two Generations of Work and Family Change," *Gender and Society,* 16 (1) (February): 8–28.

Glass, Jennifer. 1990. "The Impact of Occupational Segregation on Working Conditions." *Social Forces* 68 (3): 779–796.

————. 2000. "Toward a Kinder, Gentler Workplace: Envisioning the Integration of Family and Work." *Contemporary Sociology* 29: 129–143.

Glass, Jennifer L., and Sarah Beth Estes. 1997. "The Family Responsive Workplace." *Annual Review of Sociology* 23: 289–313.

Glass, Jennifer L., and Ashley Finley. 2002. "Coverage and Effectiveness of Family Responsive Workplace Policies." *Human Resource Management Review* 12: 313–337.

Glass, Jennifer L., and Lisa Riley. 1998. "Family Responsive Policies and Employee Retention Following Childbirth." *Social Forces* 76 (4): 1401–1435.

Gleick, James. 1999. *Faster: Acceleration of Just About Everything.* New York: Pantheon.

————. 2001. "Inescapably, Obsessively, Totally Connected: Life in the Wireless Age." *New York Times Magazine,* Sunday, April 23.

Goldberg, Jonah. 2000. "Oh, How the Tables Have Turned: Japan Needs to Become More Like . . . the United States." *National Review Online.* January 20.

Gordon, David. M. 1996. *Fat and Mean: The Corporate Squeeze of Working Americans and the Myth of Managerial "Downsizing."* New York: Free Press.

Gornick, Janet C. 1999. "Gender Equality in the Labor Market," pp. 210–242 in Diane Sainsbury, ed., *Gender Policy Regimes and Welfare States.* Oxford: Oxford University Press.

Gornick, Janet C., and Jerry A. Jacobs. 1996. "A Cross-National Analysis of the Wages of Part-Time Workers: Evidence from the United States, the United Kingdom, Canada, and Australia." *Work, Employment, and Society* 10 (1): 1–27.

————. 1998. "Gender, the Welfare State, and Public Employment: A Comparative Study of Seven Industrialized Countries." *American Sociological Review.* 63 (5): 688–710.

Gornick, Janet C., and Marcia K. Meyers. 2000. "Building the Dual Earner/Dual Career Society: Policy Lessons from Abroad." Paper presented at the Family, Work, and Democracy Conference, Racine, Wisc., December 1.

————. 2003. *Earning and Caring: What Government Can Do to Reconcile Motherhood, Fatherhood, and Employment.* New York: Russell Sage Foundation Press.

Greenhouse, Steven. 2001. "Report Shows Americans Have More 'Labor Days.'" *New York Times,* September 1, p. A-8.

Guzman, Lina, Laura Lippman, and Kristin A. Moore. 2003. "Public Perception of Children's Well-Being." Washington, D.C.: Child Trends Working Paper.

Hakim, Catherine. 1997. "Sociological Perspectives on Part-Time Work," pp. 22–70 in Hans-Peter Blossfeld and Catherine Hakim, eds., *Between Equalization and Marginalization: Women Working Part-Time in Europe and the United States of America.* Oxford: Oxford University Press.

Harrington, Mona. 1999. *Care and Equality: Inventing a New Family Politics.* New York: Knopf.

Hayes, Cheryl D., John L. Palmer, and Martha J. Zaslow, eds. 1990. *Who Cares for America's Children: Child Care Policy for the 1990s.* Washington, D.C.: National Academy Press.

Hays, Sharon. 1997. *The Cultural Contradictions of Motherhood.* New Haven: Yale University Press.

Helburn, Suzanne W., and Barbara R. Bergmann. 2002. *America's Child Care Problem: The Way Out.* New York: Palgrave for St. Martin's Press.

Henneck, Rachel. 2003. "Family Policy in the U.S., Japan, Germany, Italy, and France: Parental Leave, Child Benefits/Family Allowances, Child Care, Marriage/Cohabitation, and Divorce." New York: Council on Contemporary Families Briefing Paper.

Hertz, Rosanna. 1986. *More Equal Than Others: Women and Men in Dual-Career Marriages.* Berkeley: University of California Press.

Hetrick, Ron L. 2000. "Analyzing the Recent Upward Surge in Overtime Hours." *Monthly Labor Review* 123 (2): 30–33.

Hewlett, Sylvia A. 1986. *A Lesser Life: The Myth of Women's Liberation in America.* New York: Morrow.

———. 2002. *Creating a Life: Professional Women and the Quest for Children.* New York: Miramax.

Heymann, S. Jody. 2000. *The Widening Gap: Why America's Working Families Are in Jeopardy and What Can Be Done about It.* New York: Basic Books.

Hobson, Barbara. 1990. "No Exit, No Voice: Women's Economic Dependency and the Welfare State." *Acta Sociologica* 33 (3): 235–250.

Hochschild, Arlie R. 1989. *The Second Shift.* New York: Avon Books.

———. 1997. *The Time Bind: When Work Becomes Home and Home Becomes Work.* New York: Metropolitan Books.

Hofferth, Sandra L., and Deborah A. Phillips. 1987. "Child Care in the United States, 1970–1995." *Journal of Marriage and the Family* 49: 559–571.

Hoffman, Lois W., and Lise M. Youngblade, with Rebekah Levine Coley, Allison Sidle Fuligni, and Donna Dumm Kovacs. 1999. *Mothers at Work: Effects on Children's Well-Being.* Cambridge: Cambridge University Press.

Hulse, Carl. 2003. "House Defeats Democrats' Bid to Thwart New Overtime Rules." *New York Times,* July 11, p. A-10.

ILO (International Labour Office). 1995. *Conditions of Work Digest, Volume 14: Working Time around the World.* Geneva: ILO.

Insurance Institute for Highway Safety. 2002. "Fatality Facts: Large Trucks." Available on-line: *www.hwysafety.org/safety_facts/fatality_facts/trucks.htm.*

International Council of Nurses. 2002. "Nursing Matters: Nurses and Overtime." Available on-line: *www.icn.ch/matters_overtime.htm.*

Jackson, Robert Max. 1998. *Destined for Equality: The Inevitable Rise of Women's Status.* Cambridge, Mass.: Harvard University Press.

Jacobs, Jerry A. 1989. *Revolving Doors: Sex Segregation and Women's Careers.* Stanford, Calif.: Stanford University Press.

———. 1998. "Measuring Time at Work: An Assessment of the Accuracy of Self Reports." *Monthly Labor Review* 121 (December): 42–53.

———. 2003. "Gender and the Earnings Expectations of College Seniors." Manuscript, University of Pennsylvania.

Jacobs, Jerry A., and Kathleen Gerson. 1997. "The Endless Day or the Flexible Office? Working Time, Work-Family Conflict, and Gender Equity in the Modern Workplace." Report to the Alfred P. Sloan Foundation, New York.

———. 1998. "Who Are the Overworked Americans?" *Review of Social Economy* 56 (4): 442–459.

———. 2000. "The Overworked American Debate: New Evidence Comparing Ideal and Actual Working Hours," pp. 71–95 in Toby Parcel and Daniel B. Cornfield, eds., *Work and Family: Research Informing Policy.* Thousand Oaks, Calif.: Sage Publications.

Jacobs, Jerry A., and Janet C. Gornick. 2002. "Hours of Paid Work in Dual-Earner Couples: The U.S. in Cross-National Perspective." *Sociological Focus* 35 (2): 169–187.

Jacobs, Jerry A., and Ronnie Steinberg. 1990. "Compensating Differentials and the Male-Female Wage Gap: Evidence from the New York State Comparable Worth Study." *Social Forces* 69 (2): 439–468.

Juster, Thomas F., and Frank P. Stafford, eds. 1985. *Time, Goods, and Well-Being.* Ann Arbor: Survey Research Center, Institute for Social Research, University of Michigan.

Kanter, Rosabeth M. 1977. *Men and Women of the Corporation.* New York: Basic Books.

Kelly, Erin L. 1999. "Theorizing Corporate Family Policies: How Advocates Built 'The Business Case' for 'Family-Friendly' Programs." *Research in the Sociology of Work* (ed. Toby L. Parcel) 7: 169–202.

Kimmel, Michael. 1996. *Manhood in America: A Cultural History.* New York: Free Press.

Klatch, Rebecca. 1987. *Women of the New Right.* Philadelphia: Temple University Press.

Klerman, Jacob A., and Arleen Leibowitz. 1999. "Job Continuity among New Mothers." *Demography* 36 (2): 145–155.

Kmec, Julie A. 1999. "Multiple Aspects of Work-Family Conflict." *Sociological Focus* 32 (3): 265–285.

Kneisner, Thomas J. 1993. "Review Essay: The Overworked American?" *Journal of Human Resources* 28 (33): 681–688.

Kostiuk, Peter F. 1990. "Compensating Differentials for Shift Work." *Journal of Political Economy* 98 (5): 1054–1075.

Kurz, Demie. 2000. "Work-Family Issues of Mothers of Teenage Children." *Qualitative Sociology* 23 (4): 435–451.

Landers, Renee M., James B. Rebitzer, and Lowell J. Taylor. 1996. "Rat Race Redux: Adverse Selection in the Determination of Work Hours in Law Firms." *American Economic Review* 86 (3): 329–348.

Lareau, Annette. 2000. "My Wife Can Tell Me Who I Know: Methodological and Conceptual Problems in Studying Fathers." *Qualitative Sociology* 23 (4): 407–433.

———. 2002. "Invisible Inequalities: Class, Race, and Child Rearing in Black Families and White Families." *American Sociological Review* 67 (5): 747–776.

Lasch, Christopher. 1977. *Haven in a Heartless World: The Family Besieged.* New York: Basic Books.

Leete, Laura, and Juliet B. Schor. 1994. "Assessing the Time-Squeeze Hypothesis: Hours Worked in the United States, 1969–1989." *Industrial Relations* 33 (1): 25–43.

Lehndorff, Steffen. 2000. "Working Time Reduction in the European Union: A Diversity of Trends and Approaches," pp. 38–56 in Lonnie Golden and Deborah M. Figart, eds., *Working Time: International Trends, Theory, and Policy Perspectives.* New York: Routledge.

Leicht, Kevin T., and Mary L. Fennell. 2001. *Professional Work: A Sociological Approach.* Malden, Mass.: Blackwell Publishers.

Lerman, Robert I. 1997. "Is Earnings Inequality Really Increasing?" *Economic Restructuring and the Job Market* (1) (March): Urban Institute.

Lettau, Michael K., and Thomas C. Buchmueller. 1999. "Comparing Benefits Costs for Full- and Part-Time Workers." *Monthly Labor Review* 122 (3): 30–35.

Levine, James A., Robert Weisell, Simon Chevassus, Claudio D. Martinez, Barbara Burlingame, and W. Andrew Coward. 2001. "The Work Burden of Women." *Science* 294 (October 26): 12.

Levy, Frank. 1999. *The New Dollars and Dreams.* New York: Russell Sage Foundation.

Lorber, Judith. 1994. *Paradoxes of Gender.* New Haven, Conn.: Yale University Press.

Luxembourg Income Study. *See* De Tombeur 1995.

Manpower Global. 2000. "Companies That Exceed the 35-Hour Work Week Frequently Turn to Outside Employment Flexibility." *www.manpower.com/en/gpres_.asp?ID=68*, March 23, 2000.

Mason, Karen O., and Karen Kuhlthau. 1992. "The Perceived Impact of Child Care Costs on Women's Labor Supply and Fertility." *Demography* 29 (4): 523–543.

McCartney, Kathleen. 2001. "The *Real* Child-Care Question: How Can It Be the Best There Is?" *Boston Globe,* April 22, p. E4.

Meiksins, Peter, and Peter Whalley. 2002. *Putting Work in Its Place: A Quiet Revolution.* Ithaca, N.Y.: ILR Press.

Meyers, Marcia K., and Janet C. Gornick. 2003. "Public or Private Responsibility? Inequality and Early Childhood Education and Care in the Welfare State." *Journal of Comparative Family Studies* 34 (3): 379–411.

Miller, Dorothy. 1981. "The 'Sandwich' Generation: Adult Children of the Aging." *Social Work* 26: 419–423.

Moen, Phyllis, ed. 2003. *It's about Time: Couples and Careers.* Ithaca, N.Y.: Cornell University Press.

Moen, Phyllis, and Stephen Sweet. 2002. "Two Careers, One Employer: Couples Working for the Same Corporation." *Journal of Vocational Behavior* 61: 1–18.

Mutari, Ellen, and Deborah M. Figart. 2000. "The Social Implications of European Work Time Policies: Promoting Gender Equity?" pp. 232–250 in Lonnie Golden and Deborah M. Figart, eds., *Working Time: International Trends, Theory, and Policy Perspectives.* London: Routledge.

National Association of Elementary School Principals. 2001. *Principals and After-School Programs: A Survey of PreK–8 Principals.* Washington, D.C.: National Association of Elementary School Principals. Available on-line: *www.naesp.org/afterschool/report.pdf.*

National Opinion Research Center. 2002. *General Social Survey, 1972–2000: Cumulative Codebook.* Chicago: National Opinion Research Center.

National Survey of the Changing Workforce. 1992. *See* Galinsky, Bond, and Friedman, 1993.

National Survey of the Changing Workforce. 1997. *See* Bond, Galinsky, and Swanberg 1998.

NICHD Early Child Care Research Network. 2002. "Child-Care Structure, Process, Outcome: Direct and Indirect Effects of Child-Care Quality on Young Children's Development." *Psychological Science* 13 (3): 199–206. London: Routledge.

Nock, Steven L., and Paul William Kingston. 1988. "Time with Children: The Impact of Couples' Work-Time Commitments." *Social Forces* 67 (1): 59–85.

Nye, F. Ivan, and Lois W. Hoffman. 1963. *The Employed Mother in America.* Chicago: Rand McNally.

Nyland, Chris. 1989. *Reduced Worktime and the Management of Production.* Cambridge: Cambridge University Press, 1989.

OECD (Organization for Economic Cooperation and Development). 1994. *Women and Structural Change: New Perspectives.* Paris: OECD.

———. 1998. "Working Hours: Latest Trends and Policy Initiatives." Chapter 5 in *Employment Outlook.* Paris: OECD.

———. 1999, 2000. *Employment Outlook.* Paris: OECD.

Oppenheimer, Valerie K. 1980. "Life-Cycle Squeezes and Adaptive Family Strategies—Implications for Women's Economic Roles." *Population Index* 46 (3): 377–377.

O'Reilly, Jacqueline, and Colette Fagan, eds. 1998. *Part-Time Prospects: An International Comparison of Part-Time Work in Europe, North America, and the Pacific Rim.* London: Routledge.

Packard, Vance O. 1959. *The Status Seekers: An Exploration of Class Behavior in America and the Hidden Barriers that Affect You, Your Community, Your Future.* New York: D. McKay Co.

Padavic, Irene, and Barbara Reskin. 2002. *Women and Men at Work.* Thousand Oaks, Calif.: Pine Forge Press.

Parcel, Toby L., and Elizabeth G. Menaghan. 1994. *Parents' Jobs and Children's Lives.* Hawthorne, N.Y.: Aldine de Gruyter.

Peterson, Richard R., and Kathleen Gerson. 1992. "Determinants of Responsibility for Child-Care Arrangements among Dual-Earner Couples." *Journal of Marriage and the Family* 54 (3): 527–536.

Pfeffer, Jeffrey, and James N. Baron. 1988. "Taking the Workers Back Out: Recent Trends in the Structuring of Employment." *Research in Organizational Behavior* 10: 257–303.

Popenoe, David. 1989. *Disturbing the Nest: Family Change and Decline in Modern Societies.* New York: Aldine de Gruyter.

Poponoe, David, Jean Bethke Elshtain, and David Blankenhorn, eds. 1996. *Promises to Keep: Decline and Renewal of Marriage in America.* Lanham, Md.: Rowman and Littlefield.

Presser, Harriet B. 1994. "Employment Schedules among Dual-Earner Spouses and the Division of Household Labor by Gender." *American Sociological Review* 59: 348–364.

———. 2003. *Toward a 24-Hour Economy.* New York: Russell Sage Foundation.

Putnam, Robert. 1996. "The Strange Disappearance of Civic America." *American Prospect* 24 (Winter): 34–48.

———. 2000. *Bowling Alone: The Collapse and Revival of American Community.* New York: Simon and Schuster.

Queenan, Joe. 2001. "Life with Father Isn't What It Used to Be." *New York Times,* June 17.

Rakoff, Todd D. 2002. *A Time for Every Purpose: Law and the Balance of Life.* Cambridge, Mass.: Harvard University Press.

Rayman, Paula M. 2001. *Beyond the Bottom Line: The Search for Dignity at Work.* New York: St. Martin's Press.

Reynolds, Jeremy. 2001. "You Can't Always Get the Hours You Want: A Cross-National Examination of Mismatches between Actual and Preferred Work Hours." Ph.D. dissertation, University of North Carolina, Chapel Hill.

Risman, Barbara. 1998. *Gender Vertigo.* New Haven, Conn.: Yale University Press.

Robinson, John P., and Ann Bostrom. 1994. "The Overestimated Workweek? What Time Diary Measures Suggest." *Monthly Labor Review* 111 (8) (August): 11–23.

Robinson, John P., and Geoffrey Godbey. 1999. *Time for Life: The Surprising Ways Americans Use Their Time,* 2d ed. University Park: Pennsylvania State University Press.

Roediger, David R., and Philip S. Foner. 1989. *Our Own Time: A History of American Labor and the Working Day.* New York: Greenwood Press.

Rones, Philip L., Randy E. Ilg, and Jeffiner M. Gardner. 1997. "Trends in Hours of Work since the Mid-1970s." *Monthly Labor Review* (April): 3–14.

Rosa, R. R. 1995. "Extended Workshifts and Excessive Fatigue." *Journal of Sleep Research* 4: 51–56.

Ross, C., and D. Paulsell. 1998. *Sustaining Employment among Low-Income Parents: The Role of Quality in Child Care, a Research Review.* Final Report. Princeton, N.J.: Mathematica Policy Research.

Roth, Louise. 2000. "Making the Team: Gender, Money, and Mobility in Wall Street Investment Banks." Ph.D. dissertation, New York University.

Rubery, Jill, Mark Smith, and Colette Fagan. 1998. "National Working Time Regimes and Equal Opportunities." *Feminist Economics* 4 (1): 71–101.

Sayer, Liana. 2001. "Time Use, Gender, and Inequality: Differences in Men's and Women's Market, Nonmarket, and Leisure Time." Ph.D. dissertation, University of Maryland.

Scarr, Sandra. 1984. *Mother Care, Other Care.* New York: Basic Books.

———. 1998. "American Child Care Today." *American Psychologist* 53 (2): 95–108.

Schneider, Barbara, and Linda Waite. 2003. "Working Families: Time Apart, Time Together." Manuscript, Department of Sociology, University of Chicago.

Schor, Juliet. 1991. *The Overworked American: The Unexpected Decline of Leisure.* New York: Basic Books.

———. 1998. *The Overspent American.* New York: Basic Books.

Schumacher, Edward J., and Barry T. Hirsch. 1997. "Compensating Differentials and Unmeasured Ability in the Labor Market for Nurses: Why Do Hospitals Pay More?" *Industrial and Labor Relations Review* 50 (4): 557–79.

Schumacher, R., and M. Greenberg. 1999. "Child Care after Leaving Welfare: Early Evidence from State Studies." Report, Center for Law and Social Policy, Washington, D.C.

Schwartz, Felice N. 1989. "Management, Women, and the New Facts of Life." *Harvard Business Review* 67 (1): 65–76.

Shank, S. 1986. "Preferred Hours of Work and Corresponding Earnings." *Monthly Labor Review* (November): 40–44.

Sklar, Holly, Laryssa Mykyta, and Susan Wefald. 2001. *Raise the Floor: Wages and Policies That Work for All of Us.* New York: Ms. Foundation for Women.

Skocpol, Theda. 1999. "Associations without Members." *American Prospect* 45 (July–August): 66–73.

———. 2000. *The Missing Middle: Working Families and the Future of American Social Policy.* New York: W. W. Norton.

Skolnick, Arlene, and Stacey Rosencrantz. 1994. "The New Crusade for the Old Family. *American Prospect* 18 (Summer): 59–65.

Smigel, Erwin O., ed. 1963. *Work and Leisure.* New Haven, Conn.: College and University Press.

Soldo, Beth J. 1996. "Cross Pressures on Middle-Aged Adults: A Broader View." *Journal of Gerontology* 51 (6): 271–273.

Spain, Daphne, and Suzanne M. Bianchi. 1996. *Balancing Act: Motherhood, Marriage, and Employment among American Women.* New York: Russell Sage Foundation.

Stacey, Judith. 1996. *In the Name of the Family: Rethinking Family Values in the Postmodern Age.* Boston: Beacon Press.

Swidler, Ann. 1986. "Culture in Action: Symbols and Strategies." *American Sociological Review* 51 (2): 273–286.

———. 2001. *Talk of Love: How Culture Matters.* Chicago: University of Chicago Press.

Tagliabue, John. 1997. "Buona Notte, Guten Tag: Europe's New Workdays." *New York Times,* November 12: D1, D6.

32 Hours. 1998. "Action for Full Employment and the Shorter Work Time Network of Canada." Newsletter. Available on-line: *www.web.net/europe.htm.*

———. 2000. "Action for Full Employment and the Shorter Work Time Network of Canada." Newsletter. Available on-line: *www.web.net/32hours/btfeb00.htm.*

Thompson, Cynthia A., Laura L. Beauvais, and Karen Lyness. 1999. "When Work-Family Benefits Are Not Enough: The Influence of Work-Family Culture on Benefit Utilization, Organizational Attachment, and Work-Family Conflict." *Journal of Vocational Behavior* 54: 293–415.

U.S. Bureau of the Census. 1975. *Historical Statistics of the United States.* Washington, D.C.: U.S. Government Printing Office.

———. 1996, 1998, 2002. *Statistical Abstract of the United States.* Washington, D.C.: U.S. Government Printing Office.

U.S. Bureau of Labor Statistics. 1971, 1998. *Employment and Earnings.* Washington, D.C.: U.S. Government Printing Office.

———. 1980–1997. *Employment and Earnings.* Establishment Survey Data.

———. 2000. "Are Managers and Professionals Really Working More?" *Issues in Labor Statistics,* Summary, pp. 1–2 (May 12).

———. 2001. Union Members Summary. Available on-line: *stats.bls.gov/news.release/union2.nr0.htm.*

———. 2002a. *Current Population Survey Technical Paper 63RV: Design and Methodology.* Washington, D.C.: U.S. Government Printing Office.

———. 2002b. "Workers on Flexible and Shift Schedules in 2001." Available on-line: *www.bls.gov/news.release/flex.nr0.htm.*

U.S. Department of Education. 2000. *Working for Children and Families: Safe and Smart After-School Programs.* Washington, D.C.: U.S. Government Printing Office.

Veblen, Thorstein. 1994 [1899]. *The Theory of the Leisure Class.* New York: Penguin Books.

Vickery, Claire. 1977. "The Time-Poor: A New Look at Poverty," *Journal of Human Resources* 12 (1): 27–48.

Waldfogel, Jane. 1999. "Family Leave Coverage in the 1990s." *Monthly Labor Review* 122 (10): 13–21.

Wax, Amy. 2002. "Economic Models of the 'Family-Friendly' Workplace: Making the Case for Change." Manuscript, University of Pennsylvania Law School.

Wilensky, Harold. 1963. "The Uneven Distribution of Leisure: The Impact of Economic Growth on 'Free Time'," pp. 107–145 in Erwin O. Smigel, ed., *Work and Leisure.* New Haven, Conn.: College and University Press.

———. 1964. "The Professionalization of Everyone?" *American Journal of Sociology* 70: 137–148.

———. 1974. *The Welfare State and Equality: Structural and Ideological Roots of Public Expenditures.* Berkeley: University of California Press.

———. 2002. *Rich Democracies: Political Economy, Public Policy, and Performance.* Berkeley: University of California Press.

Williams, Joan. 2000. *Unbending Gender: Why Family and Work Conflict and What to Do about It.* Oxford: Oxford University Press.

Winslow, Sarah. 2002. "Trends in Work-Family Conflict, 1977–1997: The Influence of Demographic Factors." Master's thesis, University of Pennsylvania.

Wolfe, Alan. 1998. *One Nation, after All: What Middle-Class Americans Really Think about God, Country, Family, Racism, Welfare, Immigration, Homosexuality, Work, the Right, the Left, and Each Other.* New York: Viking.

Yeung, Jean W. 2001. "Children's Time with Fathers in Intact Families." *Journal of Marriage and the Family* 63: 136–154.

Zal, H. Michael. 2001. *The Sandwich Generation: Caught between Growing Children and Aging Parents.* New York: Perseus.

Zerubavel, Eviatar. 1981. *Hidden Rhythms: Schedules and Calendars in Social Life.* Chicago: University of Chicago Press.

———. 1997. *Social Mindscapes: An Invitation to Cognitive Sociology.* Cambridge, Mass.: Harvard University Press.

Index